Protection of the Financial Interests

of the European Communities:

The Fight against Fraud and Corruption

EUROPEAN MONOGRAPHS

Editor-in-Chief Prof. Dr. K. J. M. Mortelmans

1. Lammy Betten (ed.) *The Future of European Social Policy* (second and revised edition 1991).
2. J. M. E. Loman, K. J. M. Mortelmans, H. H. G. Post, J. S. Watson, *Culture and Community Law: Before and after Maastricht* (1992).
3. Prof. Dr. J. A. E. Vervaele, *Fraud against the Community: The Need for European Fraud Legislation* (1992).
4. P. Raworth, *The Legislative Process in the European Community* (1993).
5. J. Stuyck, *Financial and Monetary Integration in the European Economic Community* (1993).
6. J. H. V. Stuyck, A. Vossestein (eds.) *State Entrepreneurship, National Monopolies and European Community Law* (1993).
7. J. Stuyck, A. Looijestijn-Clearie (eds.) *The European Economic Area EC-EFTA* (1994).
8. R. B. Bouterse, *Competition and Integration – What Goals Count?* (1994).
9. R. Barents, *The Agricultural Law of the EC* (1994).
10. Nicholas Emiliou, *The Principle of Proportionality in European Law: A Comparative Study* (1996).
11. Eivind Smith, *National Parliaments as Cornerstones of European Integration* (1996).
12. Jan H. Jans, *European Environmental Law* (1996).
13. Síofra O'Leary, *The Evolving Concept of Community Citizenship: From the Free Movement of Persons to Union Citizenship* (1996).
14. Laurence Gormley (ed.) *Current and Future Perspectives on EC Competition Law* (1997).
15. Simone White, *Protection of the Financial Interests of the European Communities: The Fight against Fraud and Corruption* (1998).

EUROPEAN MONOGRAPHS

Protection of the Financial Interests
of the European Communities:
The Fight against Fraud and Corruption

By Simone White

KLUWER LAW
INTERNATIONAL

THE HAGUE · LONDON · BOSTON

Published by Kluwer Law International
P.O. Box 85889
2508 CN The Hague, The Netherlands

Sold and distributed in the USA and Canada by
Kluwer Law International
675 Massachusetts Avenue
Cambridge, MA 02139, USA

Sold and distributed in all other countries by
Kluwer Law International
Distribution Centre
P.O. Box 322
3300 AH Dordrecht, The Netherlands

British Library Cataloguing in Publication Data and Library of Congress Cataloguing in Publication Data are available.

Cover design: Bert Arts

Printed on acid-free paper

ISBN 90 411 9647 1

Preface and Acknowledgements

This book is directed to legal professionals, teachers, students and researchers, especially those whose interest in EU institutions and law overlaps with an interest in so-called white collar crime and the law. More generally, the book should be of interest to all those concerned with the integrity and development of the European Union. 'EC fraud' and the counter-measures to it – the protection of the financial interests of the European Community – have climbed to the top of the political agenda. And with good reason. The European Project may stand or fall depending on what is done in relation to the protection of its finances: standing, as a shining example of the continuing ingenuity of European policy-makers and legislators or, falling, discredited, into economic crime and political cynicism.

Many solutions have been proposed and some at least have been partially implemented, but fundamental legal and political questions remain. Is it possible to design anti-fraud measures that are appropriate, effective, proportionate to the harm caused to the Community, and yet which respect national sensitivities and subsidiarity? Are answers to be found in specific anti-fraud legislation and enforcement; in broader political solutions to the impasse which during the 1990s many observers diagnosed in EU justice and home affairs; and/or in fuller development of the internal market, reducing the opportunities for EU fraud? If the answer is to be found in specific legalization and enforcement then, in order to be effective, the protection of the financial interests of the European Community will require arrangements between the European institutions and the Member States for which there is no blueprint. If political breakthroughs are to provide the pivot, following the 1997 IGC, then it may turn out to be the harbinger to wider advances in justice and home affairs in the EU. And if, as the present author believes, the development of the internal market would remove much of the incentive for this form of business crime, then the protection of the financial interests of the European Community may find its place as one of the motors for the completion of the internal market, at the core of developments in the tradition of the Treaty of Rome. It is most likely that a comprehensive programme of action may be required, with action on several fronts.

The aims of this book are to present a comprehensive overview of the protection of the financial interests of the European Community, a work of legal reference and a manual for policy-makers. In researching and writing it I have had the good fortune to learn from many academics, policy-makers and officials. I gratefully acknowledge financial support from the European Commission, DG XX (Directorate General for Financial Control) in relation to work which appears here as Chapter 5. It is one of the great strengths of Francesco de Angelis, Director at DG XX, that he has encouraged all manner of stimulating debates on the protection of the financial interests of the European Community, bringing legal researchers and other experts together in pan-EU conferences and studies. Many working contacts were made possible through the UK Association of Lawyers for the Protection of the Financial Interests of the European Communities (ALPFIEC), which, like sister organizations in each of the Member States, receives a modest grant from DG XX.

All of these opportunities enhanced my ability to network and to learn from many experts from all the Member States of the EU, who are too numerous to list. Thanks are also due to the many EC and UK officials who kindly agreed to be interviewed and who supplied me with valuable information: convention demands they remain anonymous.

The study also builds upon research carried out between 1994 and 1996 at the London School of Economics and I am especially grateful to Professor Leonard Leigh for encouraging me throughout. My thanks must also go to Professor Christopher Harding of the University of Wales at Aberystwyth and Dr Mads Andenaes of King's College London. Finally, I thank and ask forgiveness from Nicholas Dorn and the two cats, the first of whom acted as a sounding board throughout and the latter two who offered silent sympathy at those times when it seemed to have no end. Developments in the area of the protection of EC finance have been very rapid and constant updating has been necessary, even as the text has gone to press.

Table of Contents

List of Tables

Introduction

'Fraus omnia corrumpit' (Julius Caesar)

There are three reasons why the protection of the financial interests of the European Communities should concern and interest all European citizens. Firstly, whether employed or not, they are tax payers and indirectly contribute to the budget. The protection of the financial interests of the European Communities is therefore a legitimate concern. Every year the Member States now pay the equivalent of between 4 and 5 per cent of their GNPs into the Community budget.[1] Although this constitutes a relatively small contribution in percentage terms, the political significance of the EC budget[2] should not be underestimated. It exists to give expression to common policies, and to implement jointly agreed programmes, which both are an integral part of the European Project. Yet every year a proportion[3] of the EC budget is misappropriated, through frauds and irregularities which increasingly involve more than one jurisdiction. Costly irregularities cast a shadow over the prospect for further integration (and enlargement), and raise political and legal issues for 'euro-sceptics' and 'euro-philes' alike.

Secondly, the sharing of competencies between the Communities and the Member States is generally a delicate matter, due to the absence of clear principles in the Treaty for the allocation of regulatory powers.[4] In no other area, perhaps, is the balance more delicate than in matters relating to the protection of the financial interests of the European Communities, where the budget is the Communities', yet the enforcement the Member States'. Ambiguity starts with the budget itself. The Member States are responsible for the collecting and making available of resources to the Community. They are also responsible for spending over 80 per cent of the same budget. Yet the Commission is responsible for the implementation of the budget in accordance with the principles of sound financial management.[5] Further-

---

1. European Court of Auditors, *The European Court of Auditors Auditing the finances of the European Union* (1995), p. 13.
2. Total estimated appropriations for 1997 show a grand total of 89,186 million ECU. In November 1996 one ECU was worth 57 pence.
3. Reported frauds entered into the Commission IRENE database point to a percentage of 1% to 3% of the budget being misappropriated, whilst much higher estimates have been ventured, to take into account unreported irregularities.
4. On this point, *see* S. Weatherill, 'Implementation as a constitutional issue', in *Implementing EC law in the United Kingdom – Structures for indirect rules*, ed. T. Daintith (1995), pp. 325–360.
5. Articles 201 and 205 EC; Article 22(1), first subparagraph of the Financial Regulation.

1

more the Community has no criminal jurisdiction, and relies entirely on the Member States for the protection of EC funds. Such an arrangement does not correspond to any of the models of public financing and of protection of public funds we already know well.[6] This means that there has been no blueprint for the protection of the financial interests of the European Communities. As a unique creative experiment in post-national rule making, it continues to be controversial.

Thirdly, in a political space that is neither wholly federal nor inter-governmental, there has been persisting concern about uneven and ineffective enforcement of EC law at national level. Fundamental issues concerning Member States' attachment to common goals and trust continue to be raised. In the field of the protection of the financial interests of the European Communities, there have been specific concerns over the assimilation of EC funds with national funds, but also, more fundamentally, over the adequacy of national measures in an internal market, in a world where formal, informal and criminal economies are increasingly seen as converging. The difficulty in preventing and sanctioning frauds affecting the EC budget, and in recovering funds, cannot be underestimated. The evolution of the informal economy, and its links with international organized crime make these tasks particularly challenging.[7] Here both Naylor[8] and Van Duyne[9] help to understand the development and extent of the 'organized crime'[10] phenomenon in question. They find it useful to start with a distinction between two broad categories of economic crime: (i) the 'unambiguously criminal', which is dealt with by police measures and (ii) the (equally, if not more difficult to detect) 'otherwise legal', where enterprises deal with legal goods or services in illegal ways. The second sector is presumed to be much larger. Its existence is usually imputed to too much (and/or too complex) regulation, and it is seen as fundamentally a problem for the political authorities to solve. Looking at this separation between a crime market where goods are illegal, and a crime market where legal goods and services are handled in illegal ways, it seems at first that frauds and irregularities affecting the EC budget fall within the second category, in the 'price-wedge' market described by Van Duyne,[11] where the regulation of taxes, excises and EU subsidies are flouted. However neat this

---

6. Such arrangements include those evident in centralized states, federal governments or international organizations.
7. *See* for example newspaper article: 'Criminal gangs exploit Union's single market', in *European Voice*, 14 November 1996, p. 4.
8. R. Naylor, 'From underworld to underground enterprise crime, "informal sector" business and the public policy response' (1996) *Crime, Law and Social Change*, Vol. 24, number 2, 79–150.
9. P. Van Duyne, 'The phantom and threat of organised crime' (1996) 24 *Crime, Law and Social Change* p. 341.
10. Most definitions of organized crime seem to be culturally specific, and range from the minimalist (a crime which involves more than one perpetrator), to the very detailed (involving particular mafias or syndicates making routine use of violence and intimidation). For this purpose, I am adopting Fijnaut's general definition of organized crime in Europe as involving 'professional criminals [who] distinguish themselves not only by the efficient and business-like way in which they commit certain crimes, but also by the close relations they have amongst themselves' (*cf.* C. Fijnaut, 'Organized crime and anti-organized crime efforts in western Europe – An overview' (London, 1991) *Organized crime and its containment, a transatlantic initiative*. For our purpose, the definition has the benefit of being sufficiently wide, and of not taking violence to be a major definitional determinant.
11. *Ibid.*, page 356.

theoretical separation may seem at first sight, we shall see that in practice it flounders. The boundary between the two sectors has become blurred, making the task of both legislators and enforcers more difficult. For these reasons the author argues simply that an approach which focuses on *reducing opportunities* for fraud and corruption should be prioritized. This means, *inter alia*, completing the internal market.

The focus of this work is on the institutional response, and the evolution of Community control, although it also contains a national study on the recovery of unwarranted payments. Although much of the literature on the protection of the financial interests of the European Communities has hitherto focused on the CAP,[12] little has been written on, for example, (i) large-scale transit fraud, (ii) procurement fraud affecting the Structural Funds, (iii) the recovery of EC funds, (iv) corruption affecting the EC budget – nor has VAT fraud been much discussed in the context of the EC budget. The present work goes some way towards addressing these gaps, although it often raises more questions than it solves.

This work does not claim to be comprehensive. For a start, it deals with the control of fraud affecting European Community finances, rather than European Union finances. This is because, notwithstanding new Treaty provisions,[13] the position of expenditure incurred under the second and third pillars has not been clarified yet. Furthermore not all expenditure or loans are audited by the European Court of Auditors (a situation they would like to see remedied, *see* Chapter 2) and as a result are not open to scrutiny. A study of GNP national contributions has not been included, although the author is aware of the present controversy over the lack of uniformity in the Member States' calculations of their contributions, and this omission should not be interpreted as a belief that generally speaking, national treasuries are beyond reproach in their handling of EC funds. The control of frauds affecting Community Initiatives (which are part of the Structural Funds) deserved more thorough treatment, but would have required a period of research at the Commission itself. It is unfortunate therefore that the author was age-barred from doing a 'stage' at DG XX or UCLAF. Because this work focuses on Community control, it does not address in detail issues of mutual assistance in criminal justice matters which, in any case, have been the subject of recent and extensive studies, to which the author would be able to add little.[14] Lastly, because it dwells on control, the work is unashamedly 'top-down', although it deals with some of the

---

12. *See* for example K. Tiedemann, 'La fraude dans le domaine des subventions – Crime et politique criminelle' (1975) *Revue de droit pénal et de criminologie*, p. 129; G. Dannecker (ed.), *Combatting subsidy fraud in the EC area* ((1993 Köln); D. Norton, 'Smuggling under the CAP: Northern Ireland and the Republic of Ireland' (1986) 32, *Journal of Common Market Studies*, p. 319; C. Harding, 'The European Communities and control of criminal business activities' (1982) *International and Comparative Law Quarterly*, p. 246.

13. Article 199 EC.

14. *See* for example C. Van den Wyngaert, *Etude espace judiciaire européen – Groupe thématique no. 2 – Règles de compétence et extra-territorialité* (1996); AERPE, *La protection du budget communautaire et l'assistance entre états* (1995); also S. Manacorda, 'La criminalité économique internationale – Un premier bilan des instruments de politique criminelle' (1995) *Le Trimestre du Monde*, p. 59.

issues relating to the rights of operators in Chapters 2 and 4, and incorporates operators' views in Chapter 3.

The structure is in four parts. Part I introduces the subject with a panoramic view of the evolution of control (Chapter 1) and outlines the role of the European institutions, without going into the intricacies of budgetary control but taking into account proposed institutional reforms (Chapter 2). Part II offers a more detailed account of Community control of income fraud (Chapter 3) and expenditure fraud, focusing on intra-Community expenditure (Chapter 4). Part III (Chapter 5) is a study of the recovery of EC funds in the United Kingdom, which ends with a comparison of the main features of its system with Denmark. Part IV is concerned with the widening of the debate. Chapter 6 deals with various aspects of corruption. Chapter 7 deals with the possible future contours of enforcement upon enlargement to Central and Eastern Europe. Chapter 8 discusses the legal space and, in particular, the ambitious proposal for a *Corpus Juris*, which has been particularly motivated by considerations around the protection of the financial interests of the European Communities. Finally, Chapter 9 deals with post-IGC considerations, and some of the implications for the European Legal Space. However, the work concludes more modestly, with a call for a balanced anti-fraud policy.

PART I

Evolution of Control and Institutions' Roles

Chapter 1. Evolution of Control: A Panoramic View

1. BACKGROUND: THE COMMON AGRICULTURAL POLICY

The setting up of a Common Market in the 1950s by the six founding Member States of the European Community meant the replacement of individual marketing structures with individual agricultural products by a Community marketing structure.[1] This in turn meant the establishment of a Common Agricultural Policy (CAP henceforth) and a common price system for which the Community took financial responsibility. The objectives of the CAP were laid down in the Treaty of Rome and were to raise agricultural productivity, to ensure a fair standard of living to the agricultural community, to stabilize markets, to assure availability of supplies and to ensure that supplies reach consumers at reasonable prices.[2]

Although the CAP has made the Community self-sufficient in food supplies, the cost has been high. Every year most of the overall budget of the EC has been spent on maintaining the CAP, which has aptly been described by Lasok and Bridge as 'a hungry sacred cow ... leaving little for the development of other well-deserving policies'.[3] Since 1978, the European Court of Auditors' annual reports show that the Guarantee Section of the European Agricultural Guarantee and Guidance Fund (EAGGF henceforth), which is concerned with the support of prices for agricultural products, although declining in overall percentage, still forms the main part of EC budget expenditure (*see* Table 1.1.).

Frauds and irregularities affecting the Guarantee Section of the EAGGF have been widely reported and discussed, particularly in the context of exports of agricultural products and market intervention (*see* Chapter 4 on expenditure fraud). Although the Commission is responsible for the integrity of the budget, the European Community has no criminal jurisdiction as such, so it is the responsibility of the Member States to investigate and to prosecute frauds and irregularities affecting the EC budget, to recover funds when necessary and to pay them back into the common purse. In December 1994, the Council stated in a resolution

> '[C]riminal provisions protecting the Communities' financial interests already exist in many areas in the Member States; there are wide variations, however,

---

1. D. Lasok and J. Bridge, *Law and institutions of the European Communities* (1991), p. 482.
2. Article 39 EEC; *see also* J. Harrop, *The political economy of integration in the European Community* (1985); J. Usher, *Legal aspects of Agriculture in the European Community* (1988), pp. 35–40.
3. Lasok and Bridge, *op. cit.*, p. 489.

as to what constitutes an offence ...; there are also gaps which may be affecting cooperation between Member States.'

Table 1.1. EC Budget and EAGGF Guarantee Section appropriations

Financial year	EC expenditure*	EAGGF Guarantee as % of total**
1977	9,584	74
1978	12,302	70
1979	14,447	72
1980	16,182	71
1981	19,986	58
1982	23,260	57
1983	26,533	60
1984	29,264	62
1985	30,616	65
1986	36,052	61
1987	37,452	61
1988	45,344	61
1989	46,426	60
1990	49,208	54
1991	59,369	55
1992	63,907	52
1993	70,408	52

* EC expenditure is cited as million UA (Unit of Account) until 1977; million EUA (European Unit of Account) from 1978 to 1980; million ECU (European Currency Unit) from 1 January 1981.

** Sources: Court of Auditors' Annual Reports, 1977–1993. The figures under 'total EC budget' are the appropriations for commitment found in the seventeen Court of Auditors' reports for the financial years in question, but have been rounded upwards. The EAGGF Guarantee Section expenditure is from the same source, shown here as percentage of total budget. It has been rounded upwards to the nearest million.

As a rule, Member States tend to think that their own national system of handling fraud affecting the Community budget is more effective than that of their neighbours.[4] Since the 1960s the nature of enforcement has evolved. Much of the fraud control measures taken at EC level have taken place against a background of a rapid succession of enlargements (and a corresponding increase in the size and complexity of the CAP), and budgetary crises (hence the need to find ways to reduce the CAP). It is within this paradox that enforcement efforts, which until recently almost

---

4. N. Passas, *Milking consumers and taxpayers – Farm frauds in the European Community* (Temple University 1993), p. 19.

entirely focused on the CAP, must be located. The reality is that, although fraud has always existed, fraud enforcement has not always been high on the political agenda. Historically, four phases can be distinguished, which are briefly outlined below.

2. FIRST (LATENT) PHASE: BENIGN NEGLECT

Although there are indications that the price equalization and compensation schemes under Articles 55 and 62 ECSC gave rise to fraud as early as the late 1950s,[5] and that the early CAP was also affected,[6] the 1960s and 1970s were characterized by weak enforcement or 'benign neglect'.

After 1962 the CAP gradually extended to cover all agricultural products. It was a time of expansion and growth, at least until 1973, when coincidentally the first accessions took place. It was not until the late 1970s that the first steps were taken by the Community institutions to try and increase budgetary control, and in the process to protect the financial interests of the Community.

The first CAP regulations[7] established a common price system for cereals and regulated trade with third countries. In the 1960s and 1970s the CAP gradually extended to cover most agricultural products, including fish. Structural and guidance measures, however, were not implemented until the mid 1970s. The years 1960–73 have been described as an era of unprecedented growth and of GNP convergence within the Community.[8] It may be that the post-war consensus and economic growth helped to buttress the phasing-in of the CAP without too many questions being asked about its eventual size. At this stage of expansion of the CAP, anti-fraud enforcement did not appear to be an urgent priority for the Member States, nor Community institutions. Political concern was limited and media interest scant.

After 1973 the rate of growth of GNP in the EC fell from 4.8 per cent to 2.5 per cent between 1973 and 1979[9] and a pattern on unequal development set in following the accession of Denmark, Ireland and the United Kingdom. This change of pattern coincided with the oil crisis. Indeed Tulkens[10] remarked that fraud became an issue around the time when economic disparities began to emerge between the

---

5. Case 23/59 *FERAM* v. *High Authority* (1959) ECR 245, O.J. (1958) 22 reported in C. Harding, 'The European Community and control of criminal business activities' (1982) *International Comparative Law Quarterly*, p. 250; also verbal testimony by Professor K. Tiedemann to the House of Lords in 1989, to the effect that the checks carried out on the steel industries in the 1960s 'revealed that one third in that type of subsidised group was fictitious' (House of Lords Select Committee on the European Communities fraud against the Community (1989), p. 88).
6. K. Tiedemann, 'La fraude dans le domaine des subventions – Criminologie et politique criminelle' (1975) *Revue de Droit Pénal et de Criminologie*, pp. 137–139 in particular.
7. Council Regulations 25/62 O.J. 1962 p. 991 establishing the EAGGF and 19/62 O.J. 1962 p. 933 for the gradual organization of the markets in cereals.
8. M. Dunford, 'Winners and losers, the new map of economic inequality in the European Union' (1994) 1(2) *European Urban and Regional Studies* 95; B. Laffan, *Integration and cooperation in Europe* (1992).
9. Laffan, *op. cit.* p. 102.
10. F. Tulkens, 'Les fraudes communautaires – Un observatoire pénal européen' (1994) XVIII *Déviance et Société*, p. 219.

Member States. In 1976 a draft convention for the protection of the financial interests of the Community was rejected by the Member States. As far as the Commission was concerned '[d]uring the sixties and the seventies [it] had its hands full with obtaining and delimiting its powers and with fleshing out and consolidating them'.[11] In fact, until the Court of Auditors was created in 1977 to work alongside Parliament in order to improve budgetary control, there was no institutional mechanism to advise on budgetary control or to review anti-fraud measures.

It also seems that the secondary legislation of the day had little impact. For example, Directive 77/435[12] left up to the Member States the scope and frequency of CAP inspections. There was no common definition of fraud and the Court of Auditors somewhat ambiguously opted for the word irregularity, 'which does not presuppose the establishment of an unlawful intention and does not, therefore as strongly as the word fraud, require irrefutable proof'.[13]

3. SECOND (TRANSITIONAL) PHASE: CONTROL COORDINATION

The 1980s were a time of constant quarrels over the budget,[14] when budgetary crises were increasingly blamed on the CAP and the costs of exports and surpluses in particular were found to be 'largely responsible for the acute financial crisis of the Community'.[15] In 1980 the European Parliament refused to ratify the proposed budget until CAP expenditure, *inter alia*, was revised. From 1983 onwards the Community had difficulties balancing the books: the upwards trend in expenditure at Community level was occurring in a climate of fiscal restraint in the Member States. These successive budgetary crises have to be put in the context of the accession of three new predominantly agricultural, poorer (in EC terms) countries: Greece in 1981 and Spain and Portugal in 1986. German re-unification in 1989 also contributed to budgetary de-stabilization.[16] Meanwhile the budget more than trebled. The period between 1985 and 1992 also corresponds to a peak in legislative activity in the lead up to the internal market.[17] It is also the time when crime prevention measures began to be incorporated into economic regulation, in order to compensate for the anticipated effects of the internal market.[18]

---

11. J. Vervaele, *Fraud against the Community: The need for European fraud legislation* (1992), p. 15.
12. Council Directive 77/435: [1977] O.J. L172/17 on scrutiny by the Member States of transactions forming part of the system of financing by the Guarantee Section of the EAGGF.
13. C. Kok 'The Court of Auditors of the European Communities – The other European Court in Luxembourg' (1989) 26 *Common Market Law Review* p. 360.
14. M. Shackleton, 'Budgetary policy in transition' in L. Hurwitz and C. Lequesne (eds.), *The State of the EC* (Colorado: Lynne Rienner Pubs 1991), p. 65.
15. R. Levy, '1992: Towards better budgetary control in the EC?' (1991) 6 *Corruption and Reform* p. 289.
16. M. Shackelton, *op. cit.*
17. T. Burns, 'Better lawmaking? An evaluation of the law reform in the European Community', 1996, W G Hart Legal Workshop, London.
18. N. Dorn and S. White, 'Beyond "pillars" and "passerelle" debates – The European Union's emerging crime prevention space' (1997) *Legal Issues of European Integration*, forthcoming.

During this period, the Commission in particular started to take a much more active role in the supervision and the detection of fraud, particularly of Guarantee Section fraud (although the same funds' share of the budget started to decrease, *see* Table 1.1.). Directives were found wanting for the purpose of enforcing an anti-fraud strategy which included increased scrutiny, so regulations began to be used more frequently. Unless they are absolutely unambiguous and precise, directives have to be transcribed into the laws of the Member States, which takes time, and requires political will. The repeal of Directive 77/435[19] in favour of Council Regulation 4045/89[20] is a case in point. The Regulation explicitly requests Member States to submit their inspection programmes to the Commission for approval (Article 10) and requires scrutiny visits to be carried out on all targeted schemes.

In 1988 UCLAF[21] was created in order to coordinate efforts to tackle fraud. All fraud prevention operations extending beyond the responsibility of a single directorate were to be prepared and monitored by UCLAF.

So in this second phase, a 'secondary crime control space'[22] was established in the Community. That is to say the Community acquired limited powers and personnel to oversee the control efforts of individual Member States, which they did mostly in respect to CAP expenditure.

4. THIRD (ACTIVE) PHASE: FROM ADMINISTRATION TO PUNISHMENT?

Since the late 1980s enforcement has been stepped up. The principle of assimilation was established, as well as the right of the Commission to introduce administrative penalties of a punitive nature. In brief the administrative-control space of the 1980s has become the administrative-penal space of the 1990s. Fraud control generally acquired an 'actuarial' flavour and institutional powers were reinforced. The emphasis of control began to shift from CAP expenditure to procurement fraud affecting the Structural Funds, and the collecting of revenue, in particular import duties. However, this shift has yet to be significantly reflected in the allocation of anti-fraud appropriations at Commission level, as illustrated in Table 1.2.

---

19. [1977] O.J. L172/17.
20. Council Regulation 4045/89 [1989] L388/18 on scrutiny by Member States of transactions forming part of the system of financing by the Guarantee Section of the EAGGF.
21. *See* Decision of 20 November 1987 SEC(87) 572.
22. J. Vervaele, 'Fraude communautaire et sauvegarde du droit communautaire – Vers un droit pénal européen' (1994) Vol. XVIII number 2, *Déviance et Société*, 201–210.

*Table 1.2. Anti-fraud appropriations – comparative table
for 1994, 1995 and 1996 financial years (in thousand ECU)*

Budget areas	Budget reference	1994	1995	1996
EAGGF Guarantee Section	B1360	86,000 (62%)	85,000 (66%)	44,000 (51%)
CAP	B2	31,000 (22%)	32,500 (25%)	28,500 (33%)
Customs/ indirect taxation	B5	15,800 (11%)	3,000 (4%)	3,200 (4%)
Coordination	(not coded)	(zero)	5,000 (4%)	99,200 (11%)
Structural Funds (incl. Cohesion Funds)	B2–150 B2–301	1,050 (1%)	2,700 (0.5%)	1,050 (1%)
Training (various)	A	5,289 (4%)	4,418 (3%)	(zero)
TOTAL		139,139 (100%)	132,618 (100%)	86,670 (100%)

Sources: European Commission reports on the fight against fraud for the years 1993, 1994 and 1995.

4.1. Assimilation

Given that the Member States deal with domestic fraud differently, shouldn't they at least treat fraud and irregularities affecting the common purse on par with those affecting domestic finance? The question was asked in the 'Greek maize' case[23] and the European Court of Justice ruled that

> '... Whilst the choice of penalties remains within their discretion, they [the Member States] must ensure in particular that infringements of Community law are penalized under conditions, both procedural and substantive, which are analogous to those applicable to infringements of national law of a similar nature and importance and which, in any event, make the penalty effective, proportionate and dissuasive. Moreover, the national authorities must proceed, with respect to infringements of Community law, with the same diligence as that which they bring to bear in implementing corresponding national laws.'

Thus the principle whereby crimes affecting the Community budget had to evoke as serious a response as those affecting the national budget was articulated for the first time. The principle was later enshrined in Article 209a of the Treaty on

---

23. Case 68/88, *Commission* v. *Greece*, ECR [1989] 2965.

European Union signed at Maastricht. The first paragraph of Article 209a states that the Member States must take 'the same measures to counter fraud affecting the financial interests of the Community as they take to counter fraud affecting their own financial interests'.

The case has two serious implications. Firstly, as Delmas-Marty pointed out in 1994, there are no reliable means of finding out whether the principle has been respected or not in the Member States.[24] That is to say, it is difficult to gauge the extent to which Member States have dealt with frauds and irregularities affecting the EC budget on an equal footing with frauds and irregularities affecting the national purse, lest a test be devised for that purpose.

Secondly, De Moor[25] noted in 1992 that even if the stipulations of the Court in the 'Greek maize' case were strictly followed, very significant discrepancies would remain as between Member States in the protection afforded to the Community interests. This is because the definition of what constitutes an offence against the Community interests is determined according to the provisions of national laws, which vary greatly in their approach to Community fraud. Furthermore sanctions provided in the Member States may not be effective, proportional or dissuasive.

It became clear that to get an adequate system for preventing and sanctioning fraud against the Community a twin-track strategy would have to be pursued. Firstly the control and sanctioning power of the EC had to be increased to ensure minimum sanctions, without prejudice to any other criminal sanctions the Member States may wish to impose in addition. Secondly national provisions, sanctions and practices had to be approximated.[26] In relation to the former, the question thus began to be asked about the Community's, and in particular the Commission's, power to impose sanctions.

4.2. The Commission's Power to Punish

In the field of competition, the Commission already has a power to impose fines under Articles 65 and 66 ECSC[27] and Article 87 EEC.[28] These provisions, however, make no reference to the Community budget. In 1991 the Theato Report[29] argued, *inter alia*, that Article 172 EEC implied that the Council had a general

---

24. M. Delmas-Marty, *Rapport Final – Etude comparative des dispositions législatives, réglementaires des états membres relatives aux agissements frauduleux commis au préjudice du budget communautaire – un rapport de synthèse, étude sur les systèmes de sanctions communautaires* (1994) SEC 1994(93), p. 1172.
25. L. De Moor, 'The legal protection of the financial interests of the European Community' (1992) in *EC fraud*, ed. J. Van der Hulst, Kluwer.
26. *See* J. Vervaele, 'Subsidy fraud' (1992) in *EC fraud*, ed. J. Van der Hulst.
27. Article 65(5) authorizes the High Authority to impose fines or periodic penalty payments for a breach of the rules. Article 66(6) lays down a scale of fines from 3 per cent to 15 per cent of the value of the assets acquired.
28. Regulations and directives can be adopted in order to ensure compliance with the prohibitions laid down in Articles 85(1) and 86 EEC by making provision for fines and periodic penalty payments.
29. European Parliament, *Report of the Committee on budgetary control on the legal protection of the European Community's financial interests*, rapporteur Diemut Theato, MEP (1991).

power to include penalties in its regulations. This power was to be later confirmed by the case law of the European Court of Justice.

The Commission started to introduce sanctions in sectoral regulations, as part of its implementing powers. It did so with increasing frequency: 'ten times in 1988, seventeen in 1989, more than 30 in 1990 and as a standard practice thereafter'.[30] In 1992 the European Court of Justice gave a ruling in *Germany* v. *Commission*[31] which clarified the power of the Community in general, and of the Commission in particular, to introduce sanctions with a punitive, rather than a purely remedial or compensatory character, in the exercise of its powers to enact regulations for the common organization of agricultural markets. In this context the Court recalled its ruling in *Köster*[32] to the effect that the imposition of penalties came within the Commission's powers if the Council had not reserved such powers to itself. The penalties laid down by Community law are meant to be enforced by the national authorities and not (as it the case in area of competition) by the Community institutions themselves.

This, in turn, raised the question as to the nature of the sanctions to be applied in the Member States. In the early 1990s, one of the burning issues raised was whether the Commission had any power to impose particular criminal sanctions to be applied in the Member States in order to protect the financial interests of the European Communities.

Community law as it stands does not give the Community the power to lay down criminal penalties, although Articles 100 and 100A enable the Council to adopt measures for the approximation of the measures laid down by law, regulation or administrative action in Member States which have as their object the establishment and functioning of the internal market. Article 100A has been used, for example, as the legal basis for the Money Laundering Directive,[33] which resulted in Member States setting up rules aimed at their financial and credit institutions, and creating specific offences. The more contentious Article 235 EC also allows the Council to take appropriate measures when the Treaty has not provided the necessary powers for doing so.

Generally the regulation of financial crime falls into the penal-administrative sphere, which means that the distinction between criminal and administrative penalties is blurred. The European Court of Justice has hitherto not been drawn into ruling on the exact nature of Community sanctions. However, it ruled in *Könecke* that what mattered was that the penalty, whatever its label, ensured the effective implementation of the regulation in question, and that it be imposed on a 'clear and unambiguous legal basis'.[34]

---

30. J. Heine, 'Community penalties in agriculture and fisheries – Legislative activity in the Commission' (1994) in *The legal protection of the financial interests of the Community: Progress and prospects since the Brussels seminar of 1989*, p. 18.
31. Case C-240/90, *Germany* v. *Commission*, [1992] ECR I-5383.
32. Case 25/70, *Einfuhr- und Voratsstelle für Getreide und Futtermittel* v. *Köster, Berodt & Co*, preliminary ruling ECR [1970] 1161.
33. Council Directive 91/308: [1991] L166/77.
34. Case 117/83, *Könecke GmbH and Co KG v Bundesanstalt für Landwirtschaftliche Marktordnung*, [1984] ECR 3291, para. 11.

The third phase of anti-fraud enforcement is also the time when surveillance is organized, and modern techniques are used to control fraud.

4.3. Actuarial Measures

Increasingly in the third phase measures with a strong actuarial flavour were incorporated into regulations and surveillance became an important feature of enforcement, with the help of funds made available to the Member States specifically for the financing of remote sensing equipment and surveillance operations.[35] Detailed information has to be provided to the Commission on detected cases of irregularities.[36] Under Regulation 4045/89,[37] for example, Member States must carry out an audit control programme on all traders in receipt of EAGGF funds. Risk analysis and targeting are methods increasingly used by the Member States' authorities responsible for enforcement, such as the Intervention Board for Agricultural Produce in the United Kingdom. Risk analysis involves the collecting and analysis of financial data, histories of irregularities and investigations and scrutiny visits.[38] Application of the technique of risk analysis together with a systems audit, makes it possible to confine inspections to sensitive areas and to 'high risk' operations and/or recipients, identifying those control structures in the Member States which ought to be strengthened.[39] In 1994 the Commission issued a further Regulation (3122/94)[40] laying down the exact criteria (with regards to products receiving refunds) according to which high risk sectors could be targeted. Sectors vary from Member State to Member State. In the UK, for example in 1995 milk quotas, beef and cereals were targeted sectors for enforcement. Finance was made available to Member States implementing these measures, through Regulation 307/91,[41] which provided for additional funds to be made available for the control of a number of high risk areas for five years. Regulation 4045/89[42] provided for funds to be made available for the training of scrutiny officers and the setting up of computer systems to carry out the scrutiny programme.

In 1990 for the first time minima were set for the inspection of goods in the Member States: Council Regulation 386/90[43] imposed a duty on Member States to inspect 5 per cent of all goods presented for export.

---

35. European Commission, *Protecting the financial interests of the European Community – the fight against fraud, 1993 Annual Report* (1994).
36. Article 3(1) of Council Regulation 595/91: [1991] O.J. L67/11.
37. [1989] O.J. L388/18, *op. cit.*
38. Intervention Board Anti-Fraud Unit, *1993 Annual Report* (1994).
39. EC (1994) *op. cit.*
40. Commission Regulation 3122/94: [1994] O.J. L330/31 laying down criteria for risk analysis as regards agricultural products receiving refunds.
41. Council Regulation 307/91: [1991] O.J. L37/5 on reinforcing the monitoring of certain expenditure chargeable to the Guarantee Section of the EAGGF. Article 2 specifies that the Community's financial contribution towards the remuneration of supplementary agents and equipment shall be 50 per cent for the first three years and 25 per cent for the fourth and fifth years.
42. *Op. cit.*
43. [1990] O.J. L42.

15

4.4. The Uneven Nature of Control in the Third Phase

The stepping up of enforcement against EC fraud in the third phase fell mostly upon the EAGGF Guarantee Section Fund. Member States were still reluctant to establish control systems for Structural Funds identical to those in place to protect the Guarantee Section Fund. In July 1993 the Council adopted six Structural Funds regulations[44] to strengthen the principles of concentration, partnership, programming and additionality. This had the effect of bringing Structural Funds fraud enforcement into a phase corresponding to the second control-coordination phase described earlier with respect to the EAGGF Guarantee Section Fund. This is because reinforced partnership means closer collaboration between the Commission and all the relevant authorities at national, regional or local level. Reinforced programming[45] means that Member States had to start submitting detailed programming documents, complete with specific objectives to be attained, and detailed financial tables showing national and Community finance. Finally, in view of prior difficulties in implementing the additionality[46] principle, the revised Coordination Regulation stipulated that each Member State had to maintain, in the whole of the territory concerned, its public structural or comparable expenditure at least at the same level as in the previous programming period, taking into account, however, 'the macro economic circumstances in which the funding takes place' – this last concept being rather difficult to unwrap. The Member States also acquired a duty to provide the financial information needed to verify additionality when submitting plans during the implementation of the Community Support Frameworks.

The principle of co-financing is considered to be an important tool in the control of fraud. It is felt that Member States have more incentive to prevent and prosecute fraud when a proportion of purely national finance is directly involved in the projects. However, specific problems remain, which are explored in Chapter 4.

As far as the control of income fraud is concerned, this remained a neglected area (*see* Chapter 3) until more ambitious plans were formulated for the protection of the financial interests of the Community.

---

44. Council Regulations 2080/93: [1993] O.J. L130/1 (FIFG Regulation); 2081/93: [1993] O.J. L193/5 (Framework Regulation); 2082/93: [1993] O.J. L193/20 (Coordination Regulation); 2083/93: [1993] O.J. L193/24 (ERDF Regulation); 2084/94: [1993] O.J. L193/39 (ESF Regulation) and 2085/93: [1993] O.J. L193/44 (EAGGF – Guidance Section Regulation).
45. The last subparagraph in Article 5(2) of Regulation 4253/88 foresees that in order to simplify and to speed up programming procedures, Member States may submit in a Single Programming Document (SPD) the information required for the regional and social conversion plan referred to in Article 9(8) of Regulation 2052/88 and information required in Article 14(2) of Regulation 4253/88.
46. The principle of additionality means that Community assistance should complement the contributions of the Member State rather than reducing them. For a discussion on the application of additionality in the Member States *see* S. White and N. Dorn, 'EC fraud, subsidiarity and prospects for the IGC: A regional dimension?' (1996) 3(3) *European Urban and Regional Studies*, 262–266.

5. FOURTH (AMBITIOUS) PHASE

The approach to fraud control until the mid 1990s has been described as 'atom-istic'[47] or 'fragmentary'.[48] In addition to possibly encouraging the possibility of displacement in criminal activities, the sector by sector approach has the drawback of adding to the complexity of the regulatory environment. This 'atomistic' response to fraud was felt to be inadequate. The main elements of the contemporaneous 'ambitious' phase are the stepping up of cooperation, the integration of control, the reinforcement of Commission powers of inspection and a recognition of the international and of the organized crime dimension of fraud and corruption, and of their money laundering implications.

5.1. The Stepping Up of Cooperation

In 1994 the cooperation between Member States and Commission was stepped up. The Commission set up an advisory committee for the coordination of fraud preven-tion, consisting of two representatives working alongside anti-fraud services in each of the Member States. In November 1994 the Commission also set up a free phone service to encourage the reporting of fraud and set aside 200,000 ECU to reward informants. According to the Commission, payments to informants are relatively modest and correspond to the value of the information, and each informant is checked against an independent source before being paid. Unlike the situation which now prevails in the competition field, participating informants who are guilty of fraud enjoy no privileges, and cannot expect a lighter fine. The free phone service has proved successful. In addition, the 'Black List' Regulation places duties on Member States to notify the Commission (who in turn notifies other Member States) and under certain circumstances, to exclude traders from funding for periods of up to five years. The political significance of the Regulation is very considerable since it establishes a Community system requiring Member States to circulate information on certain operators and to adopt preventive measures. The potential of blacklisting to damage traders' interests should not be underestimated, although it must be remembered that it is confined, in the 'Black List' Regulation, to cases of irregular-ities exceeding 100,000 ECU over a one-year period (*see* Chapter 4).

5.2. Integration of Control

Several instruments have been put forward, but not all are in force at the time of writing. Taken together, they represent a giant step forward, in that they seek to reduce control disparities between sectors (through 'horizontal' first pillar instru-

---

47. *See* for example J-C Marin, 'Legal protection of the Community's financial interests – Experience and prospects since the Brussels seminar of 1989' (1994) in *Legal protection of the Community's financial interests: Experience and prospects since the Brussels seminar of 1989*, Oak Tree Press, Dublin, pp. 204–207. [Both book and article have the same title.]
48. M. Darras, 'Le Parlement Européen et la protection juridique des intérêts financiers de la Commu-nauté Européenne' (1992) in *EC fraud*, ed. J. Van der Hulst.

ments, which cut across most sectors of the budget), and disparities between the Member States' criminalization of EC fraud (through third pillar instruments).

Council Regulation 2988/95: harmonization of administrative sanctions. In 1995 a significant step forward was taken. A 'horizontal' Regulation on the protection of the European Communities' financial interests[49] (or 'PIF'[50] Regulation) was adopted under Article 235, which framed the whole range of Community sanctions and established rules for the interface of national criminal laws and Community administrative sanctions.

The 'PIF' Regulation (*see* appendix B) sets out a legal framework for Community administrative sanctions. It starts by giving the Member States a common definition of 'irregularity'. Irregularity in this context means any infringement of Community law resulting from an act or omission by an economic operator, which has, or would have, the effect of prejudicing the general budget of the Communities or budgets managed by them, either by reducing or losing revenues accruing from own resources collected directly on behalf of the Communities, or by an unjustified item of expenditure.[51] 'Resources collected directly on behalf of the Communities' excludes VAT, a small proportion of which only comes indirectly into the budget of the Communities. For the purpose of applying the Regulation, criminal proceedings may be regarded as having been completed where the competent national authority and the person concerned have come to an arrangement.[52]

The Regulation also lists Community sanctions available to national authorities for intentional irregularities.[53] These vary from the payment of an administrative fine to a loss of security or deposit.[54] Such sanctions may be suspended if criminal proceedings have been initiated against the person concerned in connection with the same facts.[55] A limitation period of four years is set for proceedings.[56] In its third title, the Regulation adopt general rules for checks, whether they be performed by the Member States, or the Communities' institutions. In its third title, concerned with checks, it refers to more detailed provisions concerning on-the-spot checks and inspections to be adopted discreetly.[57]

'PIF' Convention: harmonization of criminal sanctions. The 1976 project[58] for a Convention on the Protection of Community Financial Interests of the European

---

49. Council Regulation 2988/95: [1995] O.J. L312/1.
50. From the French 'Protection des Intérêts Financiers'.
51. Article 1(2) of Council Regulation 2988/95: [1995] O.J. L312/1.
52. Eleventh Preamble of the 'PIF' Regulation: [1995] O.J. L312/1.
53. Article 5 of 'PIF' Regulation.
54. Article 5(1)(a) and (f) of 'PIF' Regulation.
55. Article 6(1) of 'PIF' Regulation.
56. Article 3(1) of 'PIF' Regulation.
57. *See* Article 10 of 'PIF' Regulation.
58. *See* Draft for a Treaty amending the Treaties establishing the European Communities so as to permit the adoption of common rules on the protection under criminal law of the financial interests of the Communities and the prosecution of infringements of the provisions of those Treaties and amending the Treaty establishing a Single Council and a Single Commission of the European Communities so as to permit the adoption of common rules on the liability and protection under Criminal Law of Officials and other Servants of the European Communities: [1976] O.J. C222.

Communities was resurrected in the early 1990s. The final text was agreed in July 1995 under the French Presidency of the Council, and published in the *Official Journal* in November 1995.[59] It has yet to be ratified. The Convention defines the concept of fraud affecting the EC budget, lays an obligation on the Member States to provide criminal penalties in cases of serious fraud, including custody for cases involving over 50,000 ECU. The signatories will also have to make provisions in their national laws for heads of businesses to be declared criminally liable in case of fraud. It lays a duty on the Member States to cooperate in deciding which State will prosecute. This requirement has in view the 'centralization' of prosecution in a single Member State where possible. Furthermore, Member States will have a duty to transmit to the Commission the text of the provisions transposing into their domestic law the obligations imposed on them under the provisions of this Convention. The European Court of Justice has jurisdiction to decide on disputes between Member States if no solution is found within six months.

On-the-spot checks Regulation: Commission powers reinforced. A Regulation concerning on-the-Spot Checks and Inspections was adopted in November 1996.[60]

The Regulation authorizes the Commission to send Commission officials to carry out on-the-spot checks at central, regional or local level on any economic operator directly or indirectly receiving a financial benefit from the European Communities. The Regulation also defines the powers and duties of Commission inspectors. Officials of the Member State may take part in the inspections. The Commission may ask officials of Member States other than that on whose territory inspections and checks are being performed to take part in them. The Commission may also resort to outside bodies to provide technical help.[61] All information collected is covered by the rule of confidentiality and the Community's provisions on data protection.[62] It is envisaged that this regulation will help to speed up the investigation of complex transnational cases.

> '[The] entry into force of the Regulation should make the beginning of a new phase of Community legislation designed to define more clearly the Community's powers of inquiry at sectoral level, through new regulations or the refinement of existing regulations.'[63]

The Regulation reinforces the Commission's existing powers of inspection, and some Member States believe that this places the Commission at the limit of, or

---

59. Convention on the Protection of the European Communities' Financial Interests: [1995] O.J. C316/48.
60. Council Regulation 2185/96: [1996] O.J. L192/2, concerning on-the-spot checks and inspections carried out by the Commission in order to protect the European Communities' financial interests against fraud and other irregularities.
61. Articles 3 to 6 of Council Regulation 2185/96: [1996], O.J. L292/2.
62. Article 8 of Council Regulation 2185/96.
63. European Parliament, *Report (Consultation Procedure) on the proposal concerning on-the-sport checks and inspections by the Commission for the detection of frauds and irregularities detrimental to the financial interests of the European Communities, rapporteur: Diemut Theato, MEP* (1996).

beyond its powers of direct intervention in the Member States. Notwithstanding the extension of inspection powers proposed in the Regulation, checks will continue to rest and depend on the principle of cooperation with national agencies and officials.

Protocols to the 'PIF' Convention. Two protocols have been added to the 'PIF' Convention. They deal respectively with money laundering and judicial cooperation and with the corruption of EC and national officials, in cases involving EC funds.

A proposition for a protocol to the 'PIF' Convention was adopted by the Commission in December 1995. It deals with money laundering and judicial cooperation. It lays out the responsibility of legal persons and criminalizes the laundering of fraud profits. It gives detailed rules for direct judicial cooperation and for determining which Member State takes the lead role for prosecution of transnational frauds. It lays out the competence of the European Court of Justice.

As the emphasis of control shifted to trade rather than farming, corrupt practices were increasingly highlighted in cases. For example, procurement frauds affecting the Structural Funds, and the evasion of duties were often carried with the connivance of officials. An anti-corruption protocol was added to the 'PIF' Convention. A more ambitious instrument, an anti-corruption convention still under discussion in 1997, proposes to extend the measures contained in the Protocol, whether the financial interests of the European Communities are involved or not. These measures are examined in detail in Chapter 6, which deals specifically with the fight against corruption.

5.3. Conclusion

In the 1980s it became apparent that the fast-enlarging Community budget attracted commensurate fraud, so measures to counter fraud affecting the EC budget were increasingly incorporated into sectoral regulations. These sectoral regulations place duties on the Member States to take appropriate measures to prevent irregularities, such as surveillance or checks based on risk analysis, but also to report certain irregularities and recover funds.[64] For instance a 1995 sectoral regulation agreed on the basis of Article 43, the 'Black List'[65] Regulation, targets traders claiming from the EAGGF Guarantee Section.

One effect of this sectoral approach has been that more attention has been paid to policing certain sectors of the EC budget than to others. On the income side of the budget, Member States are likely to carry on resisting any Commission interference with their sovereign right to raise taxes.

The unevenness of the control space was finally addressed through the 'PIF' Regulation,[66] which confirmed the effectiveness of this system of penalties already

---

64. Council Regulations 729/70: [1970] O.J. L94; 283/72: [1972] O.J. L36; 595/91: [1991] O.J. L67; 4253/88: [1988] O.J. L374; 1164/94: [1994] O.J. L130; Commission Regulations 1681/94: [1994] O.J. L178 and 1831/94: [1994] O.J. L191.

65. Council Regulation 1469/95: [1995] O.J. L145/1 implemented by Commission Regulation 745/96: [1996] O.J. L102/15.

66. Council Regulation 2988/95: [1995] O.J. L312/1 ('PIF' Regulation).

in place for the Common Agricultural Policy and drew on the impetus provided by the Council's call for the introduction of Community administrative penalties in areas other than agriculture.[67] Due to the near-collapse of the transit system, attention began to shift more noticeably to traders unlawfully claiming refunds or evading duties and the computerization of the transit system was planned. However, it is noticeable that anti-fraud appropriations dropped significantly in 1996. The financing for the central development of the computerization of the transit system, for example (under B5) was greatly reduced during the course of the 1996 budgetary procedure, casting doubts as to whether the system will be operational in 1998 as originally planned.[68] Thus budgetary considerations continue to play a key role in the fight against fraud.

67. European Commission, *Protecting the Community's financial interests – The fight against fraud, Annual Report for 1995* (1996), COM(96) 173, p. 11.
68. European Commission, *Rapport Intermédiaire sur le transit* (1996) SEC(96) 1739, Annex V.

Chapter 2. The Institutions and the Fight Against Fraud

1. POWERS AND RESPONSIBILITIES, AGENDA FOR CHANGE

As part of the consultation process leading to the IGC, the institutions have taken the opportunity, *inter alia*, to highlight some of the conundra and difficulties they experience in relation to the protection of EC finance. They have, at times, been able to make very specific proposals for change (*see* for example the European Court of Auditors). This chapter considers the existing powers and responsibilities of the institutions with respect to fraud control (without going into the intricacies of the budgetary process itself) and discusses the agenda for change arising from the work carried out in preparation for the IGC.[1]

2. THE COMMISSION

The Commission is the executive organ of the Communities,[2] and also its budgetary authority.[3] Its duties go beyond mere implementation of legislation, since it can make legislative proposals on its own initiative. Its power is however circumscribed,[4] since it may not make any proposals with appreciable budgetary implications unless it can guarantee that the proposal could be financed within the limits of the revenue available.

Unlike a national or a federal executive, the Commission has no tax-raising powers. The Member States are responsible for the collecting and making available of their GNP and VAT contributions, as well as Customs and other duties to the Community budget. Furthermore, the Commission only spends a small proportion of the budget directly. The Member States are responsible for the collecting and making available of revenue, and also for most of the budget expenditure. The Commission also depends on the Member States for the protection of the financial interests of the European Communities, and has endeavoured to find out how such

---

1. *See also* S. White, 'Reflections on the IGC and the protection of the financial interests of the EC' (1995) 10 *AGON*, 10–13.
2. Article 155 EC.
3. Articles 203(3) EC and 205 EC.
4. Article 201a EC.

protection works in practice.[5] In this the work of the national associations of lawyers for the protection of the financial interests of the European Communities,[6] with their journal *AGON* acting as a conduit for discussion and information, must be noted.

The Commission works closely with its budgetary control 'partners' (Council and European Parliament) through the budgetary control committee. The relationship of the Commission with the European Court of Auditors, often in the past strained by long drawn-out contradictory procedures,[7] has now improved.

2.1. IGC Agenda

The position of the Commission in relation to the protection of the financial interests of the European Communities, it suggests in its IGC report, remains paradoxical on two grounds.[8] Firstly, at the moment Council measures to control expenditure and combat fraud require an unanimous vote,[9] whereas a qualified majority is enough to act as the budgetary authority and determine expenditure and revenue levels.[10] This means that potentially one Member State can veto a measure aiming to protect the financial interests of the European Communities, whilst no such possibility exists in the determination of revenue or expenditure. Secondly, the Commission alone is responsible for budget execution,[11] whereas the management of expenditure is mostly decentralized.

Notwithstanding the paradoxical position the Commission finds itself in, it has been able to improve the coordination of its anti-fraud work through the work of UCLAF and COCOLAF.

---

5. A series of reports have been commissioned by D-G XX (Financial Control) in each Member State, followed by synthesis reports: for example, in 1993, report of the study on the systems of administrative and criminal penalties of the Member States and general principles applicable to Community penalties SEC(93) 1172 (known as the 'Delmas-Marty Report'); in 1995 Comparative analysis of the reports supplied by the Member States on national measures taken to combat wastefulness and the misuse of Community resources, November; also in 1995, report on Whistle blowing, fraud and the European Union (synthesis carried out by Public Concern at Work); in 1996, *La transaction dans l'Union Européenne, rapport de synthèse* (known as 'Labayle Report').
6. The first association was constituted in Italy in October 1990, and by 1993 all Member States had an association. *See also* L. De Moor, 'The Associations of Lawyers for the Protection of the Financial Interests of the European Community' (Speech to the founding symposium of the European Criminal Law association) (1993) in *Europäische Einigung und Europäisches Strafrecht*, ed. U. Sieber, Carl Heymanns Verlag, Bonn, 29–33.
7. This procedure involves audit letters and reports being sent to the auditee with a request for a written reply within a given time-limit. The reply may be preceded by bilateral discussions in order to clarify any matters in dispute. In keeping with this practice, the Annual Report of the ECA includes responses from the institutions.
8. *See* European Commission Préparation CIG 1996 contribution du Conseil, information aux délégations extérieures de la Commission, info-note number 20/95 (1995); also European Commission Report on the operation of the Treaty of the European Union (1995) SEC (95) 731 Final.
9. For example under Article 235 EC and 209 EC.
10. Article 203 EC.
11. Articles 205 EC and 201a EC.

2.2. The Work of UCLAF

Since 1988 the Commission has been assisted in its fight against fraud by UCLAF (the coordinating unit for the fight against fraud), set up in order to replace the inter-service group responsible for on-the-spot checks which was attached to DG XX (Financial Control). The unit's main aim when it came into existence was to coordinate anti-fraud policy and effort within the Commission. To emphasize the general broad-based nature of its duties, it was decided to place UCLAF within the Secretariat General of the Commission rather than within an existing Directorate-General.[12] The majority of the 130 UCLAF personnel have been employed, in their respective Member States, in Customs, Police services with responsibility for financial crime, national audit offices, agricultural ministries' verification departments, etc.[13]

UCLAF is responsible to the Commission for all aspects of the fight against fraud affecting the budget. It is split into six divisions, dealing respectively with legislation, intelligence gathering, Structural Funds, Own Resources, and two separate divisions handling agriculture. Its operational mission is primarily to support the Member States where they need co-ordination with other Member States and the relevant services of the Commission. UCLAF fulfils its mission mainly by investigation into suspected fraud cases with the aim of both establishing the sums at risk to be recovered and preparing a case suitable for submission to public prosecutors in the Member States. Such cases are entered into UCLAF's IRENE database and now number over 20,000.[14] Whilst UCLAF has the power to request that investigations be carried out by the competent services of the Member States involved, it may also take the lead in an investigation, while maintaining co-operation with the Member States concerned. This course of action is taken when the investigation cannot be carried out effectively without coordination with other Member States; for example, where elements of an important fraudulent operation appear to exist in various Member States simultaneously, or where evidence has to be obtained outside the Community. UCLAF also takes part in bringing forward legislative proposals which tighten legislative loopholes, seek equivalent treatment of EU fraud at both the administrative and criminal level, and give the Commission the power to undertake on-the-spot controls.

2.3. COCOLAF

In 1994 an advisory Committee for the coordination of fraud prevention was set up under Article 209a.[15] The Commission consults the Committee, made up of two representatives from each Member State, on matters relating to the prevention and

---

12. *See* B. Knudsen, 'Global programme of the European Community's fight against fraud' (1994) in *The legal protection of the financial interests of the Community: Progress and prospects since the Brussels seminar of 1989*, pp. 247–251.
13. *See* European Commission, UCLAF 17 questions on fraud (1996).
14. *See* newspaper article: 'Commission fraudbusters hot on the scent of misused Union funds' (feature) in *European Voice*, 10–16 October 1996, page 19.
15. Commission decision 94/140: [1994] O.J. L61/27.

the prosecution of fraud affecting the EC budget. This can be seen as an addition to the 'sectoral' Committee approach adopted hitherto, and thus an attempt to deal with the protection of the financial interests of the European Communities cross-sectorially.

3. THE EUROPEAN COURT OF AUDITORS

In view of the key role played by the European Court of Auditors in highlighting financial mismanagement and fraud, a slightly longer section is dedicated to its role and agenda for change.

3.1. Duties and Powers

The creation in 1977 of a Court of Auditors, with specific responsibility for the external audit[16] of Community revenue and expenditure, followed from the creation of an autonomous budget of the European Communities, separate from those of the Member States, and managed by the European Institutions.[17] Since the implementation of the Treaty on European Union, the now re-named European Court of Auditors (ECA henceforth) occupies the rank of European Institution together with the Commission, Council, the Court of Justice and the European Parliament.[18] This means, *inter alia*, that the ECA now has the power to defend its own opinions against other Community institutions in law. It acts as an external, independent auditor of European public finances. The ECA is a collegiate body[19] without judicial, or decision-making powers.[20] Notwithstanding these institutional constraints, it has been coined as 'the financial conscience' of the Union[21] and more colourfully by the media as 'the watchdog snapping at the heels of the institutions'.[22] As such it acts as a catalyst in the fight against waste and fraud. The ECA's institutional presence, however, is felt mostly through its reports and

---

16. An external audit is carried out by a body which is external to and independent of the auditee, the purpose being to give an opinion on and report on the accounts and the financial statements, the regularity and legality of operations, and/or the financial management (*see* P. Everard and D. Wolter, *Glossary Selection of terms and expressions used in the external audit of the public sector* (1989)).
17. The Court of Auditors of the European Communities (now European Court of Auditors) was created by the Treaty of 22 July 1975, signed in Brussels, but did not become operational until 25 October 1977 when it took over from the EEC and Euratom Audit Board and from the ECSC Auditor.
18. Article 4 EC.
19. Article 188c(4) EC, third indent replacing Article 206b (3) EEC states that 'It [The Court] shall adopt its annual reports, special reports or opinions by a majority of its members'.
20. *See* P. Bugnot, 'La cour des comptes des communautés européennes – Premier bilan' (1982) *Revue du Marché Commun* 609–623.
21. Court of Auditors, *op. cit.* (1995) pp. 8–12.
22. *See* newspaper article: 'Watchdog snapping at the heels of the institutions' in *European Voice*, 10–16 October 1996, page 19.

opinions,[23] and as such its power is one of persuasion in relation to the Commission in particular.

Generally speaking, the ECA has a duty to assist the European Parliament and the Council in exercising their powers of control over the implementation of the budget,[24] a task carried out mainly within the procedure for the discharge in respect of the implementation of the budget.[25] This includes submitting observations, particularly in the form of Special Reports, on specific questions and delivering opinions at the request of one of the other institutions of the Community.[26] The ECA draws up an Annual Report after the close of each financial year, which is forwarded to the other institutions of the Community and is published, together with the replies of these institutions, in the *Official Journal of the European Communities*.[27] The nature of the ECA's role and responsibilities point to a natural alliance with the European Parliament, and a constant dialogue with the Commission, whose responsibility it is to maintain budgetary discipline in accordance with the principle of sound financial management and to implement the budget.[28]

It has been suggested that the powers of the ECA, which have already helped to improve Community financial procedures, have only marginally changed since 1977.[29] Be that as it may, the bulk of the work undertaken by the ECA has increased in line with the budget. At present it employs some 250 staff to audit revenue and expenditure representing approximately 4–5 per cent of the total budgets of all the Member States.[30] The European budget alone has been multiplied by a factor of 2.7 in ten years, rising from 28,800 million ECU in 1985 to 79,800 million ECU in 1995.[31] The ECA carries out the audit[32] which is based on records, and if necessary, performed on the spot at the institutions of the Communities and in the Member States.[33] It examines the accounts of all revenue and expenditure of all bodies set up by the Community for legality and correctness in so far as the relevant constituent instrument does not preclude such examination.[34] It also examines whether financial management has been sound.[35]

---

23. The most important of these is the Annual Report, published in the *Official Journal* in November each year.
24. Article 188c (4) EC, fourth subparagraph.
25. Article 206(1) EC.
26. Article 188c(4) EC, second subparagraph.
27. Article 188c (4) EC, first subparagraph.
28. Articles 201 and 205 EC; Article 22(1), first subparagraph of the Financial Regulation.
29. J. Church and P. Phinnemore, *European Union and European Community – A handbook and Commentary on the post-Maastricht Treaties* (1994) pp. 292–294.
30. European Court of Auditors, *The European Court of Auditors – Auditing the finances of the European Union* (1995) p. 13.
31. English version of the Report by the Court of Auditors to the 'Reflection Group' on the operation of the Treaty on European Union, May 1995, page 2.
32. Article 188a EC.
33. Article 188c (3) EC, first subparagraph.
34. Article 188c (1) EC, first subparagraph. The principal bodies audited on this basis are: the general budget of the Union and of the EEA, Community loans and borrowings, the Euratom Supply Agency, the European Centre for the Development of Vocational Training in Berlin, the European Foundation for the Improvement of Living and Working Conditions in Dublin, the European Schools, JET (Joint European Torus – research project on thermonuclear fusion), the EAC (European Association for Cooperation).

The Treaty on European Union has added one new element to the ECA's tasks. It is now required to provide the European Parliament and the Council with a Statement of Assurance (SOA or DAS) as to the reliability of the accounts and the legality and regularity of the underlying transactions.[36] The specific role of the ECA in testing the integrity of financial systems takes on even more importance in the light of this new duty. The first SOA[37] was delivered in November 1995 and found that the accounts for 1994 accurately reflected the revenue and expenditure, as well as the financial situation, of the Union, although their informative value should be improved. However, it was not possible to give an assurance that all chargeable imports had actually been declared and had yielded the corresponding revenue. With regard to the expenditure part of the budget, there were too many errors in the transactions underlying the payments entered in the accounts for the court to be able to be able to give a positive global assurance of their legality/regularity. This, one would assume, sets the tone for future SOAs.

In the introduction to its 1993 Annual Report, the ECA points out that many of the problems it identified in accounting and financial management in 1983 had not yet been overcome. The ECA deplored that the development of Community activities had not been accompanied, either in the Commission or in the Member States, by a commensurate development of the necessary financial management. Furthermore, control systems and insufficient resources, both in quantity and in quality, had been allocated to ensuring the best use of public money.[38] As a rule, it seems that the follow-up of reports has been largely unsatisfactory,[39] and that the ECA's influence has left something to be desired.

3.2. The ECA's Consultative Role

The present system distinguishes between compulsory and optional consultation. Under Article 209 EC, the ECA must be consulted during the legislative process with respect to financial regulations – when they specify a procedure to be adopted for establishing the budget and for presenting and auditing accounts,[40] when the methods and procedures with regards to cash payments are being determined,[41] and finally when rules on the responsibility of financial controllers, authorizing officers, and concerning appropriate arrangements for inspection are concerned.[42] These are,

---

35. Article 188c(2) EC, first subparagraph; Article 2 of the Financial Regulation states that the budget appropriations must be used in accordance with the principles of sound financial management, and in particular those of economy and cost-effectiveness. Quantified objectives must be identified and the progress of their realization monitored.
36. Article 188c(1) EC, second subparagraph.
37. European Court of Auditors, *Statement of Assurance concerning activities financed from the general budget for the financial year 1994* (1995).
38. Court of Auditors Annual Report for the 1993 financial year, *see supra*, page 5.
39. *See* D. O'Keefe, 'The Court of Auditors', in *Institutional dynamics of European integration – Essays in honour of Henry G. Schermers* (1994) Volume II, eds. D. Curtin and T. Heukels, p. 183.
40. Article 209(a) EC.
41. Article 209 (b) EC.
42. Article 209(c) EC.

in fact, quite limited circumstances obliging the other institutions of the Union to consult the ECA.

The ECA *may* be consulted on matters not covered under Article 209. Under Article 188c(4) EC the ECA may, at any time, submit observations, particularly in the form of special reports, on specific questions and deliver opinions at the request of one of the institutions of the Community.[43] These special reports usually record the audit results obtained in specific management areas. In fact, it looks as if only moderate use is made of the option to seek an opinion from the ECA. Out of 66 opinions produced between 1977 and 1990, 48 were produced under Article 209 (the compulsory procedure) and only 18 under Article 206a EEC (the optional procedure).[44] The ECA also produces reports *sui generis.*

Sitting rather uncertainly between those circumstances when other Community bodies must consult the ECA and those when they may, there has arisen an intermediate category of uncertain obligation, which perhaps we may call *good intentions*. For example, an agreement had been concluded between the Commission and the ECA whereby the European Commission undertook, firstly, to propose that the Council should consult the ECA regarding any proposals which have a significant effect on the financial and budgetary mechanisms of the Communities and, secondly, to consult the ECA with regard to any similar measures within the scope of its own powers. But, according to Strasser, it seems that this agreement has had hardly any effect.[45] As a result the ECA was not asked for an opinion on the draft Regulation on the protection of the Community's financial interests.[46] Undeterred, the ECA produced an opinion in February 1995.[47] This opinion was not, however, published in the *Official Journal*. It is not surprising that, in its submissions to the IGC Reflection Group, the ECA asked for the compulsory procedure to be extended to any draft legislation which affects the Community's budgetary and financial mechanisms, particularly if they involve financial control.

3.3. Budgetary Control

The ECA objects to basic principles of financial control being flouted. The principle of separation of roles in financial control, and the principle of budgetary unity in particular, have an important role to play in fraud (and corruption) prevention. The separation of roles means that the different roles of the various financial officers managing the funds be clearly defined and mutually exclusive. The principle of budgetary unity requires that all financial transactions concerning a public body be

43. Article 206a (4) EEC, second subparagraph was replaced by Article 188c (4) EC, second subparagraph. The phrase 'particularly in the form of special reports' was added to the latter for clarification.
44. *See* D. Strasser, *The finances of Europe* (1991) p. 277.
45. *Ibid.* p. 277.
46. Council Regulation 2988/95 ('PIF' Regulation): [1995] O.J. L312/1.
47. European Court of Auditors, *Observations de la Cour des Comptes sur la proposition de règlement (CE, EURATOM) relatif à la protection des intérêts financiers des Communautés ainsi que sur une proposition d'acte portant établissement de la convention relative à la protection des intérêts financiers des Communautés* (1995) Document COM (94) 214 final of 15 June 1994.

brought into a single document known as its budget, which is then voted on by its budgetary authority.[48] Some attention is now paid to these principles and to their importance for the development of a Union whose activities, rather than being criminogenic, must be transparent, democratic, and cost-effective.

3.3.1. Principle of Separation of Roles in Internal Control[49]

One basic principle of financial control is that the management of funds be kept separate from the monitoring of their utilization. This basic principle of financial control is flouted when the function of independent surveillance is carried out by the same department whose expenditure is to be scrutinized.

In relation to the European budget this means that the duties of the authorizing officer, financial controller and accounting officer are mutually incompatible.[50] The authorizing officer alone is empowered to enter into commitments regarding expenditure, to establish entitlements to be collected and issue recovery orders and payment orders.[51] Each institution has an accounting officer, who is responsible for the collection of revenue and the payment of expenditure.[52] The accounting officer alone is empowered to manage moneys and other assets and is responsible for their safekeeping. The financial controller is responsible for monitoring the commitment and authorization of all expenditure and the establishment and collection of all revenue. The financial controller acts as 'internal auditor' and is thus responsible for monitoring the commitment and authorization of all expenditure and the establishment and collection of all revenue.[53]

Title V of the Financial Regulation only offers vague definitions of the roles of financial officers. However, Article 126 of the Regulation requires that '[I]n consultation with the European Parliament and the Council and after the other institutions have delivered their opinions, the Commission shall adopt implementing measures for this Financial Regulation.' This requirement is reiterated in Article 209(c) EC: '[T]he Council ... shall ... lay down rules concerning the responsibility of financial controllers, authorizing officers and accounting officers, and concerning appropriate arrangements for inspection.'

Although they have been hailed as a priority by the ECA for several years,[54] such implementing rules have yet to be agreed. As a result there sometimes occurs a 'slippage' in the separation of functions within the system of internal financial

---

48. Article 199 EC; Article 4 of the Financial Regulation; also V. Schmitt, *Dix ans de travaux de la cour des comptes européenne – Essai de typologie* (1988) pp. 282–283; Strasser, *op. cit.* p. 42.
49. Internal control is defined as 'all the procedures and means making it possible to comply with the budget and the rules in force, to safeguard assets, ensure the accuracy and reliability of accounting data and facilitate management decisions, in particular by making financial information available at the appropriate time.' (P. Everard and D. Wolter, *op. cit.*).
50. Article 21, fourth subparagraph of the Financial Regulation.
51. Article 21 of the Financial Regulation.
52. Article 25 of the Financial Regulation.
53. Article 24 of the Financial Regulation.
54. *See* for example P. Lelong, 'La cour des comptes des communautés européennes – Sa mission, son bilan' (1989) 274 *l'Europe en formation*, pp. 35–44.

control. The financial controller gives an *ex ante* approval to the authorizing officer. This prior approval all too often has the effect of encouraging the authorizing officer to offer his subsequent approval. Although the financial controller has the power[55] to submit an expert report to his institution (in particular with relation to the principle of sound management), he may be, as the ECA observes, naturally reluctant to do this in respect of expenditure for which he has already granted *ex ante* approval. As a rule, the ECA has been very critical of internal financial control. In some cases, it reports a lack of rigour. It notes that in 1993 advance payments were made by the Commission on a quasi-automatic basis and on the basis of very superficial checks,[56] without proper examination of the underlying transactions.[57] Furthermore in 1992 the Commission granted financial assistance for the organization of 20 scientific conferences concerned with the coordination of projects in the Member States. In two cases, it even made 'advance payments' even though the conferences in question had ended several weeks earlier. Despite the fact that in five cases those who received the advance payments failed to submit their final accounts, this failure did not elicit any reaction from the Commission.[58] Expenditure may also be carried out without the necessary, complementary, external audit. In 1993 the Commission adopted a plan of action in order to improve the quality of the European Development Fund's financial management, which hitherto did not come under the ambit of the ECA. The reasons advanced by the Commission for excluding the Development Fund from the external audit of the ECA was that the Directorate-General for Development Aid had built up a satisfactory financial control system of its own. The ECA opposed this view, because it found it to be contradictory to the principle of separation of functions (found in Article 21 of the Financial Regulation). The Directorate-General for Development Aid had not only assumed sole responsibility for financial control, but also for accounting. On examination of the EDF's financial management, the ECA found that there were many operations whose eligibility was questionable. The Commission was not able, for example, to identify various transactions accounting for a sum of at least 2.5 million ECU.[59] The ECA concluded that a body appointed by the institution should make an investigation to determine how far individuals were liable in the Commission's departments.[60] But in the absence of a disciplinary framework defining liability, this may be difficult.

3.3.2. Principle of Budgetary Unity

If the separation of functions has an important role to play in preventing corruption, the principle of budgetary unity helps to ensure the equally important democratic accountability and transparency in Community finance.

---

55. Article 40 of Regulation 3418/93 laying down implementing procedures for the Financial Regulation.
56. Court of Auditors Annual Report for the 1993 financial year: [1994] O.J. C327, p. 164, 9.6.
57. *Ibid.*, 9.6.
58. *Ibid.*, 11.38(e).
59. *Ibid.*, p. 271.
60. *Ibid.*, pp. 284–285, 15.117–15.126.

In 1967 the budgets of the three Communities were merged.[61] This helped to bring about the observance of the principle of budgetary unity, which requires that all financial transactions concerning a public body should be brought into a single document known as its budget, which is then voted on by its budgetary authority.[62] The ECA examines the accounts of all bodies set up by the Community only in so far as the relevant constituent instrument does not preclude such examination,[63] so it is not the case at the moment that all the Community's revenues and expenditure appear in the budget. Thus, there remain important exceptions to the principle of budgetary unity.[64] For example, in its Annual Report for the financial year 1993,[65] the ECA points out that in the context of several contracts signed with the Council of Europe in Strasbourg (about 1.5 million ECU), the Commission agreed to subordinate the ECA's audit rights to the provisions of the Financial Regulation of the Council of Europe and only to authorize them to be exercised via the Council of Europe's Audit Committee. Situations of this sort undermine the audit powers of the ECA as laid down in the Treaty and given concrete expression, in the case in point, in Article 87, fifth subparagraph of the Financial Regulation, which states that 'the grant of Community funds to beneficiaries outside the institutions shall be subject to an audit being carried out by the ECA on the utilization of the amounts granted'. This has led the ECA to argue that it should be entitled to audit all revenue and expenditure managed on behalf of the Community.[66] At present Article 188c (3) EC does not cover the inspection of records in institutions which are independent from the Member States and were not set up by the Communities (for example, the European Investment Bank)[67] or bodies set up by and managing funds for the Communities, but whose constituent instrument does not provide for control by the ECA (for example, the International Olive Oil Council). Within the context of the 1996 IGC, the ECA has proposed that the same Article be amended so as to include them (*see* Part IV).[68] In addition the field of application of the

---

61. *See* Article 20 of the Treaty signed in Brussels on April 1965, and which came into force on 1 July 1967 (known as the Merger Treaty) as amended by Article 10 of the Treaty of Luxembourg. The EEC budget, the operational budget of the EAEC and the administrative budget of the ECSC were merged into a single budget.
62. Article 199 EC; Article 4 of the Financial Regulation; also V. Schmitt and D. Strasser, *op. cit.* p. 42.
63. Article 188c (1) EC.
64. D. Strasser, *op. cit.*, pp. 44–47.
65. Court of Auditors Annual Report for the 1993 financial year: [1994] O.J. C327, p. 254, 14.90 on cooperation with the countries of Central and Eastern Europe.
66. Court of Auditors report for the IGC, *op. cit.*, p. 4.
67. Articles 198d and 198e EC; also Protocol annexed to the Treaty on European Union, 1992. The EIB's task is to contribute to the balanced and steady development of the common market in the interests of the Community. It does this by granting loans and giving guarantees which facilitate the financing of projects. This includes projects in less-developed regions, modernization or development projects and projects of common interest in several Member States. It also facilitates the financing of investment programmes in conjunction with assistance from the structural funds and other Community financial instruments.
68. The proposed amended text reads (emphasis added): 'The audit shall be based on records and, if necessary, performed on the spot in the other institutions of the Community, *on the premises of any body which manages revenue and/or expenditure on behalf of the Community* and in the Member States.' The rest of the subparagraph remains unchanged, whilst the next subparagraph

ECA's audit powers should be clarified in areas which are not, or are only partly, covered by the 1992 Treaty on European Union. The ECA is now required to audit expenditure incurred under the second and the third pillars and which is chargeable to the budget of the European Communities.[69] It has also been asked to audit expenditure chargeable to the Member States on a sliding scale basis (for example the EUROPOL budget), so it argues that these new duties should be acknowledged. It therefore suggests that it should be included under Article E EC, together with the other institutions.[70] In order to consolidate its auditing powers, the ECA argues that it should have access to the European Court of Justice for rulings on disputes arising from its lack of access to records. Although access to records must be a *sine qua non* of auditing, such access has occasionally been refused to the ECA (by the Commission, the Member States or private concerns) which is then unable to appeal against the decision.[71] Although other European institutions and their financial personnel have access to the Court of Justice, the ECA has no such access if disputes arise in the performance of its auditing duties. To guarantee the ECA access to the Court of Justice would entail two additions to the Treaty.[72]

This state of affairs has lead the ECA to prioritize budgetary unity within the framework of the 1996 IGC: 'The Court should be automatically entitled to audit all revenue and expenditure managed on behalf of the Community'[73] – so that no Community income or expenditure be outside the reach of democratic control.

4. THE EUROPEAN COURT OF JUSTICE

The European Court of Justice (ECJ henceforth) ensures that the law is observed in the interpretation and application of the EC Treaty. The Treaty on European Union broke new ground by giving the ECJ the power to fine Member States that fail to comply with its judgments [Article 171(2)], but it excluded the new fields of Common Foreign and Security Policy (CFSP henceforth) and Justice and Internal

---

reads: 'The other institutions of the Community, *any body that manages revenue and/or expenditure on behalf of the Community* and the national audit bodies or, if these do not have the necessary powers, the competent national departments, shall forward to the Court of Auditors, at its request, any document or information necessary to carry out its task'. Article 188c(3) EC does not explicitly cover access to the records of private beneficiaries.

69. Article J.11, paragraph 2, first sub-paragraph and Article K 8, paragraph 2, second sub-paragraph, first indent.

70. The proposed amended Article E EC reads (emphasis added): 'The European Parliament, the Council, the Commission (...) the Court of Justice *and the Court of Auditors* shall exercise their powers under the conditions and for the purposes provided for, on the one hand, by the provisions of the Treaties establishing the European Communities and of the subsequent Treaties and Acts modifying and supplementing them and, on the other hand, by the other provisions of this Treaty.'

71. Article 188c (3) EC.

72. The proposed additions to the Treaty read as follows. Article 280(a) EC: 'The Court of Justice shall have jurisdiction in disputes concerning such rights and prerogatives as have been conferred on the Court of Auditors by this Treaty'. Article 188c (5): 'Any infringement of the rights and prerogatives of the Court of Auditors may be placed by the latter before the Court of Justice. If the Court of Justice finds that an infringement has occurred, the persons responsible shall take such steps as may be necessary to comply with the Court of Justice's ruling'.

73. *See supra*, Court of Auditors report for the IGC, 1995, p. 4.

Affairs (JHA henceforth), save when conventions adopted by the Member States make provision for it. Within the consultation process of the IGC, the Court has made a few suggestions which are relevant to the protection of the financial interests of the European Communities.

The ECJ contribution[74] to the Reflection process prior to the IGC stresses the need for a uniform application of the law throughout the Union but notes that, under Article L, it has no competence to decide cases in the field of Justice and Internal Affairs. A recent case confirms that it has no competence to interpret Article B.[75] According to the findings of the ECJ, there is at present no way of obtaining a ruling on certain constitutional matters.

The ECJ contribution was written in early June 1995, that is to say, before the Regulation and the convention for the protection of the financial interests were agreed. It therefore looked back to an earlier convention, concerning the Simplified Extradition Procedure. This, the first Convention to be signed under the third pillar, did not grant the Court any competence in dispute resolution. But things have moved on since then, with four new conventions on third pillar matters being signed in June 1995. The present author suggests that, of these, the Convention on the Protection of the Communities' financial interests may be seen as a breakthrough. It grants the Court the competence to interpret the provisions of the Convention by way of preliminary rulings, and to determine disputes arising out of the operation of the Convention, on application from a Member State or the Commission, when disputes have not been settled within six months.[76]

Surprisingly, there are few key rulings in the area of the protection of the financial interests of the European Communities. *Commission* v. *Greece*[77] has crystallized Member States' duties and competence with regards to the application of sanctions, and *Germany* v. *Commission*[78] has clarified the competence of EC institutions in imposing sanctions. The jurisprudence has also clarified the rights of operators when Community sanctions are involved.

4.1. Member States' Duties and Competence

According to Article 5 EC, Member States have a duty to take all appropriate measures to ensure fulfilment of the obligations arising out of the Treaty. This has been compared to the German doctrine of 'Bundestreuepflicht' or duty of loyalty.[79] In particular, when governments of the Member States make decisions, they must be in accordance with the rule imposing on Member States and the Community institutions

---

74. European Court of Justice, *Rapport de la Cour de Justice sur certains aspects de l'application du Traité sur l'Union Européenne* (1995).
75. Case C-167/94, *Grau Gomis*: judgment of 7 April 1995, nyr.
76. Article 8 of the 'PIF' Convention: [1995] O.J. C316/48.
77. Case 68/88, *Commission* v. *Greece*, ECR [1989] 2965.
78. *Ibid.*
79. V. Contantinesco, 'L'article 5 CEE, de la bonne foi à la loyauté communautaire – Du droit international au droit de l'intégration' (1987) in *Liber Amicorum Pierre Pescatore*, eds: F. Capotorti, C-D Ehlermann, J. Frohwein, F. Jacobs, R. Joliet, T. Koopmans, R. Kovar, pp. 97–115.

mutual duties of sincere cooperation.[80] Those requirements include the 'obligation of general diligence',[81] as specifically embodied in Article 8(1) and (2) of Council Regulation 729/70 with regard to the financing of the CAP, according to which Member States must (i) satisfy themselves that transactions financed by the Fund are actually carried out and are executed correctly, (ii) prevent and deal with irregularities and (iii) recover sums lost as a result of irregularities or negligence.

As part of this duty of diligence, the Member States must initiate any proceedings under administrative, fiscal or civil law for the collection or recovery of duties or levies which have been fraudulently evaded or for damages.[82] In the *Amsterdam Bulb* case[83] the European Court of Justice ruled that 'In the absence of any provisions in the Community rules providing for specific sanctions to be imposed on individuals for a failure to observe those rules, the Member States are competent to adopt such sanctions as appear to them to be appropriate'. In *Hansen*[84] the Court ruled that '... [W]hilst the choice of penalties remains within their discretion, [the Member States] must ensure in particular that infringements of Community law are penalized under conditions, both procedural and substantive, which are analogous to those applicable to infringements of national law of a similar nature and importance and which, in any event, make the penalty effective, proportionate and dissuasive.[85] And, to drive the point home the Court added: '... [I]t *continues*[86] to be the task of the Member States to undertake prosecutions and proceedings for the purpose of the system of levies and refunds and to *continue*[87] to take steps to this end vis-à-vis the parties involved.'[88]

Assimilation remains a problem in some Member States, where the legal system has yet to be adapted.[89] It just means that a Member State may extend its (sometimes fairly ineffective) ways of tackling economic crime to EC funds. Predictably the question of the Commission's normative competence to impose sanctions appears in the jurisprudence of the Court, and it did in *Germany* v. *Commission*.

4.2. Commission Competence

The Community's power to create penalties to be imposed by national authorities and necessary for the effective application of the rules in the sphere of the CAP, based on Articles 40(3) and 43(2) EC, has repeatedly been recognized by the

---

80. *See* case 230/81, *Luxembourg* v. *European Parliament* ('seat' case), [1983] ECR 255, at 37.
81. Case C-34/89, *Italy* v. *Commission*, [1990] ECR I 3603, at 12.
82. Case C-352/92, *Milchwerke Köln/Wuppertal EG* v. *Hauptzollamt Köln-Rheinau*, [1994] ECR I-3385, at 23.
83. Case 50/76, *Amsterdam Bulb BV* v. *Produktschap voor Siergewassen*, [1977] ECR 137, [1977] 2 CMLR 218.
84. Case 148/77, *Hansen* v. *Hauptzollamt Flensburg*, [1978] ECR 1787; [1979] 1 CMLR 604.
85. *Ibid.*, at 2, second paragraph.
86. Author's emphasis.
87. *Ibid.*
88. *Ibid.*, at 16.
89. *See* for example N. Courakis, 'Greece Coping with EU fraud' (1996) 4:1 *Journal of Financial Crime*, pp. 78–84.

Court,[90] be it in the form of a requirement to refund a benefit unduly received,[91] the loss of security equivalent to that benefit,[92] or the forfeiture of a security.[93] In *Germany* v. *Commission*,[94] the Court went one step further and held that exclusion from a scheme within the CAP came within the implementing powers which the Council may delegate to the Commission under Articles 145 and 155 EC. This is because penalties such as a surcharge on the reimbursement with interests of a subsidy paid, or exclusion for a certain period of a trader from a subsidies scheme, are measures intended to further CAP goals and the proper financial management of the Community funds designated for their attainment.

Following the ruling in *Germany* v. *Commission*,[95] which established Community competence to impose penal-administrative sanctions, two questions arose in relation to the Community's powers to impose sanctions. The first concerns its competence to impose sanctions beyond the CAP (i.e. to other parts of the EC budget), and the second relates to its competence to impose penal, rather than purely administrative, sanctions.

The 'PIF' Regulation[96] now extends the Community's competence to impose penalties beyond the sphere of the CAP.[97] This means that the Community now has competence to impose the types of penalties enumerated in Article 5 of the 'PIF' Regulation (ranging from fines to loss of deposit) to other parts of the budget. This now makes it possible, for example, to extend a specific regime of penalties to affect the collection of import duties, which as we shall see is badly affected by fraud.

With regard to the Community's competence to impose penal sanctions, the Court has consistently declined to be drawn into the distinction between penal sanctions (the sole preserve of the Member States) and administrative sanctions (where the Community has a normative competence). Administrative sanctions apply without prejudice to criminal sanctions imposed in the Member States. The fact that fraud is due to the negligence of a producer, is not sufficient to invest the sanction with a penal character, given that fraud, and even more so negligence, is as much a concept of the civil as of the criminal law.[98]

4.3. Rights of Operators

Penalties such as fines are imposed under both criminal and civil/administrative law in the Member States. In criminal law, the defendant's behaviour is the main issue

---

90. Cases 357/88, *Oberhausener* v. *BALM*, [1990] ECR 1669; 25/70, *EVGF* v. *Köster*, ECR [1970] 1161.
91. Case 288/85, *Hauptzollamt Hamburg-Jonas* v. *Plange Kraftfutterwerke*, [1987] ECR 611.
92. Case C-199/90, *Italtrade* v. *AIMA*, [1990] ECR I-5545.
93. Cases 11/70, *Internationale Handelsgesellschaft* v. *Einfuhr- und Vorratstelle für Getreide und Futtermittel*, [1970] ECR 1125; 137/85, *Maizena* v. *BALM*, [1987] ECR 4587, at 12; C-155/89, *Philipp. Brothers* [1990] ECR I-3265, at 40; C-199/90, *Italtrade* v. *AIMA*, [1991] ECR I-5545, at 10; 122/78, *Buitoni* v. *FORMA*, [1979] ECR 677; *Man (Sugar)* v. *IBAP*, [1985] ECR 2889.
94. Case C-240/90, *Germany* v. *Commission*, [1992] ECR I-5385.
95. *Ibid.*
96. Council Regulation 2988/95 ('PIF' Regulation) [1995] O.J. L312/1.
97. *Ibid.*, 12th preamble.
98. Case C-240/90: *op. cit.*, at 16.

in court, whilst in administrative decisions what is at stake is the legitimacy of the decision.

Administrative sanctions have increasingly been incorporated into regulations since a landmark case,[99] which acknowledged the Commission's power to introduce penalties with a punitive, rather than merely remedial or compensatory character into regulations. Such penalties are not meant to replace criminal proceedings in the Member States, but rather they set minimal sanctions to be applied, irrespective of criminal proceedings.

The question has arisen whether or not increasing the share of administrative penalties against reprehensible behaviour does not tilt the balance of powers in favour of the executive.[100] At the national level, although there have been studies concerned with the change of relationships between the judiciary and the legislature, little has been formulated on the consequences for the rule of law resulting from such a shift of judicial functions from the judiciary to the executive. Administrative sanctions do not automatically fall under the ambit of Article 6(1) ECHR.

In the *Könecke*[101] and *Maizena*[102] cases, the Court ruled that 'a penalty, even of a non-criminal nature, cannot be imposed unless it rests on a clear and unambiguous legal basis.' Furthermore, a penalty must not be retroactive.[103] It must be appropriate and necessary and proportionate to the objectives to be attained,[104] and must only be applied after the person concerned has had an opportunity to make known his/her views.[105] The requirement of judicial control also applies to administrative decisions.[106] According to Schockweiler,[107] the requirement of judicial control should apply, particularly when sanctions are involved.

But there has been more uncertainty whether the principle of equality of arms derived from Article 6(1) ECHR applies in administrative proceedings of a penal nature. The Court of First Instance has ruled that companies involved in antitrust proceedings, where the Community has the power to impose penalties directly, have a right to defend themselves,[108] since the European Court of Justice has a duty to ensure that the procedural safeguards granted by ECHR are respected within the

---

99. Case 240/90, *op. cit.*

100. H. De Doelder, 'The enforcement of economic legislation' (1994) in *Administrative law application and enforcement of Community law in The Netherlands*, ed. J. Vervaele, pp. 133–142.

101. Case 117/83, *Könecke* v. *Balm*, [1984] ECR 3291.

102. Case 137/85, *Maizena* v. *BALM*, [1987] ECR 4587.

103. Case 63/83, *R* v. *Kirk*, [1984] ECR 2689, at 22: '[T]he principle that penal provisions may not have retroactive effect is one which is common to all the legal orders of the Member States and is enshrined in Article 7 of the European Convention for the Protection of Human Rights and Fundamental Freedoms as fundamental right; it takes its place among the general principles of law whose observance is ensured by the Court of Justice.'

104. Cases C-319/90, *Pressler* v. *Germany*, [1992] ECR I-203, at 12; C-326/88, *Anklagemyndigheden* v. *Hansen*, [1990] ECR I-2911; 15/83, *Denkavit*, [1984] ECR 2171; 122/78, *Buitoni* v. *Forma*, [1979] ECR 677; 66/82, *Fromençais* v. *Forma*, [1983] ECR 395.

105. Case 85/76, *Hoffman-La Roche* v. *Commission (vitamins)*, [1979] ECR 461.

106. *Johnston* v. *Chief Constable of the RUC*, [1986] ECR 1651 at 18.

107. F. Schockweiler, 'La répression des infractions au droit communautaire dans la jurisprudence de la Cour, La protection du budget communautaire et l'assistance entre états' (1995) in *Proceeds of Luxembourg Conference*, 12 May 1995, Luxembourg ARPE.

108. Case T-36/91, *ICI*: judgment of 29 June 195, nyr.

Community's legal order.[109] This clarifies matters as far as competition hearings are concerned,[110] but what of administrative proceedings conducted in the Member States themselves, and which have for their objective the protection of the financial interests of the European Communities? There may be three (related) levels of difficulties in this area. Firstly, the case law of the Court of Human Rights is far from unequivocal as to whether penal-administrative sanctions should attract the same guarantees under Article 6(1) as criminal sanctions do. Secondly, learned commentators have argued that, because the Community itself has not acceded to ECHR,[111] the Member States could conceivably 'find themselves in a situation in which they are required to take actions according to Community law which the ECHR forbids'.[112] This sounds rather far-fetched in view of the present incorporation of human rights into Community law, but it must be conceded that De Doelder may well have a point, since the implementation of the 'Black List' Regulation has come very close to creating such problems in the UK (*see* Chapter 4). Thirdly, national administrative proceedings in general do not automatically ensure fulfilment of the same guarantees.[113] De Doelder has summarized the situation thus:

> 'The "message" of both courts [ECJ and ECHR] is therefore not the same: the Court of Luxembourg gives Member States the task of imposing certain predetermined sanctions, while the Court in Strasbourg speaks in terms of "reasonableness" and "fairness". The States are caught between two fires without a right-of-way rule.'[114]

4.4. Cooperation

The duty of 'sincere cooperation' must extend to Commission checks which are carried out in the Member States. This means that Commission officials have access to the same premises and to the same documents as national officials.[115] With respect to access to evidence, the Commission can be assimilated to the national authorities. National rules limiting access therefore also apply to the Commission. When the Commission has autonomous powers of inspection, national authorities

---

109. *See* cases C-260/89, *ERT*, [1991] ECR 2925; also 46 and 227/87, *Hoechst*, [1989] ECR 2859.
110. *See* J. Van Der Woude, 'Hearing officers and EC antitrust procedures – The art of making subjective procedures more objective' (1996) 33 CMLR, pp. 531–546.
111. In Opinion 2/94, [1996] 2 CMLR 265, the ECJ subsequently opined that as Community law stands, the Community had no competence to accede to the European Convention for the Protection of Human Rights and Fundamental Freedoms.
112. B. Vermeulen, 'The issue of fundamental rights in the administrative application and enforcement of Community law' (1994) in *Administrative law application and enforcement of Community law in the Netherlands*, p. 47.
113. H. De Doelder, 'The enforcement of economic legislation' (1994) in *Administrative law application and enforcement of Community law in the Netherlands*, ed. J. Vervaele, p. 141.
114. *Ibid.*, p. 141.
115. *See* case 267/78, *Commission* v. *Italy*, [1980] ECR 31; also Article 6(4) of Council Regulation 595/91 [1991] O.J. L67/11.

have a duty to assist.[116] Member States also have a duty to cooperate with their national authorities by communicating information which is necessary for ensuring that Community law is applied.[117] This duty is mutual, and the Commission also has a duty to cooperate with national authorities:

'... [T]his duty of sincere cooperation is of particular importance vis-à-vis the judicial authorities of the Member States who are responsible for ensuring that Community law is applied and respected in the national legal system.'[118]

This requirement was added by the Treaty on European Union to the EEC Treaty:

'Without prejudice to other provisions of this Treaty, Member States shall coordinate their action aimed at protecting the financial interests of the Community against fraud. To this end they shall organize, with the help of the Commission, close and regular cooperation between the competent departments of their administrations.' (Article 209a, second paragraph).

5. THE COUNCIL

The Council has a general duty to enact legislation, and indeed most laws are enacted by Council.

Under Article 209 EC, the Council acts unanimously on a proposal from the Commission and after consulting the European Parliament and obtaining the opinion of the Court of Auditors. Like the Commission and the European Parliament, it has budgetary duties. It makes financial regulations specifying the procedure to be adopted for establishment and implementation of the budget and for presenting and auditing accounts. It also determines the modalities for the payment of own resources into the budget. These tasks are carried out through the Budget Committee, which in turn reports to COREPER.[119] Importantly, it also lays down the rules concerning the responsibility of financial controllers, authorizing officers and accounting officers, and concerning appropriate arrangements for inspection.

---

116. Joined cases 46/87 and 227/88, *Hoechst AG* v. *Commission*, [1989] ECR 2859, at 4 second paragraph '... If the undertakings concerned oppose the Commission's investigation, its officials may, on the basis of Article 14(6) of Regulation 17 and without the cooperation of the undertaking, search for any information necessary for the investigation with the assistance of the authorities, which are required to afford them the assistance necessary for the performance of their duties. Although such assistance is required only if the undertaking expresses its opposition, it may also be requested as a precautionary measure, in order to overcome any opposition on the part of the undertaking.'

117. Case C-9/89, *Spain* v. *Council*, [1990] ECR 1383.

118. Case C-2/8, *Imm. J.J. Zwartveld and others*, [1990] ECR I-3365, at 1.

119. Comité des Représentants Permanents; Committee of Permanent Representatives.

6. THE EUROPEAN PARLIAMENT

Generally, the European Parliament's power over the budget as a whole is limited. It does, however, have the right to reject the budget as a whole. But if it rejects the budget, the Community can continue to spend at the same monthly rate as in the previous year.[120] It is also responsible for granting discharge for the whole budget.[121] The EP only refused discharge once in November 1984, when it refused discharge for the 1982 financial year. The Treaty on European Union strengthened the role of the EP by giving it power to demand information from the Commission about its execution of financial control, and by requiring the Commission to act on the EP's observations.[122] The EP has the right to dismiss the Commission by a two-thirds majority,[123] thus ensuring that the Commission pays a great deal of attention to its views. The EP generally wants to play a greater institutional role and this is reflected in its IGC proposals.

The European Parliament's IGC proposals[124] can be divided between general concerns, those relating to budgetary control, those concerning other institutions and others.

6.1. General Concerns

Generally the EP argues that it should have equal status with the Council in all fields of EU legislative and budgetary competence.

- Its role should be reinforced in those areas where there is currently inadequate scrutiny at European level, for example in Justice and Internal Affairs. It stresses that the unanimity requirement has lead to delays and to ineffective legislation in the past, and that consequently further extension of qualified majority voting is required if the EU is to function effectively. However, for certain areas of particular sensitivity, unanimity will remain necessary, i.e. Treaty amendment, 'constitutional decisions' (enlargement, own resources, uniform electoral system) and Article 235.
- Public access to EU documents should be greatly improved.
- The Union's powers in the agricultural sector largely evade the direct scrutiny of national parliaments and must be subject to greater democratic control by the European Parliament; in fact, responsibility for agricultural markets and prices policy, and thus for farm incomes policy, has long been outside the control of national parliaments.
- The democratic principle of the final adoption of the budget by the European Parliament must be maintained.

---

120. Article 204 EC.
121. Article 206 EC.
122. Article 206 EC.
123. Article 144 EC.
124. European Commission, *Préparation CIG 1996 – Contribution du Parlement Européen* (1995) info-note number 26/95.

– Finally, the Treaty should be revised to permit tougher measures to be taken to combat fraud and other infringements of EU law, to permit wider-ranging investigations within the Member States (by means, for example, of a reinforced Article 138c) and to enable dissuasive penal and administrative sanctions to be imposed at EU level (with an article to permit harmonization directives in the area of relevant criminal law, and specifically obliging Member States to apply effective, proportionate, harmonized and deterrent penalties for breach of Community law).

6.2. Budgetary Control

The EP finds budgetary legislation confusing and asks that it be rationalized to distinguish between own resources decisions, financial regulation and budgetary discipline. Multi-annual financial programming should be incorporated into the Treaty. The income of the EIB should be treated as an own resource of the Community. The Union's budget should be the sole instrument for realizing the Union's objectives. The unity of the budget should be established, the Union budget incorporating the European Development Fund and CFSP and JHA expenditure and Community borrowing and lending.

The budgetary procedure should be simplified, more transparent and effective; the Commission's draft budget proposals should be the basis for the European Parliament's first reading.[125]

The distinction between compulsory and non-compulsory expenditures should be abolished within a defined period; the European Parliament should be an equal partner for all expenditure.

6.3. Proposals Concerning Other Institutions

The competence of the ECJ should be extended to areas relating to Justice and Internal Affairs and those covered by the Schengen agreement. The conditions for referring matters to the ECJ should be enlarged so that each institution of the Union should have the possibility (in addition to the means of redress in Article 173) of bringing an action in the Court where it considers that its rights have been infringed by the failure on the part of another institution or a Member State to fulfil a Treaty obligation.

6.4. Other Proposals

The EP proposes that when the Council is acting in its legislative capacity, its proceedings should be public and its agenda binding. The ECA should play its proper role in all the areas of EU activity.

---

125. European Commission, *Tableau comparatif des contributions du Conseil, de la Commission, du P.E.* (1995) info-note number 32/95.

6.5. The Meaning of the EP Agenda

The EP strongly supports the Commission in its efforts to control fraud affecting the budget. It even goes as far as recommending the constitutionalization of the powers of the Commission to perform checks in the Member States, and to harmonize criminal laws. On budgetary unity, it reflects the ECA's views (*see* above). Generally, the EP wishes to have equal access to all parts of the budget, in order to establish better accountability for the tax payer. This forward-looking agenda has it roots in the early concern the EP has shown in fraud control, and in its increasing involvement in matters relating to it.

6.6. The EP and Fraud Control

Historically, the European Parliament first showed concern for the protection of the financial interests of the European Communities in 1973, and subsequently through a number of reports.[126] It also supported the 1976 proposal for a convention, which was subsequently shelved. At that time, the 1977 de Keersmaker report[127] had already highlighted the need for sanctions, and in particular the need to ensure that Community fraud be given due consideration in the national laws of the Member States. In 1991 the Theato report reiterated the same concerns and deplored the fact that little progress had been made in that direction.

Of late, the EP's scrutiny of the Structural Funds, in particular, has increased. Whilst respecting the division of rule between the institutions as laid down by the Treaty, the revised Structural Funds legislation of 1993[128] provides for a greater involvement of Parliament in the implementation of Community structural measures and as a result entails:

– forwarding to Parliament lists of the areas concerned in respect of Objectives 2 and 5b, the development plans submitted by the Member States, the Community Support Frameworks and the texts of the implementing regulations concerning monitoring and publicity;
– notifying Parliament of the Community initiatives before their adoption, in order to enable the Commission to take note of Parliament's requests before each initiative;
– providing regular and detailed information on the implementation of the funds.

---

126. De Keersmaeker Report (1977), EP document 531/76; Gabert Report (1984), EP document 1–1346/83; Guermeur Report 1987), EP document A2–251/86; Dankert Report (1989), EP Document A2–20/89; Theato Report (1991), EP document A3–0250/91.
127. *Ibid.*
128. *See* Articles 9(3), 11b(4), 16 of Council Regulation 2081/93 [1993] O.J. L193/5 (Framework Regulation) and Articles 10, 11, 23, 26(5), 32(2) of Council Regulation 2082/93 [1993] O.J. L193/30 (Coordination Regulation).

6.6.1. The Budgetary Control Committee

Since 1973 the European Parliament (EP henceforth) has had a Committee for budgetary control. The Committee's powers were determined by Parliament on 19 May 1983 and subsequently amended on 26 July 1989. The Committee is competent to examine, *inter alia*, the conditions of appropriations, the financing mechanisms and the administrative structures for putting them into effect, through a study of the cases of fraud and irregularity. Every quarter it reviews cases of fraud which are of interest. The Committee gives opinions on request or on its own initiative, to the parliamentary committees and other bodies of Parliament on matters within the field of budgetary control. Its busiest period is at the time of the discharge of the budget, at the beginning of every autumn. The Committee, acting like the proverbial grit in the oyster, has been actively pressing the Commission to come up with credible strategies to fight fraud, the Council to pronounce on proposals for legislation, and has worked to improve communication strategies with the European Court of Auditors.[129]

6.6.2. The Temporary Committee of Inquiry[130]

With fraud being high on the EP's agenda, it is not wholly surprising that the first Committee of Inquiry, set up under Article 138C EC, should be dedicated to it. The EP decided in 1995 that the subject of the inquiry should be to consider allegations of offences committed or of maladministration under the Community Transit System.[131] The TCI is due to report in January 1997 at the earliest,[132] and its work programme has included gathering evidence from all quarters (national Customs authorities, freight forwarders, national permanent representatives, commissioners, the International Chamber of Commerce, etc.). It will be interesting to see whether as a result of the inquiry, the Commission's anti-fraud programme is amended.

129. *See* European Parliament, *Rapport de la Commission du Contrôle Budgétaire sur les relations entre les organes de contrôle de budget communautaire, rapporteur John Tomlinson* (1993) A3–0320.
130. On the setting up of the Committee and the necessary changes to the rules of procedure, *see* the following European Parliament reports: *Les commissions parlementaires d'enquête des états membres de la CE* (1993) W3; *Commission de règlement, de la vérification des pouvoirs et des immunités* (1994) PE 210.750 and (1995) PE 212.084; *Document de travail* (1995) PE 211.818 and (1995) PE 210.700; also S. Boyron, *Un pouvoir de contrôle confirmé: les commissions temporaires d'enquête, rapport à la Commission Institutionnelle* (1995); also S. Boyron, *Les commissions temporaires et les adaptations réglementaires nécessaires* (1995).
131. Decision 96/C, [1996] O.J. C7.
132. According to the Rules of Procedure two to three months extension is possible.

7. DISCUSSION

The main function of the Commission, and in particular DG XX (Financial Control), has been to raise awareness, to make proposals, and to put forward implementing measures for existing secondary legislation. However, because the Commission's legislative proposals have to be adopted by a unanimous vote, they have often been shelved for long periods (e.g. the 'PIF' Convention). Occasionally, the Commission's implementing efforts have seemed over-zealous to the Member States, as in the Code of Conduct attached to Council Regulation 4253/88,[133] which was subsequently annulled by the European Court of Justice (*see* Chapter 4). Whether the handicap provided by the unanimity requirement is remedied through constitutional reform remains an open question at the moment. In this the EP's suggestion that certain powers of the Commission (in the field of inspection and harmonization of criminal laws) be constitutionalized, and that qualified majority be extended to more areas, pays lip service to the Commission.

But what are we to think of the ECA's quite detailed proposals, which are technical in as much as they deal with budgetary control, but nevertheless go to the heart of the problem? The ECA is playing an increasingly important role in the protection of the financial interests of the European Communities. Cynics might see in the ECA proposals merely an instance of a more general tendency for Community institutions to extend their powers. Be that as it may, specific proposals seem hard to fault – for example the need for all bodies handling EU funds to be subjected to an external audit must be heeded. A role for the Court of Auditors in investigations, an acknowledgement of its role under the second and third pillars, and the possibility of appeal to the ECJ should also be given serious consideration. The request that the ECA be consulted in the legislative process when anti-fraud legislation is considered is difficult to rebut, yet may fail to gain a hearing amongst the cacophony of other, more politically visible issues projected for debate at the Inter-Governmental Conference.

If anything, pre-IGC reports should help to open up the discussion on fraud prevention through sound financial management, epitomized by the SEM 2000[134] initiative. The initiative[135] has already examined the possibility of extending the clearance of accounts procedure to the non-compulsory part of the budget, and has come to the conclusion that a new clearance procedure should be created for own resources.

This signals the beginning of an era in which financial management promises to play a more dominant role in the fight against fraud.

---

133. [1988] O.J. L374/1.
134. SEM 2000 is the acronym for the programme to improve financial management launched by the Commission in January 1995. Its full name is Sound and Efficient Financial Management, SEM 2000.
135. *See* for example European Parliament, Budgetary Control Committee, *SEM 2000 Working document – Rationalising controls – Preventing fraud* (1996) PE 219.146; European Parliament, Budgetary Control Committee, *SEM 2000 Working document – Evaluation* (1996) PE 218.773; European Parliament, Budgetary Control Committee, *SEM 2000 Working document, Defining a methodological approach* (1996).

PART II

The Control of Income and Expenditure Fraud

Chapter 3. The Control of Fraud Affecting EC Revenue

This chapter focuses on the control of fraud affecting traditional own resources (§ 2) and VAT-based own resources (§ 3), which are collected and controlled by the Member States themselves. First their respective history is examined briefly, and examples of fraud are given. This is followed by an expose of the Community control framework and Member States' responses. Proposed solutions are examined thereafter. The last part of the chapter (§ 4) deals with recent developments and prospects for improvement of the protection of the financial interests of the European Communities. Readers should note that the question of recovery of EC revenue has not been dealt with in any depth in this chapter, since a detailed case study has been included separately in Part III.

1. INTRODUCTION: OWN RESOURCES

Community revenues are referred to as 'own resources'. This technically is a misnomer since the Community resources are collected by the Member States, and subsequently made available to the European Communities, as we shall see. The Council Decision of 21 April 1970 gave the Community for the first time 'financial autonomy through fiscal power',[1] by establishing a system of 'own resources' under Article EEC. At first own resources consisted of VAT, Customs duties and agricultural and sugar levies. In 1989 the own resources system was changed in order to accommodate a proportion of national GNPs, thus creating a regime of EC revenue raising which was felt to be more equitable. Decision 88/376[2] was closely followed by Council Regulations 1552/89[3] and 1553/89[4] laying down rules for the implementation of the amended regime. The regime was finally enshrined in the EEC Treaty when 201 EEC was amended by the Treaty on European Union to read:

> 'Without prejudice to other revenue, the budget shall be financed wholly from own resources. The Council, acting unanimously on a proposal from the Commission and after consulting the European Parliament, shall lay down provisions relating to the system of own resources of the Community, which

---

1. *See* D. Strasser, *op. cit.*, p. 85.
2. Council Decision 88/376, [1988] O.J. L185/24, on the Communities' own resources.
3. Council Regulation 1552/89 [1989] O.J. L155/1 implementing Decision 88/376 on the system of the Communities' own resources.
4. Council Regulation 1553/89 [1989] O.J. L155/9, on the definitive uniform arrangements for the collection of own resources accruing from value added tax.

it shall recommend to the Member States for adoption in accordance with their respective constitutional requirements.' (Article 201 EC)

In the absence of a Community tax-collecting authority[5] the system of 'own resources' means that Member States must make available to the Community budget a small proportion of their VAT and GNP, as well as various levies and duties. Levies, premiums, supplementary or compensatory amounts, additional amounts of items and other duties established at present or in the future by the institutions of the Communities in respect of trade with non-member countries, within the framework of the CAP and any other contributions and other duties established within the common organization of the markets in sugar have been described by the Commission as 'traditional own resources' in order to distinguish them from (VAT-based) own resources. The payment of traditional own resources into the EC budget derives from the application of the Common Customs Tariff[6] (CCT) to the Customs value of goods imported from third countries. It is to traditional own resources that we turn first.

2. FRAUD AND TRADITIONAL OWN RESOURCES

Revenue frauds are prevalent in particular in the area of agricultural and Customs levies. The administration of sugar levies, however, is held to be relatively straightforward and leaves little scope for exploitation.[7] Agricultural levies and Customs duties are collected by the Member States' Customs authorities from traders importing goods into the Community. Fraud occurs when a trader evades paying duty to the Customs authorities by, for example, misleading the authorities about the source of the goods, or the nature of the product he is transporting. The Common Customs Tariff alone contains over 4,000 product codes,[8] so the scope for fraud (and error!) due to misdescription alone is vast. It is generally acknowledged that inward transits (i.e. imports to the Community) are more susceptible to fraud than outward transits (exports).[9]

Levies and duties are designed to bring the prices of imported goods to the level of Community prices. The product's country of origin does not generally affect the size of the levy. However, the system is complicated by preferential arrangements such as the Generalised Scheme of Tariff Preferences,[10] which

---

5. Article 8(1) of Council Decision 88/376, *op. cit.*
6. Council Regulation 950/68 [1968] I O.J. Spec. Ed. 275. The CCT was established even before the dated provided for in the Treaty (1 January 1970), namely on 1 July 1968. The combined nomenclature of the system, which is based on the Harmonized Commodity Description and Coding System (Council Regulation 2658/87 [1987] O.J. L256), is reviewed annually.
7. A. Sherlock and C. Harding, 'Controlling fraud within the European Community' (1991) 16, ELR 20–36, p. 22.
8. 'For processed goods, a further 932 product codes exist, 1,416 recipes and 14,000 non-standard recipes'. *See* L. Leigh and A. Smith, 'Some observations on European fraud laws and their reform with reference to the EEC' (1991) 6 *Corruption and reform*, p. 268.
9. European Parliament, *Committee of Inquiry into the Community Transit System*, Response from the Irish Permanent Representation to the European Union (1996) p. 2.
10. The GSP was first adopted by the Community in 1971.

allows goods from certain developing countries discounts on levies and duties. Imports from third countries are regulated by Council Regulations 3285/94[11] and 519/94.[12] The Regulation includes a simplification and standardization of the import formalities to be fulfilled by importers when surveillance or safeguard measures are applied.

2.1. Fraud Cases

In external transit frauds, goods are sometimes released onto the Community market *qua* Community goods, in order to evade duties (*see* cases 3 and 4). In all cases the correct determination of origin, following Article 24 of the Community Customs Code[13] and the jurisprudence of the Court,[14] is of crucial importance to the integrity of Community revenue, as illustrated by the four cases below.

Case 1: False Community origin: dairy products. In 1994 Spanish Customs found that certain companies had been purchasing dairy products from the Czech and Slovak Republics and releasing them onto the Community market with a false Spanish Customs' declaration. As a result some 15.7 million ECU of duties were evaded.[15]

Case 2: False preferential origin: bicycles from Vietnam.[16] In 1995 the Commission[17] found that all the components used to make over 520,000 bicycles which were subsequently released onto the Community market (in particular the UK, Belgium, Germany and Denmark), did not actually originate from Vietnam, but from China and Hong Kong. The certificates of preferential origin from the Vietnamese authorities were therefore incorrect and the Customs duties evaded ran

11. Council Regulation 3285/94 [1994] O.J. L349/53.
12. Council Regulation 519/94 [1994] O.J. L67/89. The countries listed in the Regulation include countries whose economies are in transition towards a market economy, except where the Community has entered into an Association Agreement or a free trade agreement with the country concerned.
13. Council Regulation 2913/92 [1992] O.J. L302/1.
14. Disputes over the origin of goods have often arisen in relation to fish and shell fish, for example in case 100/84, *Commission* v. *United Kingdom*, [1985] ECR 170 and more recently in joined cases C-153/94 and C-204/94, *Faroe Seafood*, ruling of 14 May 1996, nyr; or in relation to products acquiring added value through processes of manufacture, for example cases 49/76, *Überseehandel* v. *Handelskammer Hamburg*, [1977] ECR 41; 34/78 and 114/78, *Yoshida*, [1979] ECR 115 and 151; 162/83, *Cousin*, [1983] ECR 1101; C-26/88, *Brother International* v. *HZA Giessen*, [1989] ECR 4253.
15. European Commission, *Protecting the Community's financial interests, the fight against fraud – Annual Report for 1995* (1996) COM(96) 173, p. 51.
16. *See also* newspaper article '"Mafia gangs involved" in 1 billion pounds EU frauds', in *The Guardian* 9 May 1996, p. 10.
17. Under Article 15b of Council Regulation 945/87 (amending Regulation 1468/81) O.J. [1987] L90/3, the Commission may carry out administrative and investigative missions in third countries in coordination and close cooperation with the competent authorities of the Member States.

to 6.85 million ECU. In view of the circumstances in which the products were assembled, anti-dumping duties totalling 9.78 million may also be payable.[18]

Case 3: External transit fraud: sugar. In 1994 the German authorities informed the Commission about a case of fraud involving the dispatch of sugar originating in the Czech Republic and Poland to Morocco and Angola in transit through the Community. The goods, transported under the TIR system, were in fact released in Spain and Portugal, after Customs documents with forged stamps were presented. Evaded duties amount to 9 million ECU.[19]

Case 4: External transit fraud: beef. Beef from Argentina was unloaded in Rotterdam and placed under the external Community transit arrangements for carriage to Croatia. Forged Italian Customs documents were presented in Nice, and the beef was subsequently released onto the Italian market. Some 700 tonnes of beef were involved and the duty evaded totalled around 3 million ECU.[20]

Fraud in EU transit forms an important part of the fraud with Customs duties. In contravention of transit arrangements, goods are not presented at the Customs office of expected destination. Instead, they are released onto the Community market without payment of the duties and other taxes which are due. Alternatively, Customs documents certifying the presentation of goods at the office of destination, or guarantees are forged, using stolen or counterfeit stamps. Up to now there has been no way of cross-checking the authenticity of Customs stamps. At the moment itineraries are not binding,[21] so it is possible for cargoes to get 'lost' in this way. In the 'Greek Maize' case,[22] for example, maize originating from (the then) Yugoslavia was presented to the Belgian authorities, complete with a false declaration of origin from Greece. The fraud had been carried out with the complicity of some Greek senior civil servants – hence the relevance of the fight against corruption in order to protect EC revenue (*see* Chapter 6 on corruption).

The practices mentioned above (non-reporting, forgery of certificates) are particularly lucrative to the fraudster when the goods are, as the Commission describes them, 'sensitive'.[23] Sensitive goods fall into two categories. Firstly, some goods are sensitive because they attract a high level of indirect taxation, for example tobacco or alcohol. A single container load of cigarettes, for example, can attract duties and taxes of approximately 1 million ECU. This situation has prompted some commentators to suggest that cigarette smuggling was now more lucrative, and certainly less risky than illegal drug smuggling. Other sensitive or high-risk goods

---

18. European Commission, *Protecting the Community's financial interests, the fight against fraud – Annual Report for 1995* (1996) COM (96) 173, p. 62.
19. *Ibid.*, p. 54.
20. *Ibid.*, p. 55.
21. *See* for example *European Parliament Committee of Inquiry into the Community Transit System*, Contribution submitted by the Danish Freight Forwarders Association in Copenhagen (1996) point 12.
22. Case 68/88, *op. cit.*
23. S. White, 'The transit system in crisis: argument for European Customs?' (1996) 2 *Irish Journal of European Law* pp. 225–237.

attract high levels of subsidy or refund under the CAP (*see* Chapter 3). Since the opening up of the borders to Central and Eastern Europe in particular, the transit of sensitive products seems to have been targeted by criminal networks.[24]

2.2. Transit in the EU and Beyond

Since the opening of the internal market in 1993, under the Community Transit System, all goods transported within the Customs territory of the Community have been treated as Community goods unless demonstrated otherwise.[25] This has had the effect of eliminating Customs formalities on such goods whilst on the territory of the Community. The Common Transit System, an extension of the Community Transit System to EFTA countries[26] (Iceland, Norway and Switzerland), will include 22 participants after the Visegrad[27] countries (Poland, Hungary, the Czech Republic and the Slovak Republic) join in July 1996,[28] in the first stage of an extension to Central and Eastern Europe.[29] Another transit regime also exists for countries outside the Common Transit System and which are signatories of the TIR Convention.[30] Fifty-eight countries world-wide are currently signatories of this convention, including all EU Member States taken both individually and as the European Union.[31]

Main features of transit. The Common Transit System works according to a relatively simple principle. It allows for the suspension of duties and other charges during transit within the Common Transit territory, for goods coming from or going to third countries. The goods must be produced intact at the Customs office of destination within a prescribed time limit. This means that Customs controls are concentrated at the office of destination. The office of destination is therefore

---

24. European Commission, *Fraud in the transit procedure, solutions foreseen and perspectives for the future* (1995) COM(95) 108 p. 5; also J. Rump, 'The legal protection of the Community's financial interests as seen by Customs investigators in Germany' (1993) in *The legal protection of the financial interests of the Community – Progress and prospects since the Brussels seminar of 1989*, pp. 133–138.
25. Commission Regulation 1214/92 [1992] O.J. L132/1 on provisions for the implementation of the Community transit procedure and for certain simplifications of that procedure.
26. Convention on a common transit procedure [1987] O.J. L226/1.
27. In February 1991 at Visegrad, in Hungary, the leaders of Hungary, Poland and what was then Czechoslovakia met to discuss their approach to European integration. They confirmed their wish for 'total integration into the European political, economic, security and legislative order' and agreed to cooperate in the progressive achievement of such integration.
28. Commission Decision 1/95 [1996] O.J. L117/13 of the EC-EFTA joint Committee on Common Transit concerning invitations to the Republic of Poland, the Czech Republic and the Slovak Republic to accede to the Convention of 20 May 1987 on a common transit procedure.
29. *See* Council Resolution [1995] O.J. C327/2 on the computerization of customs transit systems, 11th preamble.
30. Customs Convention on the International Transport of Goods under Cover of TIR Carnets signed in Geneva, 1975.
31. Council Regulation 2112/78 [1978] O.J. L252. Implementing provisions for the TIR Convention and the Community Transit System are now both included in the Community Customs Code [1992] O.J. L302 and [1993] O.J. L253.

where most of the information on the consignment is, or should be, available. In practice, the procedure starts with the presentation of goods and the validation of a transit document at the Customs office of departure. One copy of the document[32] is kept there. When the goods arrive at destination, the Customs authorities carry out the necessary controls, note the outcome on the document and return a copy to the office of departure. According to Article 96 of the Community Customs Code,[33] the 'principal' (usually the forwarding agent) is responsible for ensuring that the goods are presented at the office of destination. If he fails to do so, a Customs debt is incurred. Guarantees may be lodged in order to ensure the collection of duties and other charges in the event of irregularities. The most common type of guarantee is the comprehensive guarantee,[34] which allows its holder to carry out an unlimited number of transit operations, involving any Community Customs office.[35]

The TIR system works on similar lines. It enables road haulers to seal their vehicles in the country of origin, travel across national frontiers without interference, and have all Customs clearance and documentation processed at the final delivery point. It does this through a system of 'carnets'. A system of guarantees is also in place, with a flat-rate guarantee of $50,000 applying to each journey.[36] The TIR system is administered centrally in Geneva by the IRU (International Road Transport Union) and operates through a chain of Guaranteeing Associations, which are normally national trade associations representing freight movers and/or the industry generally. Most associations have a dual function in that they guarantee to meet claims by their own national Customs authorities where these arise from irregularities in the use of carnets, irrespective of the nationality of the carrier or the origin of the carnet. At the same time the majority of Associations also issue carnets to their own national members. According to the IRU, some three million TIR carnets are now issued per year, 70 per cent of which are issued in Eastern Europe.[37] Table 3.1. compares the main features of TIR and Common/Community transit.

---

32. Commission Regulation 2453/92 [1992] O.J. L249/1 implementing Council Regulation 717/91 concerning the Single Administrative Document.
33. Community Customs Code, *op. cit.*
34. European Parliament, *Committee of Inquiry into the Community Transit System*, Progress Report number one, rapporteur: Mr Edward Kellett-Bowman, MEP (1996) p. 7.
35. Article 360 of Commission Regulation 2454/93 [1993] O.J. L253 implementing the Community Customs Code.
36. European Parliament, *Committee of Inquiry into the Community Transit System*, Revised note on the TIR carnets and the 'Community' and 'Common' transit procedures (1996).
37. European Parliament, *Committee of Inquiry into the Community Transit System*, Hearing with Commissioners Mario Monti and Anita Gradin (1996).

Table 3.1. TIR/Common Transit procedures: main differences

TIR	Common/Community Transit
58 member countries	15 EU Member States + EFTA + Visegrad countries
Single numerically identified document issued and administered centrally	T1/T2 forms
Managed by IRU and national affiliated authorities	Managed by Customs
2.3 million carnets issued annually	18 million documents issued annually
Guarantee arranged through IRU – Carnet holder responsible (usually transporter)	Principal responsible for guarantee (but usually indemnity arranged by national association)
Obligatory approval of vehicles	No approval of vehicles
Obligatory sealing of vehicles	No obligatory sealing of vehicles
TIR plate identifies vehicle	No specific identification
Period of transit fixed by transporter	Period of transit fixed by office of departure: normally 8 days

Source: reproduced with adaptations from European Parliament Committee of Inquiry into the Community Transit System (1996) Revised note on the TIR carnets and the Community and Common Transit procedures, 18 March, PE 216.559, page 4.

The Community Transit System was originally put in place in a Community of six members, three of which (the Benelux countries) already had a Customs union. Since then the Community has grown and the number of trade transactions has increased enormously, to the point where Customs have been unable to cope with the sheer volume of administrative formalities. One important aspect affecting Customs' ability to respond is that the abolition of internal frontiers has tended to lead to a reduction in the number of Customs personnel, and in funding for equipment. This has had a 'disarming' effect on Customs, with morale running particularly low in some regions.

Not unlike the Common Transit System, the TIR system too has acquired new contracting parties, and in particular countries from the ex-Soviet block, with weak and disorganized Customs administrations.[38] In such an environment, Customs services often fail to investigate suspected cases of frauds and irregularities and do little more than submit claims under the (flawed) guarantee system when irregularities (*see* below). The TIR system guarantee chain is at present receiving 500 Customs claims per day.

38. *See* European Parliament, *Committee of Inquiry into the Community Transit System*, Contribution by Jean Duquesne, president of ODASCE, Paris (1996).

2.3. Community Control Framework

Council Regulation 1552/89[39] lays down the rules for implementing Decision 88/376[40] on the system of the Communities' own resources. This Regulation supersedes Council Regulation 2891/77. It lays down rules for the making available of traditional own resources, but also for the reporting of irregularities and the recovery of sums due. It empowers the Commission to carry out joint checks with the national competent authorities, or to carry out their own on-the-spot checks. Council Regulation 1552/89[41] was amended in 1993[42] and 1994,[43] mainly in order to tighten up the arrangements whereby the Member States make available to the Commission the own resources assigned to the Community.

2.3.1. Notification, Keeping of Records, Crediting to Communities' Account

Regulation 1552/89[44] first establishes a framework for the establishment of amounts payable to the EC budget. According to Article 6(2) of Council Regulation 1552/89,[45] the own resources that are to be made available to the Community are established entitlements which have been collected or for which securities have been provided. These entitlements are entered by the Member States into 'A' accounts kept in the Treasury of each Member State.[46] Entitlements not entered in the accounts because they have not yet been recovered and no security has been provided must be shown in separate 'B' accounts. However, some Member States have been slow in establishing this system.

2.3.2. Reporting Fraud

The situation prior to the adoption of Council Regulation 1552/89[47] was one where Member States could communicate to the Commission 'information of particular interest' under Council Regulation 1468/81, which deals with mutual assistance. This had resulted in scant reporting and difficulties in accounting for own resources.[48] From 1 January 1990 each Member State has had to submit to the Commission a brief half-yearly report on any fraud or irregularity involving an amount exceeding 10,000 ECU stating the measures adopted in order to prevent the

---

39. [1989] O.J. L155/1.
40. [1988] O.J. L185/24.
41. [1989] O.J. L155/1.
42. Council Regulation 3464/93 [1993] O.J. L317.
43. Council Regulation 2729/94 [1994] O.J. L293.
44. [1989] O.J. L155/1.
45. *Ibid.*
46. Article 2(1) of Council Regulation 1552/89, *op. cit.*
47. [1989] O.J. L155/1.
48. House of Lords Select Committee on the European Communities, *Fraud against the Community*, session 1988–89 fifth report (1989) p. 12.

recurrence of cases of fraud and irregularities.[49] Yet the Commission wishes more detailed reporting. It has submitted proposals to improve the present quality of reports by amending Regulation 1552/89.[50] The amendment would have the effect of strengthening the present system of documentary checks and thus provide additional information.[51]

2.3.3. Checks

Joint inspections were the first form of Community inspection to be introduced by the Commission, and to be carried out in accordance with Council Regulation 165/74.[52] The distinguishing feature of joint inspections is that the prime responsibility for carrying out the inspection (i.e. fixing the dates and purpose) rests with the Member States. The choice of site of inspection rests with the Member State concerned. Article 18 of Council Regulation 1552/89[53] provides that the Member States must carry out checks and enquiries concerning the establishment and the making available of own resources, and any additional checks requested by the Commission.

The Commission can also conduct its own on-the-spot checks.[54] But the conditions under which the Commission may carry out those checks are severely restricted: the Commission must notify the Member State in advance, specifying the reasons, so that, for the sake of efficiency, the Member State in question can appoint its own officials to participate in the checks. As for the nature of such checks, the Commission found in 1992 that 'in 1991 most man-days of inspectors were spent in monitoring the introduction of the B accounts [separate accounts for uncollected debts] in the Member States'.[55] A later Commission report[56] (1994) shows that the areas covered in its on-the-spot inspections carried out between 1990 and 1992 were as follows.

---

49. Article 6 (3) second subparagraph of Council Regulation 1552/89, *op. cit.*
50. [1989] O.J. L155/1.
51. European Commission, *Report of the Committee of Budgets on the Commission Proposal to the Council for amending Council Regulation 1552/89* (1993); European Commission, *Report from the Commission on the functioning of the inspection arrangements for traditional own resources* (1994) COM(93) 691.
52. Council Regulation 165/74 [1974] O.J. L20/1 determining the powers and obligations of officials appointed by the authorities of the Member States.
53. [1989] O.J. L155/1.
54. Article 12 of Council Regulation 1552/89, *op. cit.*
55. European Commission, *Report on the application of Council Regulation 1552/89 implementing Decision 88/376 on he system of the Communities' own resources* (1992) COM (92) 530.
56. European Commission, *Report on the functioning of the inspection arrangements for traditional own resources* (1994) COM(93) 691.

Table 3.2. On-the-spot inspections carried out
by the Commission in 1990, 1991 and 1992.

1990		1991		1992	
Inward process-ing	29%	Separate accounts	92%	Imports under preferential agreements	56%
Presentation at Customs – release into free circulation of fishery products	29%	Special desti-nation	8%	Sugar and iso-glucose levies	33%
Separate accounts	14%			Imports of cattle from Eastern Europe	14%
Imports of cattle from Eastern Europe – Com-munity transit	14%				
Postal traffic	14%				
Total	100%	Total	100%	Total	100%

Source: European Commission (1994) Report on the application of the inspection arrangements for Traditional Own Resources, COM(93) 691.

It has been an on-going concern of the Commission that the national authorities responsible for the collection of own resources should be able to produce to authorized Commission officials the documents substantiating the own resources collected.[57] Access to documents has occasionally proved problematic to the Commission. In case 267/78,[58] the Court found that a Member State may not contest the Commission's power to exercise its supervision as soon as the Communities' own resources have been established by the competent national authorities. However, rules which in the national systems of criminal law prevent the communication to certain persons of documents in criminal proceedings may be relied upon against the Commission.

Article 20 of Council Regulation 1552/89[59] sets up the Advisory Committee consisting of representatives from the Member States and the Commission. One of the aims of the Committee is to examine and discuss the problems raised in inspection reports. The procedure is designed to ensure equal treatment for the Member States, at least for those affected by the issues concerned. Following

57. Amended proposal for a Council Regulation amending Council Regulation 1552/89, [1994] O.J. C382/6.
58. Case 267/78, *Commission* v. *Italy*, [1980] ECR 31.
59. [1989] O.J. L155/1.

discussion in the Committee, the Commission adopts its final position and informs the Member State concerned accordingly.

2.3.4. Mutual Assistance in Administrative Matters

Council Regulation 1468/81[60] lays down rules for mutual assistance and cooperation with the Commission in agricultural and Customs matters. Council Regulation 945/87 amending Regulation 1468/81 allows the Commission to carry out 'Community administrative and investigative missions in third countries in coordination and close cooperation with the competent authorities of the Member States'.[61] In practice these regulations and the Naples Convention of 1967[62] are sometimes used simultaneously when third countries are involved. According to Article 209 EC, which was added to the EEC Treaty by the Treaty on European Union, Member States should take the same measures to combat fraud prejudicial to the financial interests of the Community (*see* Chapter 1). Also,

> 'Without prejudice to other provisions in this Treaty, Member States should co-ordinate action aimed at protecting the Community's financial interests against fraud. To this end, they should organise, with the assistance of the Commission, close and regular collaboration between the competent services in their administrations.'

In the synthesis report regarding measures to combat wastefulness and the misuse of Community resources in the Member States,[63] the author concluded that cooperation instruments were not ignored by the Member States, who found this type of cooperation satisfactory. This assertion is supported by the European Court of Auditors. The number of cases involving Customs fraud and irregularities that have been the subject of exchange of information under Regulation 1468/81 between the Commission and the Member States has risen from 33 in 1988 to 534 in 1994 (114 cases were new in 1994). The Commission estimated that the total amount of traditional own resources at stake in these cases was more than 600 million ECU as of 31 December 1994 – the equivalent of 2 per cent of net traditional own resources collected that year.[64] However, response times remain slow. Differences of all kinds (administrative, legal, technical) hamper the movement of information between Member States. A number of suggestions were made by the Member States in order to improve this state of affairs. In particular the need for a basic require-

---

60. Council Regulation 1468/81 [1981] O.J. L144/1 (mutual assistance).
61. Article 15b of Council Regulation 945/87 amending Regulation 1468/81.
62. The Naples Convention of 1967 was concluded between the six original EC Member States and later extended to the other Member States, still with the exception of Portugal. The Convention also covers judicial assistance to a certain extent.
63. European Commission, *Protection of the Community's financial interests, Synthesis Document of the comparative analysis of the reports supplied by the Member States on national measures taken to combat wastefulness and the misuse of Community resources* (1995) COM(95) 556.
64. European Court of Auditors Annual Report for the financial year 1994, [1995] O.J. C303, p. 25.

ment for rapid information on transnational fraud emerged from the 'wastefulness' report mentioned earlier,[65] since fraud rarely developed in isolation in one country.

There are several instruments on Customs co-operation included in various treaties between the Community and its Member States and third countries: the Treaty on the European Economic Area, association Treaties with Central and Eastern European countries[66] and treaties on co-operation with other third states.[67] These instruments are relevant for the prevention and detection of EC fraud, and it is expected that they will lead to more information being exchanged. Now is the time to think of a monitoring system that measures the effectiveness of such cooperation agreements.[68]

2.4. An 'Immature' Regulatory Framework?

Clearly, until recently the regulatory framework has focused mainly on the making available of the correct amount of resources, rather than the fight against fraud. Council Regulation 1552/89[69] introduced Commission on-the-spot checks, and has upgraded mutual assistance requirements. However, on-the-spot checks remain limited in scope, and mutual assistance slow.

It is only in 1994 that a new GSP system was conceived, which allowed for the temporary withdrawal of preferences in cases of fraud or lack of administrative cooperation from the beneficiary country in checking certificates of origin. In December 1995 Council Regulation 2988/95[70] on the protection of the Community's financial interests was adopted. The Regulation has the effect, *inter alia*, of extending to traditional own resources the Commission's approach to administrative penalties already in place for the Common Agricultural Policy (*see* Chapters 1 and 2), and which the Court of Justice has consistently upheld.[71] One of the Regulation's main features is the list of penalties, which can already be found in earlier CAP (sectoral) regulations. It also gives a much-awaited definition of irregularity in the context of EC fraud. The main strength of the Regulation is to set a basic legal framework for the formulation of uniform administrative penalties with the same force throughout the Union. The penalties can be set for fraud relating to

65. European Commission (1995) *Comparative analysis ... op. cit.*

66. The European Agreements with the Czech Republic, Slovakia, Romania and Bulgaria entered into force on 1 February 1995, thus extending mutual assistance in the customs field beyond the confines of the Community.

67. In 1995 instruments containing protocols on mutual assistance in the customs field were initialled or signed with Tunisia, Morocco, Israel, Slovenia, and the trans-caucasian republics. Interim agreements were also signed with Belarus, Kyrgystan, Moldova, Russia and Ukraine. Negotiations are continuing with the Faroes, Jordan, Egypt, Lebanon, South Africa, the United States, Canada and South Korea. Lastly, the Customs Union with Turkey, which entered into force on 1 January 1996, also includes a protocol on mutual assistance in Customs matters.

68. J. Schutte, 'Administrative and judicial co-operation in the fight EC fraud' (1995) in *The Dutch approach in tackling EC fraud*, eds. M.S. Groenhuijsen and M.I. Veldt, pp. 127–134.

69. [1989] O.J. L155/1.

70. [1995] O.I. L312.

71. Cases 240/90, *Germany* v. *Commission*, [1992] ECR I-5383 and 104/94, *Cereal Italia Srl*: judgment of 12 October 1995, nyr.

any area of Community policy where they are required and for which there is a legal basis (except VAT-based own resources). The need to set up a system of sanctions has been highlighted by the Commission.[72] Another horizontal regulation under consideration is a Council Regulation concerning on-the-spot checks and inspections by the Commission for the detection of frauds and irregularities detrimental to the financial interests of the European Communities.[73] This Regulation would empower the Commission to ask officials of Member States other than that on whose territory inspections and checks are being performed to take part in them. The Commission would also be able to call on outside bodies to provide technical help to perform inspections. These officials or nominated bodies would work closely with the national authorities. This proposal has met with considerable resistance from certain Member States' governments, who have complained about the 'multiplicity of controls' and have invoked subsidiarity against its adoption.[74]

Nevertheless both horizontal instruments are particularly important in the field of fraud control for traditional own resources. This is because Community control has tended to lag behind other areas, particularly those concerned with the CAP. However, the widening of the Commission's inspection powers is delicate, since it involves a degree of interference with national tax-raising authorities.

Guarantees: scope for reform. At the moment, about 18 million transit declarations (in quadruplicate) per year are processed manually by Customs under the Common Transit System[75] and 2.3 million TIR carnets are issued every year, also manually. As a result Customs authorities have found it increasingly difficult to cope with the sheer volume of work, and, not surprisingly, have accumulated a backlog. With the extension of Common Transit to the Visegrad countries, the pressure on the system can only increase. Criticisms of the administration of the present system have already been voiced by the European Court of Auditors[76] and by the Commission.[77] These criticisms seem to fall broadly into two categories. Firstly they highlight poor administration of the system generally. Secondly they note failure by the Member States to notify and to recover sums due. The two categories are briefly examined below.

72. European Parliament, *Committee of Inquiry into the Community Transit System*, Hearing with commissioners Mario Monti and Anita Gradin (1996), p. 20.
73. European Commission Proposal for a Council Regulation concerning on-the-spot checks and inspections by the Commission for the detection of frauds and irregularities detrimental to the financial interests of the European Communities (1995) SEC (95) 9151 Final.
74. J. Myard, *Combattre la fraude: Un défi pour les quinze – Rapport d'information déposé par la délégation de l'Assemblée Nationale pour l'Union Européenne sur la proposition de règlement du conseil relatif aux contrôles et vérifications sur place de la Commission aux fins de la constatation des fraudes et irrégularités portant atteinte aux intérêts financiers des communautés européennes* (1996) French National Assembly Publications Kiosk.
75. European Parliament, *Committee of Inquiry into the Community Transit System*, Contribution from FENEX, Nederlandse Organisatie voor Expeditie en Logistiek inzake communautair douane-vervoer, Rotterdam (1996) p. 4.
76. Court of Auditors Annual Report for 1994, [1995] O.J. C303, 1.45 – 1.89; also previously Court of Auditors for 1987, [1988] O.J. C316, 3–17 *et seq.*
77. European Commission (1995) *op. cit.*

Generally speaking, the Commission[78] finds that Customs authorities in the Member States do not appear to give sufficient priority to transit controls. This means that investigations are not always carried out with the urgency required. Operators must present goods and documents to the Customs office of destination within certain time limits.[79] However, in practice, these time limits do not appear to be respected. In addition, there is failure to impose penalties where the time limits are also not respected.

The late presentation to the Customs office of departure of the copy to be returned results in an accumulation of uncleared documents. In some cases, delays in transferring documentation between Customs offices seem so great that it would be impossible to respect the time limits laid down by Community legislation without a major effort to clear the backlog, bearing in mind the accumulated delays.

The two main criticisms in this area are that the amounts recovered on the basis of Regulation 1552/89[80] are very small and that only a few cases notified on the basis of the Regulation are subject to legal proceedings.

Three comments can be made in relation to the dearth of court proceedings, which according to the Commission only number 22 out of 1000 cases. Firstly, the difficulties involved in getting different jurisdictions, and/or administrations to cooperate, in what is still basically a collection of national-territorial judicial spaces, should not be underestimated. Initiatives to improve cooperation have already been launched by the Commission. Secondly, the impact of insolvencies should not be overlooked, nor the relative ease with which economic operators – in some jurisdictions – can be discharged of their financial obligations, or alternatively just 'disappear' and 'resurrect'. In understanding this, a comparative analysis of the Member States' insolvency regimes might help to assess the situation better. Thirdly, a recent study commissioned by the Commission's Directorate of Financial Control and carried out in each of the Member States has shown that extra-judicial settlements were commonplace, particularly in northern Member States.[81] It follows that the number of court cases may not be even an approximate indicator of the effort exerted in order to recover funds, so in future the Commission may need to refine this particular indicator.

In some circumstances, recovery may be hindered by specific aspects of the regulatory framework.[82] In particular, there are shortcomings in the rules concerning guarantees and connected with the time limit of three years imposed by the Customs Code.[83]

---

78. European Commission (1995) *op. cit.*
79. Twenty days in the case of air transport and 45 days in the case of sea transport.
80. Council Regulation 1552/89 [1989] O.J. L155/1 implementing Decision 88/376 on the system of the Communities' Own Resources.
81. *See* H. Labayle, *La transaction dans l'Union Européenne* (Synthesis report of the studies carried out in the fifteen Member States concerning the settlement of fraud in cases affecting the EC budget, 1996)
82. *See* European Commission, *Report on the recovery of Traditional Own Resources in cases of fraud and irregularities* (1995) COM(95) 398 Final, pp. 10–11.
83. Article 218(3) and 221(3) of the Customs Code, 2913/92 [1992] O.J. L302.

The rules concerning guarantees. One way in which the authorities can recover duties and charges, in the event of an irregularity, is through guarantees (securities),[84] which can be provided either by a cash deposit, or through a guarantor. Guarantees can apply on a fixed-rate basis, for a single operation, or be comprehensive. In some cases, securities are optional, that is to say required at the discretion of the Customs authorities in so far as they consider that a Customs debt which has been or may be incurred is not certain to be paid within the prescribed period. But in practice, Customs sometimes fail to demand guarantees when sensitive or high-risk goods are involved, or guarantees are sometimes insufficient to cover any debt which might be incurred.[85] '[T]oo often, Customs administrations have been too slow to take action and have allowed guarantees to be unduly liberated or have failed to act against the Principal or against the other parties involved.'[86]

Particular problems arise in connection with the 'comprehensive' guarantee. A comprehensive guarantee document allows the holder to carry out an unlimited number of transit operations by road simultaneously. It is therefore the most flexible arrangement for traders, since it allows a series of operations by the same principal over a period of time. The amount of the guarantee is calculated according to a percentage of the import duties and other charges payable on the goods carried under the transit system on average during a week of the preceding year. The percentage varies according to the degree of risk involved. One criticism of this procedure is that there is no monitoring of the balance not yet committed or available. As a result, a comprehensive guarantee is often used to cover fresh transit operations although part or even all of the amount concerned has already been committed to cover non-discharged operations or operations under inquiry.[87] Member States may request an authorization from the Commission to ban comprehensive guarantees for certain exceptional risk products,[88] but in 1996 this possibility had only been used on two occasions. In 1995 the Commission adopted a Decision[89] authorizing the Customs administration in Spain to take specific measures to forbid temporarily the use of the comprehensive guarantee for external Community transit operations involving cigarettes. In 1996 another Decision[90] was adopted authorizing Germany to forbid temporarily the use of comprehensive guarantees for external Community transit for a list of goods such as bovine animals, frozen bovine meat, dairy products and oils, bananas and plantains, cereals and meslin, rye, sugar, undenatured ethyl alcohol of 80 per cent vol. or higher and spirits, liqueurs and other spirituous beverages.

---

84. Articles 189–200 of the Community Customs Code; also Council Regulation 3712/92 [1992] O.J. L378/15.
85. European Commission, *Report on the functioning of the inspection arrangements for traditional own resources* (1994) COM(93) 691.
86. Commissioner Liikanen's statement, *op. cit.*
87. European Parliament, *Committee of Inquiry into the Community Transit System*, Reply from the Court of Auditors (1996) p. 5.
88. Article 360 of Commission Regulation 2454/93, *op. cit.*
89. Commission Decision 95/521 [1995] O.J. L299/24 adopting specific measures to temporarily prohibit use of the comprehensive guarantee for certain transit procedures.
90. Commission Decision 96/37 [1996])O.J. L10/44 adopting specific measures to temporarily prohibit use of the comprehensive guarantee for certain transit procedures.

Principals (who are usually the freight forwarders themselves), according to some representations made to the European Parliament, often lose both cargo and security.[91] That is because in the absence of fixed itineraries, it is impossible for the Customs authorities to establish where the irregularity took place. The guarantee is often the only realistic chance of recovering lost revenue. As a result guarantors can find themselves responsible for a Customs debt, when in fact a third party is responsible for the fraud committed. In a communication of February 1996, the Commission noted the general reluctance of Customs to take action against debtors other than the principal.

The predicament of principals can be worse when high-risk goods are involved. Securities, in the case of 'high-risk' goods such as cigarettes, were thought at one stage to be too low. In 1994, a 'special carnet' was established in the TIR system, requiring higher guarantees for alcohol and tobacco products. This measure backfired because, as a result of this increase, insurance companies are now refusing to insure such cargoes. Consequently the national associations and International Road Transport Union have now stopped the supply of carnets. Notwithstanding this near-collapse of the system, the Commission still insists that higher guarantees are part of the answer to the transit crisis. But if one lesson has to be learned from the position of insurance companies, it is that commercial enterprise will not buttress an ailing system.

Another feature of the guarantee system is that if all goes well, the guarantor is released from his obligations twelve months after the date of registration of transit declaration. After three years the guarantor is automatically discharged if he has not been informed of the amount for which he is liable.[92]

In practice Customs authorities often wait for 9 months or more to have elapsed before issuing the principal with a notification of non-discharge. The Court of Auditors found that some Customs authorities even waited until the end of the three-year period after which, under Article 221(3) of the Customs Code, Customs debts cease to be enforceable, before they attempted to recover the guarantee.[93] As a consequence a percentage of claims are time-barred.

Delays of several months are frequent in all the Member States, at the different stages of both the mutual assistance and the recovery procedures. The lack of procedures for coordination of recovery between the Member States contributes to this state of affairs. In complicated cases, there are signs that the three-year time limit may be too short. Furthermore, Member States do not interpret this deadline in a consistent manner. In several Member States, national laws make provision for an extension of that period. This is not however the case in Denmark and the United Kingdom.

---

91. European Parliament, *Committee of Inquiry into the Community Transit System*, Contribution submitted by the Bundesverband Spedition und Lagerei e.V., Bonn (1996); also from the Freight Transport Association, United Kingdom (1996).
92. Commission Regulation 2454/93 [1993] L253, Articles 359–379.
93. European Court of Auditors Annual Report for 1994, *op. cit.*, pp. 28 and 34.

2.5. Solutions Foreseen

The solutions foreseen by the Commission can be divided into medium-term and long-term measures. Short-term solutions include measures aimed at improving and strengthening transit legislation, and improving the detection of fraud. Long-term solutions include the computerization of the transit system, and a timetable has been established for the central development of this project (*see* Table 3.3.).

Table 3.3. Computerization of transit system:
implementation, timetable and cost for central development

Phases	Period	Tasks	Projected cost (ECU)
phase 0	1993–94	feasibility study	1,153,774
phase 1	1994–97	development of system specification	4,133,774
phase 2	1998–99	implementation and extension	10,526,000
phase 3	from 99	operation and maintenance	n/k

Source: European Commission (1996), *Rapport Intermédiaire sur le transit*, SEC(96)1739 annex V, page 5.

Medium-term measures advocated are:

(a) the introduction of the necessary flexibility to forbid throughout the Union the use of the comprehensive guarantee for those sensitive goods which present high risks of fraud;
(b) the introduction of an expedited procedure for returning and discharging transit documents concerning sensitive products, possibly including special identification of these documents;
(c) prohibiting a change of office of destination for sensitive goods (or at least allowing a change only on fulfilment of conditions which would enable the transport operation to be monitored);
(d) the drawing up of binding itineraries;
(e) the reduction of the time limits and stages provided for under the inquiry procedure;
(f) the strengthening of the special Task Group set up by the Commission's Anti-Fraud Unit, UCLAF, charged in cooperation with Member States with taking all appropriate measures in the operational frameworks necessary to combat fraud in this sector;
(g) fuller involvement of economic operators in action to defeat fraud (including clear legal provisions to create a shared financial responsibility for transporters); and
(h) strengthening administrative and operational cooperation with countries neighbouring the European Union.

As far as longer term measures are concerned, computerization of the transit system has been put forward. This would mean that consignment details would be entered at departure. Those details would be transmitted electronically over an international network, to an office of destination in another country. The system would provide inquiry procedures for consignments which had not been discharged within the time allowed for their movement. Additionally, the system would be used for a better management of the system of guarantees, and risk analysis techniques would be applied to particular consignments. It is understood that such a system would have to be backed up by a number of physical controls at offices of destination. The system is not expected to be finalized before 1998 at the earliest.

2.6. Responses from the Council and the European Parliament

In its Resolution[94] of November 1995 the Council agreed that computerization of transit systems was the most important measure in the medium term to alleviate the serious problems currently affecting the system and that achieving it must be accorded absolute priority. It also called upon the Commission to proceed with work within its competence related to the same computerization and called upon the Member States to allocate resources to the project in order to make it operational by 1998. Finally it called upon the Member States and the Commission to cooperate closely and coordinate their efforts with a view to attaining common objectives, and to make use of modern Customs techniques, such as risk analysis and audit-based controls.

In December of the same year, the European Parliament exercised its right, under Article 138c EC, to set up a Committee of Inquiry to investigate alleged contraventions or maladministration in the implementation of Community law.[95] According to the Parliament's Rules of Procedure,[96] the temporary[97] committee submits to Parliament a report on the results of its work, including minority opinions if appropriate. The report is due to be published in January 1997. It will recommend improvements with regard to the detection and prevention of fraud, the safeguarding of the Community's economic and financial interests and the recovery of sums due.[98]

2.7. A Question of Integration?

The transit system offers a considerable challenge to the integrity of EC revenue. The Commission has put forward proposals to deal with the present crisis, which

---

94. Council Resolution [1995] O.J. C327/2 on the computerization of customs transit systems.
95. *See* European Parliament, *Request for the setting up of a temporary committee of inquiry to consider allegations of offences committed or of maladministration under the Community Transit System* (1995) PE 195.288/9.
96. Under Article 4(3) of the Decision of the European Parliament, the Council and the Commission of 19 April 1995 on the detailed provisions governing the exercise of the European Parliament's right of inquiry, and Rule 136(10) of Parliament's Rules of Procedure.
97. Article 136(4) of the Parliament's Rules of Procedure.
98. European Parliament Decision [1996] O.J. C7/1 setting up a Temporary Committee of Inquiry, at 3.

include reforms to the regulatory framework in the near future, and computerization of the system in the longer term. The Council and the Commission have both pointed out that pending the computerization of transit systems, it is essential for up-to-date Customs techniques to be applied, in order to improve the operation of current procedures. It is to be hoped that, meanwhile, these measures will go some way towards addressing some of the shortcomings in the regulatory framework and thus towards stopping the haemorrhage of EC funds, and reassuring the tax payer.

Computerization has been the standard response to problems of international control in the past ten years, so it is not surprising that it has been advocated in this case. The author suggests that this, at best, can only be a partial solution.

The present manual system is slow, partly because of the sheer volume of work involved, but also because of the complexity of the present EC regulatory framework. This point has been made repeatedly by the European Parliament.[99] Complex legislation, unavoidably borne out of political compromise, often leads to hesitancy in the Member States with regard to implementation. Unfortunately the level of complexity is not set to lessen with computerization. Furthermore, computerization will not ease the need for more physical checks, for it will not, for instance, resolve the problem of fraud by means of substitution of goods en route. Nor will it improve mutual assistance *per se*.

In 1990 Delmas-Marty[100] found that most EC frauds were discovered by Customs authorities and prosecuted as absence of declarations or false declarations to the authorities. We have seen that these authorities have now often been depleted and reorganized after the abolition of fiscal frontiers, and in some regions suffer from low morale. Another problem is that, entrusted as they are with the sovereign duty of collecting indirect taxation, their outlook has remained 'national-territorial'. But how long can it remain so?

The Member States have been accused of not giving enough priority to checks. When a consignment does not arrive at the office of destination within the agreed limits, the onus is placed on the office of destination to investigate. Two ingredients seem vital for success: 'ownership' of the task (i.e. feeling concerned about the outcome), and good cooperation networks. These attributes are evident in cases where attachments, and cooperative efforts between national Customs authorities are already taking place (for example France and the UK, The Netherlands and France, within the Benelux, as part of the Matthaeus Programme,[101] and as proposed under Customs 2000). In view of the success of these recent developments, and bearing in mind the duty of Member States to cooperate in order to combat fraudulent practices and the forgery of certificates in respect of the carriage of goods between Member States,[102] the time seems ripe to take existing cooperation networks one step further.

---

99. European Parliament Committee on Institutional Affairs, *Working document on measures to combat fraud* (1996).
100. M. Delmas-Marty, *Droit Pénal des affaires* (1990) Paris, p. 144 ff, second volume.
101. The Matthaeus Programme is a Community Action Programme for the training of Customs officials, organized by DG XXI.
102. *See* Article 3(1) second subparagraph of Council Directive 83/643 [1983] O.J. L359/8; Article 16 of Commission Regulation 1214/92 [1992] O.J. L132/1; also Council Regulation 1468/81 O.J. [1981] L144/1.

One way of fostering task ownership amongst Customs would be by creating a European Customs, who would properly own the task of protecting the financial interests of the European Communities.

In its first progress report, the above-mentioned European Parliament's Committee of Inquiry asked whether the existence of fifteen different Customs authorities militated against the effective control of the transit system. This concern is reflected in the attempts which are currently being made to give national Customs authorities a more 'European' outlook. It has been suggested that, as part of the proposed Customs 2000 programme, Customs officers should wear an emblem bearing the twelve stars. It is hoped that from this humble beginning, a change of orientation may occur. It is a moot point whether more cohesiveness would resolve the problem of administrative overburdening and low morale. It is improbable that it would resolve the problem of third country civil servants on low pay scales who have to supplement their earnings through routine, small-scale corruption[103] (*see* Chapter 6 on corruption).

More controversial is the proposal for a 'joint European Customs academy' which has been proposed in order to supplement the training of Customs officers of the Member States, as part of the same 'Customs 2000' action programme. This programme is at the time of writing (July 1996) under discussion.[104] This could be the first step towards a European Customs Authority – an authority who would 'own' the task of recovering EC funds fully.

This type of 'consolidation' exercise is already planned in other areas. The 'free movement of judges' is something we can now look forward to. This will involve a small number (at first) of liaison judges working in Member States other than their own, as required.[105]

3. FRAUD AND VAT-BASED OWN RESOURCES

3.1. Background: Harmonization

The proportion of VAT revenues Member States make available to the Community is small: 1.4 per cent, destined to fall gradually to 1 per cent by 1999.[106] It is not until the budget for 1979 that VAT became an 'own resource'[107] and it is now the main source of EC revenue. VAT fraud affects national revenues foremost. Much

---

103. *See* D. Spinellis, 'The phenomenon of corruption and the challenge of good governance' (1995) in *Proceeds of OECD Symposium on corruption and good governance*, p. 12.
104. European Parliament Session document, *Recommendation for second reading* on the Common Position established by the Council with a view to the adoption of a European Parliament and Council Decision adopting a Community action programme on Customs (Customs 2000), Committee on Economic and Monetary Affairs and Industrial Policy (1996).
105. Article 9(2) of Draft Protocol, on the basis of Article K.3 supplementary to the Convention on the protection of the European Communities' financial interests (1995) SEC (95) 9296 PEN.
106. Article 3 of Council Decision 94/728 [1994] O.J. L293/9 on the system of the European Communities' own resources.
107. Decision of 21 April 1970 O.J. L94/19; Council Regulation 2891/77 [1977] O.J. L336/1; Council Regulation 2892/77 [1977] O.J. L336/8.

of the Community control framework deals with the correct establishment of own resources *per se* rather than the fight against VAT fraud. Since 1 January 1993 fiscal frontiers have been abolished,[108] VAT rates have been (somewhat) harmonized and transitional arrangements have been in operation, pending a move to the definitive system. It has been argued that, by pressing ahead with the abolition of frontier controls without VAT or excise harmonization, the Commission did in fact relegate the common interest in effective collection.[109]

The original provisions on tax harmonization in the Treaty of Rome (Article 99 EEC) left to the Council to consider how taxes could be harmonized in the interest of the Common Market. The Single European Act required the Council to adopt proposals for the harmonization of legislation regarding turnover taxes and indirect taxation, for the purpose of the process of harmonization and functioning of the internal market. The first and second VAT directives[110] required Member States to 'replace their present system of turnover taxes by a common system of value added tax'. This goal was postponed to 1972 by the third VAT Directive.

The primary purpose of the sixth VAT Directive in 1977 was to provide a uniform basis of taxation.[111] However, the Directive contained many derogations and left the Member States with complete freedom to set their own rates of VAT.

The removal of the insulating effect of the fiscal frontiers required some harmonization of rates in order to avoid significant diversions of trade due to tax-induced price variations.[112] Rules were agreed for the approximation of VAT rates.[113] This meant that from 1 January 1993, rates no lower than 15 per cent were applicable in the Member States, although two reduced rates remained applicable, neither of which may be lower than 5 per cent, on specified categories of goods and services. Higher rates were abolished, although zero rates and special reduced rates could be retained during the transition period. There is, as yet, no uniform rate of VAT in the European Union, nor for that matter of excise duties. Standard VAT rates still vary between 15 per cent in Luxembourg to 25 per cent in Sweden. In addition, the Member States apply increased, reduced, super-reduced rates (less than 5 per cent) and exemptions according to national policies. This has resulted in a number of asymmetrical characterizations[114] (i.e. similar economic transactions which are treated in different ways by the Member States as far as the application of the place of supply is concerned), which in turn have led to distortions in competition, as predicted.

---

108. *See* written question number 190/93, [1993] O.J. C264/19 (93/C 264/34) by Sotiris Kostopoulos concerning VAT payments after 1 January 1993.
109. P. Levy, '1992: Towards better budgetary control in the EC?' (1991) 6 *Corruption and Reform*, p. 292.
110. First VAT Directive 67/227 [1967] O.J. L71 and second VAT Directive 67/228 [1967] O.J. L71.
111. Sixth VAT Directive 77/388 [1977] O.J. L145.
112. P. Farmer and J. Lyal, *EC tax law* (1994), Oxford.
113. Directive 92/77 [1992] O.J. L316/1.
114. C. Amand, 'The future VAT regime in the European Union – the opinion of the tax consultants' (1995) *European Taxation*, 219–222.

3.2. The Removal of Fiscal Frontiers: Impact on Intra-Community Collection of VAT

As a result of the abolition of fiscal frontiers on 1 January 1993, the concept of import and export within the Community has been replaced by the concept of intra-Community acquisition and supply of goods. The Commission proposed a switch to a system under which goods and services would be taxed in their country of origin but the tax would be redistributed between Member States through a clearing house system. Without such a clearing house system, exporting Member States (The Netherlands in particular) would gain revenue. This has been described as the 'origin' system since the tax is collected by (but does not accrue to) the Member State of origin. The Neumark Report[115] noted in 1962 that the origin principle usually applies in the fields of company tax and personal income tax for reasons both of administrative efficiency and equity. This contrasts with a system based on the 'destination' principle where the vendor invoices his intra-Community supplies to purchasers who are identified for VAT in another Member State at a zero rate. It is then the purchaser's responsibility to declare the VAT on their intra-Community acquisitions. The principal case for applying the destination principle to VAT rests on the need to avoid distortions of competition. That is to say, a consumer in country A should always pay a price containing the same element of tax, no matter in which country the goods have been produced.

Following a lengthy legislative process, the Commission decided to retain a modified version of the destination system following the abolition of fiscal frontiers. This hybrid solution can be found in Directives 91/680[116] and 92/111.[117] These arrangements were still in existence at the time of writing (July 1996). Although the transition arrangements are applicable until 31 December 1996, their period of application will automatically be extended pending the entry into force of definitive arrangements based on collection of tax in the country of origin. So far, the move to the 'origin' principle has proved highly contentious.

3.3. Transitional Arrangements: Problems

As mentioned earlier, the transitional VAT system which came into effect at the beginning of 1993 has been described as a hybrid.[118] Its main features can be summarized as follows:

> 'As far as most final consumers are concerned, the origin principle applies. Once VAT has been paid in one Member State, the goods are in free circulation throughout the Community.

---

115. European Commission, *Rapport du Comité Fiscal et Financier* (1962).
116. Article 28 of Directive 91/680 [1991] O.J. L376/1 on the abolition of fiscal frontiers.
117. Council Directive 92/111 [1992] O.J. L384/47 amending Directive 77/388 and introducing simplification measures with regard to value added tax.
118. European Parliament, *Options for a definitive VAT system*, Economic Affairs Series (1995) executive summary.

In the case of commercial transactions, and also of certain sales to final consumers under three "special regimes" (distance sales; cars, boats, planes and sales to exempt bodies) the destination principle applies. Traders must keep records of all sales to another Member State and all acquisitions from other Member States. Every trader must have a VAT number, so that sellers are able to check the tax status of the customers through VIES (the computerized VAT Information Exchange System).'[119]

In practice, this means that the delivery of goods to another Member State is exempt from VAT, and that the purchase of goods in the Member State of destination is subject to VAT, with the tax payable by the purchaser.

The three likeliest types of fraud under such a system are (i) the diversion of goods, allegedly sold to a trader in another Member State, for illegal sale on the domestic market, (ii) the suppression of untaxed purchases from traders in other Member States for illicit sales in the country of destination and (iii) collusion between purchasers and suppliers to suppress intra-Community transactions.[120] It is the problem of collusion between traders in different Member States which seems to put the greatest amounts of VAT at risk. Indeed all the purchaser has to do to release goods untaxed is to suppress the final stage of the transaction documentation.

3.4. Community Control Framework

Although Regulation 2891/77[121] was repealed and replaced by Council Regulation 1552/89,[122] Council Regulation 2892/77 was merely amended by Council Regulation 1553/89, which lays down the definitive arrangements for the collection of own resources accruing to value added tax. As a rule, Member States pay VAT-based own resources to the Commission monthly.[123]

Under Article 11 of 1553/89 the Commission's checks are carried out at the offices of the relevant authorities in the Member States. The Commission uses these checks to verify that the correct methods are used to centralize the basis of assessment and to determine the weighted average rate and the total amount of the net VAT revenue collected. Council Regulation 165/74[124] which determine the powers and obligations of officials appointed by the Commission also apply to checks relating to VAT resources.[125]

119. Article 6 of Council Regulation 218/92, *op. cit.*
120. R. Levy (1991), *op. cit.* p. 293.
121. Regulation 2891/77 [1977] O.J. L336/1.
122. [1989] O.J. L155/1.
123. Article 10(3) of Council Regulation 1552/89, *op. cit.*
124. Regulation 165/74 [1974] O.J. L20/1–3.
125. Article 12(2) of Council Regulation 2982/77 [1977] O.J. L336; Article 11(2) of Council Regulation 1553/89 [1989] L155/9.

Article 8(2) of Decision 88/376[126] stipulates that the checks, which are also provided for under Article 18 of Council Regulation 1552/89,[127] are mainly concerned with the reliability and effectiveness of national systems and procedures for determining the base for own resources accruing from VAT and GNP.

Compared to the control framework of the EAGGF Guarantee Section Fund, for example, Community control of VAT seems slight. Vervaele[128] has argued that Member States' reticence can be explained by the fact that unlike agricultural expenditure, failure to collect own resources is in principle the responsibility of the Member State, which then owes money to the Community. The only exception to this case is *force majeure*.[129] Although traditional own resources are 100 per cent Community resources, only a small proportion of VAT accrues to the Community. It follows that it is in the area of VAT that the most resistance is likely to be encountered with regard to Commission 'interference' in fighting fraud by way of extending the penal-administrative sphere that is already established in all other sectors, and in the recovery of funds.

As mentioned earlier, the transitional VAT system involves goods leaving one Member State without payment of VAT. It therefore relies on the full cooperation of all operators involved and, in cases of suspected irregularities, on good communication channels between the Member States' competent authorities. Council Regulation 218/92 replaces Directive 79/1070[130] extending the application of Directive 77/799 on administrative cooperation in the field of taxation. Council Regulation 218/92 introduced the VIES (VAT Information Exchange System).[131] The Regulation lays down rules for computer-based information exchange between Member States concerning the intra-Community movement of goods. This is to ensure that intra-Community supplies and movements of goods are properly registered for VAT in the Member States of destination.

One criticism of the Regulation is that it only makes provision for the very minimum of requirements with regard to exchange of information. It makes no provision for automatic exchange of information for certain categories of transactions where there may be loss of revenue. Information has to be requested and 'the requested authority shall provide the information as quickly as possible and in any event no more than three months after receipt of the request'.[132]

3.5. Collection and Tax Debt Policies in the Member States

The administrative procedures, material resources and human resources dedicated to the collection and control of VAT vary greatly in the individual Member States, as do procedures for remitting, or writing off the tax. In addition the Member States

---

126. [1988] O.J. L185/24.
127. [1989] O.J. L155/1.
128. J. Vervaele, *La fraude communautaire et le droit pénal européen des affaires* (1994), Paris.
129. Article 17(2) of Regulation 2892/77 [1977] O.J. L336/8.
130. Directive 79/1070 [1979] O.J. L331/8.
131. Council Regulation 218/92 on administrative cooperation in the field of indirect taxation (VAT) [1992] L24/1.
132. Article 5(1) of Council Regulation 218/92, *op. cit.*

vary in their individual approach to debt settlement. For example, some Member States have a 'bargaining' system of tax settlement, whilst others do not. Remission involves the decision to waive, either wholly or partially, an amount of payable tax. Under Article 22(9) of Directive 77/388, the Member States may exempt taxable persons from payment of VAT where the amount in question is insignificant. National legislation applies in determining in which cases remission may occur. For example Denmark, The Netherlands and the United Kingdom have legislation which authorizes the remission of tax debts. Greece and Italy only have measures having equivalent effect, whilst Belgium, Spain and France have no such provision. As for writing off (the cancelling of part or the whole of the tax payable in the accounts by the relevant administration), it occurs in all the Member States when a debtor has disappeared or when a forced recovery procedure has not succeeded, but in varying proportions. The European Court of Auditors found that the variability of such an accounting procedure did have an impact on net revenue collected – from very little in Belgium to 4 per cent in the new German Länder. Taking data obtained in eight of the Member States, it estimated the amount concerned to be around 3,400 million ECU (which had not been included in the calculation of the Community own resource base).[133]

Prosecution. The Member States have important responsibilities in the area of fraud affecting the EC budget. They must take 'the same measures to counter fraud affecting the financial interests of the Community as they take to counter fraud affecting their own financial interests'.[134] Clearly the principle of assimilation, so described, is not an issue when it comes to collecting national income, a small proportion of which becomes 'own resources'. The problem is that although fiscal frontiers have been abolished, the Member States retain very different approaches to tax evasion/fraud.

Consequences for fraud control. The cumulation of the system's main features, such as the non-harmonization of VAT regimes, the nature of the transitional system itself, the minimalist character of the present mutual assistance requirements, and the different prosecution policies produce an environment where revenue can easily be lost to the Member States and the Community. Indeed it has been recognized that the present shortfall in revenues in some of the Member States could partly be the result of opportunities for fraud offered by the present tax regime.[135]

The impact of the non-harmonization of VAT regimes (rates, collection, remission and write-offs practices) should not be underestimated. At the very least it has a distorting effect:

> 'The Commission agrees with the Court that the current diversity of national approaches could result in inequality of treatment of taxpayers and distortions of competition and could also impair the proper collection of the VAT own

---

133. Court of Auditors Annual Report for the 1992 financial year [1993] O.J. C327, 1.61 *et seq.*
134. Article 209a EC.
135. *See* newspaper article 'Value Added Tax EU may offer fraud opportunities' in *Financial Times* 14/15 September 1996, p. 4.

resource. It therefore undertakes to look closely at the matter in conjunction with the Member States, with a view to arriving at a uniform approach ...'.[136]

The nature of the transitional system itself means that the possibility exists for operators to acquire goods without paying VAT in order not to account for subsequent transactions. With minimalist mutual assistance requirements, the investigating authorities in the Member States are often left with a cold paper trail, if any at all.

The differing approaches to the prosecution of VAT evasion or fraud within the Union also create 'zones of leniency', which have been likened, more dramatically, to 'internal fiscal havens' by Caraccioli.[137] Cumulatively, this diversity helps to create an uneven control space, which a skilled operator can take advantage of.

'[Knowledgeable] economic operators would be led to choose fictitious domiciles for their businesses with an aim to setting up evasive or avoidance-type operations in those [Member States] that best suit them.'[138]

Over fifty percent of the EC budget comes from a proportion of the Member States' VAT. Each Member State has a unique constellation of VAT rate, collection and remission procedures and prosecution policies. Some of these constellations create potential 'internal tax havens' within the internal market. The author argues that an effective strategy to protect the finances of the Community requires (i) the harmonization of some of the collection procedures, (ii) improved mutual assistance and (iii) the setting of some minimum standards of prosecution throughout the Community.[139]

3.6. Perspectives: Indefinite Postponement of the Definitive System?

It had been envisaged that at the end of 1996 the transitional system would give way to a system where VAT is paid at source, i.e. in the Member States in which goods originate. In a 'State of origin' system VAT is deductible in the Member State of destination. This, according to the German Ministry of Finance, would take us closer to 'an internal market [where it is] just as easy to deliver from Cologne to Paris as from Cologne to Munich'.[140] Powerful arguments for a swift move to

---

136. Court of Auditors (1993) *op. cit.*, p. 296, 1.45, second paragraph.
137. I. Caraccioli, 'Vers un droit fiscal européen', paper given at a Conference on the protection of the financial interests of the European Community, Dublin 1–2 June 1995; also I. Caraccioli, 'Verso un diritto penal tributario europeo' (1995) 26, *Il Fisco* 6660–6663 and I. Caraccioli, 'L'importanza del dirito penale tributario in ambito europeo' (1995) 30, *Il Fisco* 7525–7526.
138. I. Caraccioli, 'Vers un droit fiscal européen', paper given at a Conference on the protection of the financial interests of the European Community, Dublin 1–2 June 1995, p. 6, author's translation.
139. *See* note 125.
140. Bundesministerium der Finanzen, *Formulation of the definitive scheme for imposing turnover tax on the intra-Community trade in goods and services and for a functional clearing procedure* (1994) Bonn, p. 110.

the definitive system have been made anew in 1996. Firstly, the present 'destination' VAT has been found to be unsatisfactory as an equitable 'own resource'. This is because despite the provisions in the sixth Directive, VAT has always been challenged as a foundation for equitable national contributions to Community expenditure. Since imports are included, but not exports, it penalizes countries with trade deficits. More seriously, it does not take account of variations in the proportion of national economies that are VAT-registered. This was clearly recognized by the Community itself when, in 1992, it brought into being the GNP-related 'fourth resource' and reduced the maximum VAT rate from 1.4 per cent to 1 per cent. Since total contributions are now governed by a GNP ceiling, the case for a separate VAT element is not now obvious.

Secondly, it has been argued in a report from DG XXI that one of the drawbacks of the destination system presently in operation, with its tangle of complex administration procedures, is that it opens the door to tax fraud and so reduces the overall tax take of governments[141] and hence their fiscal power.[142] It has also been argued elsewhere that to omit accounting for intra-Community transactions would be potentially less attractive in the definitive system, since this would result in the non-deductibility of the input tax.[143] Furthermore the effect on the revenue departments of Member States, if transactions are not reported, would be less severe under the final system as compared to the transition period, since at lest the non-deducted input tax is collected.[144]

However, the differences in VAT rates between Member States would continue to create problems under the origin principle. There are currently 27 different VAT rates in the Community (plus exempt supplies), which would greatly complicate the deduction of input tax by purchasers. The multiplicity of reduced rates and derogations, and the selection and definitions of categories to which a reduced rates can apply, are the main problems.

The new system requires a 'clearing house' to avoid the swelling of tax revenues in exporting Member States. However, the setting up of a clearing system has proved a major stumbling block in moving on to the 'State of origin' system and the implementation of the definitive system had been postponed for what seemed to be an indefinite period.[145] The Commission has now presented a proposal[146] for a Directive amending the sixth Directive, which would have the effect of fixing

---

141. *See* M. Bridges, 'Tax evasion – A crime in itself: The relationship with money laundering' (1996) 4:2 *Journal of Financial Crime*, pp. 161–168; also newspaper article: 'Labour voices fears over VAT', *Financial Times*, 11 November 1996, p. 11. According to the article: 'In 1995–96 VAT receipts were about £5 bn lower than projected [...] a related reason for this fall has been the cut in staffing levels at Customs'.

142. *See* newspaper article: 'Monti sets out radical plan for VAT shake-up' in *European Voice*, 20–26 June 1996, p. 1.

143. D. Raponi, 'L'I.V.A comunitaria: Le tappe per il passaggio al regime definitivo', paper given at a conference held in Venice and entitled 'L'I.V.A e l'Unione Europea, Frodi, Controlli, Sanzioni' on 24 February 1996.

144. *See* J. Terra and P. Wattel, *European Tax Law* (1992), chapter on mutual assistance.

145. *See* newspaper article: 'Senior EU tax official faces sack in VAT row' in *Financial Times*, 27 October 1995, p. 22.

146. VAT – proposed change to standard-rate system, European Commission Press Release IP/95/1437, 20 December 1995.

the minimum and maximum rates at 15 per cent and 25 per cent respectively, for the period from 1 January 1997 to 31 December 1998. At present Member States must apply a standard VAT rate of not less than 15 per cent, with no upper limit. This harmonization is part of a programme to culminate in a common clearing system by mid 1998, closely followed by the definitive system. Goals to be achieved by the end of 1996 include, *inter alia*, measures to improve the collection of taxes and the cooperation between Member State administrations.

4. PROTECTING EC REVENUE AGAINST FRAUD: THE FUTURE

According to UCLAF,[147] from cases reported by the Commission, it is known that up to two per cent of the EU budget (of over 70 billion ECU in 1995) is subject to fraud and irregularities. There is, as far as the irregularities affecting the EC budget are concerned, a belief that they occur mostly on the expenditure side, for example with regard to subsidies to farmers and exporters. But the reality is that irregularities involving larger amounts also exist on the 'income' side of the budget. In fact, in 1994 the cost of reported irregularities amounted to 3.4 per cent of the traditional own resources budget (import duties).[148] One of the main areas under attack is that of Community transit, where the guarantee system is faltering. Of the 12,000 cases reported by the Member States between 1991 and 1995, 120 (1 per cent of the total) by themselves accounted for 50 per cent of the total budgetary impact. Fraud cases involving organized crime are few and far between, but their effect on the budget is considerable: out the 273 cases under investigation coordinated by the Commission, 20 per cent involved sums of more than 100,000 ECU, and in half of them the amounts involved were more than 1 million ECU.[149] It is no wonder therefore that the transit system has been repeatedly described as 'in deep crisis' and 'near collapse'. The scale of fraud demonstrates that illegal transactions are no longer isolated cases. They illustrate the establishment of a 'grey market' involving also the laundering of profits from drug trafficking, the provision of funds for the drugs market and the progressive contamination of all commercial sectors. Generally there is a considerable political impetus to deal with this problem at the level of the European institutions, since the credibility of the European project seems to be implicated (*see* Chapter 1). But the legal, administrative, organizational and technical difficulties involved in keeping one step ahead of fraudsters should not be underestimated, as I hope the present chapter has made clear.

There are hopeful signs that the problem of loss of revenue and fraud are being tackled. Transit fraud has been put very firmly on the agenda, with a myriad of medium-term measures envisaged, and a vast computerization project is at the horizon, which is expected to be operative by 1998. The Community control

---

147. Unité de Coordination pour la Lutte Anti Fraude, the Commission's anti-fraud coordination unit, Directorate F.
148. *See* C. Goybert, 'La fraude communautaire: Mythes et réalités' (1995) 388, *Revue du Marché Commun*, 281–283; UCLAF, 'Seventeen questions on fraud' (1996), p. 1.
149. European Commission, *Protecting the Community's financial interest, The fight against fraud – Annual Report for 1995* (1996) COM(96) 173, pp. 48–49.

framework to protect Community revenue is 'immature', compared to the framework in place to protect EAGGF Guarantee Section expenditure, as the next chapter will demonstrate. Until recently the emphasis of Community regulation with regard to own resources has been on the making available of the correct sums to the Community. It is not until 1990 that Member States acquired a duty to report frauds and irregularities exceeding 10,000 ECU to the Commission. In this area of tax raising and levies collecting, which is the sole prerogative of the Member States, it is difficult for the Commission to make proposals which are likely to meet with the approval of the Council in particular, unless they are confined to the improvement of technical matters. That is why an embryonic European Customs Authority would be a major breakthrough.

It is hoped that the new horizontal instruments will help to 'streamline' fraud control at Community level. But it is the short term which, perhaps, should give cause for concern. Some parliamentarians have expressed grave concerns about the extension of the Common Transit System to the Visegrad countries.[150] Concerns centre around the adequacy of Customs infrastructure and the ability to police eastern borders of countries where, historically, there has been a fair degree of tolerance of the growth of the 'second economy'.[151] One question that must be raised in this respect is whether EU citizens will ultimately have to bear the cost of fraud through their GNPs (at the moment any loss of income incurred through traditional own resources or VAT is made up through the GNP contribution of the Member States). This extra burden put on GNPs would mean that the burden would rest, ultimately, on the wealthier Member States: a purely unplanned form of redistribution!

In the field of VAT, it is hoped that further harmonization and the change to the definitive system will eventually erase some of the opportunities for fraud built into the present system. The Commission is also looking at the possibility of harmonizing some of the VAT collection procedures in the Member States – a move which some commentators argue is at the very limit of, or beyond its competence. VAT is excluded from the competence of Council Regulation 2988/95, and from the 'PIF' Convention. VAT seems set to remain an area where the Commission has difficulties in asserting any competence in terms of fraud control. However, the challenge remains one of trying to make tax havens created by the different VAT constellations less attractive, by means of a directive. Much work remains to be done in order to protect the financial interests of the European Community in this difficult area. Community efforts are likely to be resisted in some of the Member States on the grounds of interference with sovereign tax-raising powers. Finally, it must also be recognized that, within the Union, some of the opportunities for fraud are created by the uneven nature of integration. Economic integration has raced ahead for over forty years, whilst fiscal, monetary, political and judicial integration and other forms of cooperation have lagged behind. As long as VAT rates are not fully harmonized, and the definitive system in place, the present danger of collusion

---

150. *See* for example written question E-0275/96, [1996] O.J. C185/47.
151. R. Naylor, 'From underworld to underground enterprise crime – "Informal sector" business and the public policy response' (1996) 24:2 *Crime, Law and Social Change*, p. 85.

between seller and buyer in order to avoid VAT will remain.[152] The extreme variation in excise duty rates also invites fraud, particularly in the UK and the Republic of Ireland where excise duties represent a higher proportion of national revenues.[153] The complexity of the EC regulatory framework, and the uneven nature of integration, seem set to continue posing difficulties for the collection of both EC and national revenues.

At Community level there is no doubt that efforts are being made to protect the EC budget from loss of revenue, although the main responsibility will continue to rest with the individual Member States.

---

152. *See* S. White, 'EC fraud- What is VAT?' (1996) 3:3 *Journal of Financial Crime*, pp. 255–259.
153. *See* A. Easson, *The elimination of tax frontiers in 1992: One European Market* (1989) EUI Florence.

Chapter 4. The Control of Fraud Affecting EC Expenditure

This chapter focuses on the control of expenditure fraud, that is to say fraud affecting the EAGGF Guidance Section Fund (§ 1) and the Structural Funds (§ 2). The structure is similar to that of Chapter 3, although the chapter is, of necessity, longer. In each section the origins of the funds are examined briefly and examples of fraud are given. The Community's control framework follows, together with the latest developments. The last part of the chapter (§ 3) offers a summary and deals with recent developments and prospects for improvement of the protection of the financial interest of the European Communities.

1. THE EAGGF GUARANTEE SECTION

Article 40(4) of the EC Treaty expressly provides that, in order to enable the common organizations to attain their objectives, one or more Agricultural Guidance and Guarantee Funds may be set up. As a result the EAGGF Guidance and Guarantee Section was established in 1962[1] in order to cover agricultural market support and to assist farm modernization schemes. Under Regulation 17/64[2] the fund was later split up into a Guarantee Section[3] which includes (i) expenditure relating to refunds on exports to third countries and (ii) intervention intended to stabilize the agricultural markets, and a Guidance Section (*see* § 2) which includes expenditure relating to measures undertaken in order to attain the objectives of the CAP set out in Article 39, in particular matters of structural policy.[4]

1.1. EAGGF Guarantee Section Fraud

There is a well-established typology of fraud. Reported frauds under the Guarantee Section include the famous carrousels, re-export and classification frauds. A *carrousel* occurs when a good quality product is exported from the EU, attracting a high rate of subsidy. The same product is then re-imported as a low-quality product, thus attracting low duties. Traders may repeatedly carousel in and out of the Union until the product is unfit for human consumption. In a *destination fraud*

---

1. Council Regulation 25/62, [1962] O.J. L991.
2. [1964] O.J. L586.
3. Articles 1, 2 and 3 of Council Regulation 729/70 [1970] O.J. L94/13.
4. *See* J. Usher, *Legal aspects of agriculture in the European Community* (1988) Oxford, p. 104.

a consignment is described, for example as going to a third country destination attracting a high subsidy. In fact it goes to a destination which should attract a small subsidy, or no subsidy at all. *Re-export fraud* relies on goods being brought back within EC borders without Customs being aware of it.[5] Additionally frauds often involve the *substitution or alteration of foods*, when for example goods held in intervention storage are of lower quality than declared to the authorities, or disguised. *Ghosting* is also common. In Italy, for example, durum wheat stocks were found in 1994 to be 25 per cent smaller than those declared. Products exported may also be hazardous to health. Another 1994 case involved a consignment of 3,000 tonnes of beef destined to the former Soviet Republics which was found not to have been adequately sterilized. The sum involved was estimated at 11.5 million ECU.[6] Examples of imaginative schemes abound which nearly always involve the forgery of documents, the misclassification or misrepresentation of goods,[7] and the connivance of officials. For example, in 1995 an Italian olive oil company was investigated for unlawfully claiming export refunds through a parent company since 1990. The olive oil thus exported was 'sweetened', and thus did not qualify for aid. The estimated total cost to the Community was 4 million ECU.[8]

1.2. EAGGF Guarantee Section Control Framework

It is in this area that the most advanced control framework can be found. The legislation places requirements on the Member States to notify, check and recover sums due. These requirements are found in other areas of the EC budget and are therefore un-surprising. The difference here is that requirements have been refined over a longer period, and have become quite exacting. The framework also goes well beyond what has been attempted in other areas of the budget, with for example the 'Black List' Regulation, which is examined below in some detail.

1.2.1. Budgetary Control

The EAGGF Guarantee Section is subject to the clearance of accounts procedure. Under Articles 98 to 104 of the Financial Regulation, the EAGGF Guarantee Section budget is implemented in three stages. The first stage is the payment of advances to the Member States. The second stage is when the payments are charged to each budget heading, on the basis of the returns submitted by the Member States showing the expenditure incurred. The third stage is the clearance of accounts. Article (2)(b) of Council Regulation 729/70 makes provision for the clearance of

5. *See* for example D. Ruimschottel, *The EC budget: Ten per cent fraud?* (1994) EUI Florence; N. Tutt, *Europe on a fiddle* (1989) London.
6. European Commission, *Protecting the financial interests of the European Community, The fight against fraud* (1994) pp. 28–30.
7. A. Doig and M. Graham, 'Fraud and the Intervention Board' (1993) 1:3, *Journal of Asset Protection and Financial Crime*, pp. 225–233.
8. European Commission, *Protecting the Community's financial interests, The fight against fraud*, Annual Report 1995 (1996) COM(96) 173, p. 71.

accounts. This means that, once a year, the Member States send their annual accounts of expenditure, as well as all relevant certificates and reports to the Commission.[9] The clearance account decision then determines the amount of expenditure effected in each Member State, during the financial year in question, which is chargeable to the EAGGF. This decision is reached with the help of a committee. This system ensures that the Directorate-General for agriculture verifies the manner in which the appointed national authorities have used the appropriations for the CAP.

1.2.2. Notification, Checks and Inspections

The Member States have to provide detailed information on cases of irregularities.[10] Under Council Regulations 729/70[11] and 595/91,[12] the Commission may take part in relevant inspections and inquiries by the Member States.[13] It may also carry out autonomous inspections.[14] Member States have a duty to carry out systematic scrutiny of documents, in order to give the best possible assurance of the effectiveness of the measures for preventing and detecting irregularities.[15] This applies without prejudice to inspections undertaken under Article 9 of Council Regulation 729/70.[16] Regulation 3122/94[17] lays down the exact criteria for risk analysis as regards products receiving refunds, and Council Regulation 307/91[18] makes additional funds available for the control of a number of high risk areas. Council Regulation 386/90[19] places a duty on Member States to inspect 5 per cent of all goods presented for exports.

   With respect to aids to the crop and livestock sectors, Council Regulation 3508/92[20] establishes an Integrated Administration and Control System (IACS) in the Member States to replace the hitherto sectorial approach to control. This means that the system comprises, in each Member State, a computerized data base, an alphanumeric identification system for agricultural parcels, a harmonized control system and, in the livestock sector, a system for the identification and recording of animals. Commission Regulation 3887/92[21] lays down rules for the implementation of IACS. In particular, on-the-spot checks must cover 10 per cent of livestock aid

   9. Article 4 of Commission Regulation 1663/95 [1995] O.J. L158/6.
  10. Articles 3 and 5 of Council Regulation 595/91 [1991] L67/11, concerning irregularities and the recovery of sums wrongly paid in connection with the financing of the CAP and the organization of an information system in this field and repealing Regulation 283/72.
  11. [1970] O.J. L94/13.
  12. Council Regulation 595/91, *op. cit.*
  13. Article 9(2) of Council Regulation 727/70; also Article 6(1) of Council Regulation 595/91.
  14. Article 9(1) of Council Regulation 727/70.
  15. Article 2 of Council Regulation 4045/89 [1989] O.J. L388/18.
  16. [1970] O.J. L94/13.
  17. [1994] O.J. L330/31.
  18. [1991] O.J. L37/5.
  19. [1990] O.J. L42.
  20. Council Regulation 3508/92 [1992] O.J. L355/1.
  21. Commission Regulation 3887/92 [1992] O.J. L391/36 laying down detailed rules for applying the integrated administration and control system for certain Community aid schemes (IACS).

applications and 5 per cent of area aid applications.[22] Applications subjected to on-the-spot checking are selected by the competent authority in the Member State on the basis of risk analysis.

1.2.3. Penalties

Farmers and fishermen. Under IACS, there are time limits for the presentation of aid applications and late presentation triggers a cut of one percent per working day of delay, and eligibility is lost altogether after 20 days.[23] If the area determined by the authorities is found to be less than that declared in the 'area' aid application, the aid is reduced. If the difference is more than 20 per cent of the determined area, no aid is granted. In the case of a false declaration made intentionally or as a result of serious negligence, the farmer is excluded from the aid scheme for the calendar year in question, or from any aid scheme for the following calendar year.[24]

Notwithstanding the ruling of the Court in case 240/90,[25] in the context of fisheries, penalties were at first rejected. Articles 35 and 36 (relating to penalties) of Council Regulation 2847/93[26] were deleted following difficult Council discussions.

Traders. An exporter who requests a refund in excess of that applicable, sees his refund reduced by (a) half the difference between the refund requested and the refund applicable to the actual exportation or (b) twice the difference between the refund requested and the refund applicable, if the exporter has intentionally supplied false information.[27] Where the reduction results in a negative amount, the exporter shall pay that negative amount. Where reimbursement is covered by a security not yet released, seizure of that security shall constitute recovery of the amounts due. Where the security has been released, the beneficiary has to pay the amount of the security which would have been forfeit plus interest calculated from the date of the release to the day preceding the date of payment.[28]

These penalties apply without prejudice to supplementary national penalty arrangements.

1.2.4. Recovery and Member States' Liability

Member States have a duty to recover sums lost as a result of irregularities or negligence, and to inform the Commission of the measures taken for those purposes and in particular of the state of the administrative and judicial procedures.[29]

---

22. Article 6(3) of Commission Regulation 3887/92, *op. cit.*
23. Article 8 of Commission Regulation 3887/92.
24. Article 9(2) of Commission Regulation 3887/92.
25. Case C-240/90, *Germany* v. *Commission* [1992] ECR I-5383.
26. Council Regulation 2847/93 [1993] O.J. L261/1.
27. Article 11 of Commission Regulation 2945/94 [1994] O.J. L310/57.
28. Article 3 of Commission Regulation 2954/94.
29. Article 8(12) of Council Regulation 729/70 [1970] O.J. L94.

When the amounts recovered are placed at the Fund's disposal, the Member State may retain 20 per cent.[30] Article 8(2) of Council Regulation 729/70[31] states that in the absence of total recovery, the financial consequences of irregularities or negligence must be borne by the Community, with the exception of irregularities or negligence attributable to administrative authorities or other bodies of the Member States. On the question of Member States' liability, the European Court of Justice has ruled, in this context, that where the incorrect application of Community law is attributable to a Community institution, the Community should bear the financial consequences. In the majority of cases, however, the Court has found that the EAGGF was not liable for the expenditure, that is to say that the Member State had to accept financial responsibility for over-spent or missing funds.[32]

1.3. The 'Black List' Regulation

In 1995 the 'Black List' Regulation introduced a system for the identification and the communication, between the relevant authorities of the Member States, of commercial operators who have committed irregularities or against whom there are well-founded suspicions, with a view to excluding them from the Guarantee Section of the EAGGF. The commercial operators targeted are those who, for example, claim export refunds or sell intervention products. Due respect to the principle of subsidiarity means that Member States retain considerable discretion with regard to the detailed implementation of this Regulation in this sensitive area, which touches closely on the rights of operators. The author examines the scope of the Regulation, raises questions concerning the rights of operators, discusses selected implementation problems and finally examines the two diametrically opposed perceptions of the Regulation.

The 'Black List' Regulation[33] and its implementing Regulation,[34] which took effect in the Member States on 1 July 1996 must be put in the wider context of the protection of the financial interests of the European Communities, which has intensified since the late 1980s.[35] In 1995 a Regulation for the Protection of the European Communities[36] or 'PIF' Regulation came into effect. A Convention of the same name[37] has yet to be ratified. Other measures enhancing scrutiny, or

---

30. Article 7(1) of Council Regulation 595/91 [1991] O.J. L67.
31. [1970] O.J. L94/13.
32. *See* for example case 18/76, *Germany* v. *Commission (EAGGF)*, [1979] ECR 343.
33. Council Regulation 1469/95 [1995] O.J. L145/1 on measures to be taken with regard to certain beneficiaries of operations financed by the Guarantee Section of the EAGGF.
34. Commission Regulation 745/96 [1996] O.J. L102/15.
35. S. White, 'A variable geometry of enforcement? Aspects of European Community budget fraud' (1995) 23 *Crime, Law and Social Change* 235–255, p. 240.
36. Council Regulation 2988/95 [1995] O.J. L312/1, on the Protection of the European Communities' Financial Interests.
37. Council Act of 26 July 1995 drawing up the Convention on the Protection of the European Communities' Financial Interests, [1995] O.J. C316/48.

developing cooperation, are under discussion.[38] The level of fraud in the transit system, which allows the elimination of Customs formalities within the transit areas,[39] has reached alarming proportions, with a reported figure of over 1 billion ECU of revenue lost through fraud between 1990 and 1995,[40] whilst a small percentage of operators are responsible for over 80 per cent of amounts defrauded. It has been recognized that organized criminal networks are now involved.[41] The present crisis in the transit system has made it more difficult for the Member States to discharge some of the specific duties connected with the running of the EAGGF Guarantee Section. Member States have a duty to take all the measures necessary to ensure that transactions financed by the EAGGF Guarantee Section are actually carried out and properly executed, and to prevent and follow up irregularities.[42] A further duty concerns the need to check the reliability and probity of operators, as highlighted in case 240/90.[43]

In the circumstances, the prospect of the Member States being able to blacklist certain operators has proved an attractive legislative goal, and one the European Parliament in particular has pursued vociferously. The technique of blacklisting has been used successfully in other areas, in order to deny access to the market to economic operators who either failed to conform to minimum standards of safety or who made regular use of dubious practices.[44]

The 'Black List' Regulation, which concerns us here, has two aims. The first is to make known throughout the Community certain fraudulent or suspected traders who are drawing funds from the Guarantee Section of the EAGGF. This is achieved through the inclusion of the same operators into an EU-wide information system. The second aim is to specify measures to be taken to prevent the same fraudulent or suspected operators from committing further irregularities.[45] The measures, which can be cumulative, include reinforced checking, suspension of payments relating to current operations and exclusion from future operations for a period of up to five years. The Commission has excluded itself from the field of application of the Regulation: only the 'competent national authorities of the Member States' are provided with information available under the new system. The political significance of the Regulation is, however, very considerable since it establishes a

---

38. In June 1996 the ECOFIN Council agreed in principle a Regulation concerning on-the-spot checks and inspections by the Commission for the detection of frauds and irregularities detrimental to the financial interests of the European Communities; two protocols to the 'PIF' Convention and an 'Anti-Corruption' Convention have yet to be agreed.

39. Commission Regulation 1214/92 [1992] O.J. L132/1 on provisions for the implementation of the Community Transit procedure and for certain simplifications of that procedure; Convention on a Common Transit Procedure [1987] O.J. L226/1; Customs Convention on the International Transport of Goods under Cover of TIR Carnets, 1975.

40. European Parliament, *Temporary Committee of Inquiry into the Transit System*, Written statement by Commissioner Liikanen (1996).

41. *See* newspaper articles: 'EU cheesed off by tax scam', in *The Guardian*, 23 May 1996, p. 3; 'Traffic de cigarettes: l'Etat roulé', in *l'Express*, 9 May 1996 p. 39; 'Mafia gangs involved in £1 billion EU frauds', in *The Guardian*, 9 May 1996, p. 10.

42. Article 8 of Council Regulation 729/70 [1970] O.J. L94/13.

43. Case 240/90, *Germany v. Commission*, [1992] ECR I-5383, at 26.

44. *See* newspaper article: 'A hidden hand of corruption', *Financial Times*, 6 June 1996, p. 27.

45. The definition of 'irregularity' can be found in Article 1(2) of Council Regulation 2988/95 or 'PIF' Regulation [1995] O.J. L312/1.

Community system requiring Member States to distribute information on certain operators and to adopt preventive measures.

Here the legal basis and scope of the 'Black List' Regulation are examined first. The protection of the rights of operators is followed by a discussion on the potential impact of the Regulation.

1.3.1. Scope of 'Black List' Regulation

The only provision in the Treaty with regard to the protection of the financial interests of the European Communities (Article 209a) was added by the Treaty on European Union. It requires the Member States to take the same measures to counter fraud affecting the financial interests of the Community as they take to counter fraud affecting their own financial interests and has yet to be used as a legal basis. Most anti-fraud measures nevertheless are found within the first pillar. The legal basis for the 'Black List' Regulation, for example, is Article 43 EC, which enables the Commission to submit proposals for working out and implementing the Common Agricultural Policy. Notwithstanding its place in the architecture of the Union Treaty, the Regulation 'polices' since its scope extends to measures which can have serious economic consequences for traders, as we shall see.

Two distinct groups of operators. For practical purposes, operators are divided into two distinct groups in the 'Black List' Regulation. Operators 'A' are those who have committed an irregularity or irregularities either deliberately or through serious negligence and have unjustly benefited from a financial advantage, or attempted to benefit therefrom. Operators 'B' are those who have been the subject, on the basis of established facts, of a preliminary or judicial report by the competent authorities of the Member States.[46] A 'preliminary or judicial report' is defined in the implementing Regulation as 'the first written assessment, even if only internal, by a competent administrative or judicial authority based on concrete facts that an irregularity has been committed, deliberately or through gross negligence, without prejudice to the possibility of this being revived or withdrawn subsequently on the basis of developments in the administrative or judicial procedure'.[47] Operators who have participated in committing an irregularity, or who are under a duty to take responsibility for one or to ensure that it is not committed may fall under either category 'A' or 'B'.[48] Member States apply their relevant national legislation in order to determine whether an irregularity has been committed or attempted, deliberately or through gross negligence.[49]

Notification. The 'Black List' Regulation targets operators who have committed or are suspected of having committed irregularities which involve amounts in excess

---

46. *See* Article 2(3) of Commission Regulation 745/96 [1996] O.J. L102/15 and Article 1(2) of Council Regulation 1469/95 [1995] O.J. L145/1.
47. Article 1(2) of Commission Regulation 745/96, *op. cit.*
48. Article 1(4) of Commission Regulation 745/96, *op. cit.*
49. Article 1(5) of Commission Regulation 745/96, *op. cit.*

of 100,000 ECU, over a period of one year[50] starting to run on the date on which the first irregularity was committed.[51] The Member States are responsible for implementing procedures relating to notification.[52] Each Member State designates a single competent authority to make and receive notifications. The said authority, using a standard form, transmits its notifications to the Commission, which transmits them to the competent authorities of the other Member States.[53] As part of the notification, the following must be transmitted to the Commission:[54] (i) their category ('A' or 'B'), (ii) details of the inquiry, (iii) facts leading to measures being taken under the 'Black List' Regulation and (iv) cross-references to notifications already made under previous legislation.[55]

Previously, Member States have interpreted the requirement to notify, which can already be found in Article 4 of Council Regulation 595/95[56] and Article 14 of Council Regulation 1468/81,[57] in a 'minimalist' manner.[58] It is anticipated that the more detailed implementation measures contained in the 'Black List' Regulation will induce the Member States to identify traders. But should a Member State fail to implement rules relating to notification, the implementing Regulation[59] now empowers the Commission to ensure that the identification and notification system is implemented by the Member State concerned. This provision was entered as a request of the European Parliament,[60] concerned that the Regulation should not be 'vague and toothless'.

Reinforced checking. According to the 'Black List' Regulation and its implementing Regulation, any operator ('A' or 'B') presenting a risk of non-reliability may be subjected to reinforced checking with respect to any EAGGF Guarantee Section transactions.[61] This gives the competent authorities *carte blanche* to increase the level of checks when in doubt.

Suspension. The Regulation provides for payments for current operations to be suspended, or guarantees to be held back.[62] This sanction can apply to both categories of traders ('A' or 'B').[63] The scope of sanction(s) is determined on a

---

50. Article 2(1) of Commission Regulation 745/96, *op. cit.*
51. Article 2 of Commission Regulation 745/96, *op. cit.*
52. Article 2(1) of Council regulation 1469/95, *op. cit.*
53. Article 5(1) of Commission Regulation 745/96, *op. cit.*
54. Article 5(2) of Commission Regulation 745/96, *op. cit.*
55. Council Regulation 1468/81 [1981] O.J. L144/1; Council Regulation 595/91 [1991] O.J. L67/11; also Council Regulation 1469/95 [1995] O.J. L145/1.
56. Council Regulation 595/91, *op. cit.*
57. Council Regulation 1461/81 [1981] O.J. L144/1 on mutual assistance.
58. *See* articles: 'Parliament wants to increase sanctions against fraud in the framework of the CAP', in *Europe*, 17 February 1995, p. 10; 'The Council adopts the "Black List" of companies that defraud, allocation of preventive community means to combat fraud in the EAGGF', in *Europe*, 26 June 1995, p. 10.
59. Article 2(2) of Commission Regulation 1469/95, *op. cit.*
60. *See* COM (95) 194 Final including the amended proposal.
61. Article 3(1) of Commission Regulation 745/96, *op. cit.*
62. Article 3(b) of Council Regulation 1469/95 which echoes Article 5(d-f) of the 'PIF' Regulation ([1995] O.J. L312/1).
63. Article 3(2) of Council Regulation 1469/95, *op. cit.*

case-by-case basis by the competent authority, taking due account of the real risks of possible further irregularities, as well as the following:

(a) the stage of the inquiry being held, depending on whether an operator 'A' or operator 'B' is involved;
(b) the volume of his operations within the EAGGF field;
(c) the amount of Community funds involved in the suspected or established irregularity;
(d) the seriousness of the irregularity according to whether it has been committed or attempted, deliberately or through gross negligence.[64]

Exclusion. Exclusions only apply to operators 'A', and to the product sector of the EAGGF Guarantee Section in which the irregularity has been committed or attempted. Exclusions can vary between 6 months to five years and are to be determined in the Member States, using the four criteria (a-d) above.[65]

1.3.2. Rights of Operators

The rights of operators have been considered in the Regulation with respect to retroactivity, confidentiality, data protection, the right to be heard, the right to be removed from the black list and proportionality.

Exclusion measures may not be applied to irregularities before the entry into force of the 'Black List' Regulation. Article 5(2) of the implementing Regulation states that notifications exchanged must be confidential. Member States must take all necessary precautions to ensure that the information they exchange remains confidential and is not sent to persons other than the Member States or institutions whose duties require that they have access to it, unless the Member State has agreed to such disclosure. The relevant provisions laid down in the rules on mutual assistance in Customs and agricultural matters[66] and in Directive 95/46 apply *mutatis mutandis.*[67]

Article 4(1)(a) of the 'Black List' Regulation stipulates that operators have the right to a prior hearing and a right of appeal in respect of exclusion and suspension where appropriate. A 'prior hearing' in this context means an opportunity to offer explanations to the authority administering the EAGGF Guarantee Section, not access to an independent court. The question of what right of appeal traders would have against direct Commission measures is also left open.[68] This may, in time, raise challenges under Article 6(1) and 6(2) of the European Convention of Human Rights.

---

64. Article 3(3) of Commission Regulation 745/96, *op. cit.*
65. Article 3(4) second subparagraph of Commission Regulation 745/96 [1996] O.J. L102/15; also Article 5 (d) of 'PIF' Regulation 2988/95 [1995] L312/1.
66. Article 4(2) of Council Regulation 1469/95, *op. cit.*
67. Directive 95/46 [1995] L281/31 on the protection of individuals with regard to the processing of personal data and the free movement of such data.
68. *See* European Parliament, *Opinion of the Committee on Agriculture and Rural Development for the Committee on Budgetary Control*, point 1.15, 24 January 1995.

In the case of a Member State finding that an operator had been wrongfully blacklisted, the Commission must be informed, and must in turn relay this fact to the other Member States, which must in turn immediately inform those to whom they had notified these personal data under Regulation 1469/95. Clearly transmission involves several steps, and re-instatement may be protracted. Furthermore the Regulation does not say whether, in case of loss of profits due to wrongful blacklisting or delays involved in removing names from the black list, damages would be available, and from where. There remains the question of whether, in the event of loss of profit or injury to a trader, a Member State would have to make damages available under *Brasserie du Pêcheur/Factortame III.*[69] The first of several pre-conditions for the award of reparation under the above-mentioned case is that the breach of Community law must be attributable to the national legislature acting in a field in which it has *a wide discretion to make legislative choices.*[70] It is a moot point whether, put together, the 'Black List' Regulation and its implementing Regulation leave the Member States a wide discretion to make legislative choices, although an element of choice is involved.

Although the 'Black List' Regulation places a duty on the Member States to comply with the principle of proportionality with respect to the measures it makes available and the irregularity, whether it is committed or suspected, it may be more difficult to apply the principle if traders are already subject to, for example, financial penalties under other specific provisions of the CAP.[71] It must also be remembered that the measures contained in the 'Black List' Regulation can be cumulative.

In addition to this, authorities who recover extra-judicially[72] (as is more common in most of the northern Member States)[73] may have to juggle existing requirements in order to make blacklisting possible. For example, in the UK it seems that blacklisting could become part of the compounding contract possible under Article 152 of the Customs and Excise Management Act 1979. This means an addition to the 'already astonishing' powers of Customs,[74] which may give rise to problems of proportionality.

Discussion. Although the Regulation is precise in what it seeks to achieve, most of the implementation details are left to the competent authorities in the Member States. This means that competent authorities are not subjected to a 'legislative straightjacket', but on the other hand, they have to deal with the absence of detailed implementing guidelines. This creates a tension at the implementing level.

For example, when operators 'B' are involved, notification is triggered by the first written assessment (even if just internal) based on concrete facts that an

---

69. Cases C-46/93 and C-48/93, *Brasserie du Pêcheur* v. *Germany and R V Secretary of State for Transport, ex parte Factortame*, judgment of 5 March 1996, nyr.
70. Author's emphasis.
71. Article 6 of Council regulation 1469/95, *op. cit.*
72. *See* S. White, 'Black listing: three questions' (1996) 12 *AGON*, 8–9.
73. H. Labayle, *La transaction dans l'Union Européenne – Rapport de synthèse* ('Labayle Report') (1996).
74. 'The powers entrusted to Her Majesty's Customs and Excise are in themselves astonishing', Forbes, J in *R v HM Customs and Excise, ex parte Haworth*, 17 July 1985.

irregularity has been committed either deliberately of through gross negligence. Clearly the Member States will have various 'trigger points'. It must be noted that although the notification of an operator who has been convicted of fraud does not raise any particular legal problem, the notification of a suspect does raise problems, particularly since the level of proof is not specified.

The Economic and Social Committee was not slow in underlining the seriousness of the injury to an operator unjustly identified by a Member State as presenting a risk of 'non-reliability'.[75] It is likely, therefore, that the competent authorities will exercise extreme caution before notifying. The length of exclusion, too, is at the discretion of the sole competent authority. There is no detailed criterion or 'yardstick' to be used throughout the Community. Put together, these factors alone may lead to an uneven 'black list' enforcement area. However, in view of the high threshold (100,000 ECU) and the relatively small number of notifications expected, this may not cause a significant problem within the internal market.

1.3.3. Conclusion: Blacklisting, an Important Step in the Fight Against Fraud?

There are two differing perceptions of the 'Black List' Regulation. One view is that it is only a superficially attractive measure, with limited potential impact on the protection of the financial interests of the European Communities. This is so, it has been argued, because the Regulation duplicates existing provisions, particularly those now contained in the 'PIF' Regulation, which now frames Community sanctions. Secondly, a combination of factors may ensure that notifications remain as 'minimalist' as they were under Regulations 1468/81 and 595/91 because of (i) the high pecuniary threshold (100,000 ECU), (ii) the need for competent authorities to pay the fullest attention to the rights of operators and (iii) the (linked) need of competent authorities to exercise due caution in order to avoid any possible claims for damages. This diminishes the potential impact of the Regulation.

Another view is that the Regulation is in fact 'filling an important legislative lacuna'. This is because, in the internal market, it has been too easy for unscrupulous traders, when they are known or suspected of being involved in irregularities by a Customs authority, to claim export refunds from another EU Customs authority where they are not suspected. The present prescribed level of checks (not less than 5 per cent according to Article 3(6) of Council Regulation 386/90[76] and Commission Regulation 2221/95),[77] and the absence hitherto of a EU-wide computerized system to monitor transit have meant that the same 'mobile' operators could remain undetected by Customs authorities. The Regulation 'sends the right message' to traders who, if detected, have much to lose.

---

75. *See* Opinion on the Proposal for a Council Regulation on measures to be taken in dealing with certain beneficiaries of operations financed by the Guarantee Section of the EAGGF, [1994] O.J. C393/81, p. 82.
76. Council Regulation 386/90 [1990] O.J. L42 on the monitoring carried out at the time of export of agricultural products receiving refunds or other amounts.
77. Commission Regulation 2221/95 [1995] O.J. L224 laying down detailed rules for the application of Council Regulation 396/90 as regards physical checks carried out at the time of export of agricultural products qualifying for refunds.

The author feels that there is no need at this stage to take an unnecessarily pessimistic view of the Regulation. As John Tomlinson, MEP, recently pointed out in an address to the UK Association of Lawyers for the Protection of the Financial Interests of the European Communities, the 'freephone' line, established in 1994 in all the Member States to encourage informants to report fraud affecting the EC budget was also greeted with much scepticism at first.[78] It is now well established and proving an invaluable tool in the fight against fraud affecting the EC budget. The same fate may await blacklisting.

The 'Black List' Regulation will be subjected to a review no later than July 1997.[79] It may be that this revision process will help to 'iron out' uncertainties and ambiguities. If this is the case, blacklisting may be successfully extended to cover Structural Funds, and thus help to deal with the equally serious problem of procurement fraud[80] which is presently affecting them.

2. STRUCTURAL FUNDS

The tasks of the Structural Funds are defined in Council Regulation 2081/93 (Framework Regulation). The European Development Fund (ERDF henceforth) finances measures aimed at the modernization of infrastructure, in accordance with Article 130c of the EC Treaty.[81] Within the framework of Article 123 of the EC Treaty, The European Social Fund (ESF henceforth) finances various measures to combat unemployment.[82] The EAGGF Guidance-Section promotes rural development in line with the principles set out in Article 39 of the EC Treaty.[83] The tasks of the Financial Instrument of Fisheries Guidance[84] (FIFG henceforth) are set out in Articles 1–3 of Council Regulation 2080/93 in accordance with Article 43 of the EC Treaty.[85] The most recent of the Structural Funds is the Cohesion Fund, set up in 1993 under Article 235 EC to finance key environmental and transport infrastructure projects in the four poorest Member States – Spain, Portugal Greece and Ireland – whose per capita GDP is less than 90 per cent of the EU average. The tasks of the Cohesion Fund are set out in Council Regulation 1164/94.[86]

The total expenditure on Structural Funds will add up to approximately 170 billion ECU between 1994 and 1999 – around a third of the overall budget – compared with 64 billion between 1989 and 1993. Around 90 per cent of the funds are paid out to Member States' initiatives (national or regional initiatives), whilst

78. ALPFIEC Conference 16 May 1996, London School of Economics.
79. Article 7 of Council Regulation 1469/95 [1995] O.J. L145/1.
80. S. White and N. Dorn, 'EC fraud, subsidiarity and prospects for the IGC: a regional dimension?' (1996) 3(3) *European Urban and Regional Studies* 262–266; also I. Battistotti, 'Protection des intérêts financiers et fonds structurels', seminar paper, March 1995.
81. Article 3(1) of Council Regulation 2081/93 [1993] O.J. L193/5.
82. Article 3(2) of Council Regulation 2081/93, *op. cit.*
83. Article 3(3) of Council Regulation 2081/93, *op. cit.*
84. Article 3(3a) of Council Regulation 2081/93, *op. cit.*
85. Council Regulation 2080/93 [1993] O.J. L193/1 laying down provisions for implementing Regulation 2058/88 as regards the financial instrument of fisheries guidance.
86. Council Regulation 1164/94 [1994] O.J. L130, establishing a Cohesion Fund and repealing Council Regulation 792/93 establishing a cohesion financial instrument.

9 per cent is spent directly by the Community, with a 1 per cent reserve for innovative measures (Community initiatives).[87]

Table 4.1. Breakdown of Structural Funds by Objective and by Member State (in million ECU)

	Objectives						C.I.	Total
	1994-1999					1995-1999	1995-1999	
	1	2	3	4	5	6		
B	730	341	465	191.6	77	N/A	346.8	2,151.4
DK	zero	119	301	262.5	54	N/A	117.4	853.9
D	13,640	1,566	1,942	1,133.8	1,227	2,557	N/A	22,065.8
GR	13,980	zero	zero	zero	zero	zero	1,241.9	15,221.9
E	26,300	2,415	1,843	431.6	664	N/A	3,129.3	34,782.9
F	2,190	3,773	3,203	1,912.7	2,238	N/A	1,813.1	15,129.8
IRL	5,620	zero	zero	zero	zero	N/A	591.4	6,211.4
I	14,860	1,462	1,715	798.6	901	N/A	2,121.4	21,858
L	zero	15	23	40	6	N/A	21.2	105.2
NL	150	650	1,079	159.2	150	N/A	603	2.791.2
P	13,980	zero	zero	zero	zero	N/A	1,127	15,107
UK	2,360	4,580	3,377	439.3	817	N/A	1,782.2	13,355.5
A	185.5	101	395	388	411	N/A	163.5	1,644.1
FIN	zero	183	343	354	194	526.81	171.4	1,772.2
S	zero	160	520	198	138	280	142.4	1,438.4

Source: *European Voice* newspaper, 18–14 July 1996, page 19, National and Community initiatives.

For national initiatives, the Member States, acting in conjunction with the regional authorities, submit to the Commission a development plan setting out their priorities for action. A Community Support Framework (CSF) is then negotiated between the Commission and the authorities of the Member State which reflects Community priority objectives. The Commission then adopts the programmes proposed by the Member State. An alternative route is for the Member State to submit a Single Programming Document (SPD) which brings together priorities and programmes. A single decision is then taken by the Commission on the SPD. A far as Community initiatives are concerned, the Commission relies on its Green Paper and the subsequent guidelines to adopt programmes proposed by the Member States. For the period 1994 to 1999, these programmes concentrate on seven themes: (i) cross-border cooperation (INTERREG); (ii) local development in rural areas (LEADER); (iii) support for the most remote regions (REGIS); (iv) the integration into working life

---

87. Article 11 of Council Regulation 4253/88 [1988] O.J. L374/1, laying down provisions for implementing Regulation 2052/88 as regards coordination of the activities of the different Structural Funds between themselves and with the operations of the EIB and the other existing financial instruments.

of women, young people and the disadvantaged (EMPLOYMENT); (v) adaptation to industrial change (ADAPT, SME, RECHAR, KONVER, RESIDER, RETEX); (vi) urban policy (URBAN) and (vii) restructuring the fisheries sector (PESCA).

2.1. Background: Two Major Reforms

The first reform of the Structural Funds was effected as part of a larger political and economic plan to reduce economic disparities in anticipation of an internal market. The Single European Act introduced Title V into the EEC Treaty, which deals with economic and social cohesion. Article 130d in particular requires the Commission to submit a proposal to amend the structure and operational rules of the Structural Funds. In the 1988 revised regulations, the emphasis was put on (i) concentration of Structural Funds on priority objectives, (ii) participation or partnership with the Member States, (iii) coherence with the Member States' economic policies, (iv) sound financial management, and (v) monitoring involving simplification, surveillance and flexibility.

The Structural Funds were reformed a second time in 1993. In July of that year the Council adopted six revised regulations governing the Structural Funds. With a budget of 141 billion ECU for a six-year period, the Structural Funds became the favoured instrument to improve economic and social cohesion in the Community. Firstly, guiding principles were clarified and reinforced[88] to include:

- The concentration[89] of measures on six priority objectives (*see* below) for development.
- Programming,[90] which results in multi-annual development programmes.
- Partnership,[91] which implies the closest cooperation possible between the Commission and the appropriate authorities at national, regional or local level in each Member State for the preparatory stage to implementation of the measures.
- Additionality,[92] which means that Community assistance complements the contributions of the Member State rather than reducing them. This requires that

---

88. *See* European Commission, *Community Structural Funds 1994–99* (1993) pp. 10–25.
89. Reinforced concentration: Articles 1 (1,2,3,4,5) [priority objectives]; 8 (1,2,3) [eligibility of objective 1 regions]; 9 (1,2,3,4,5,6) [eligibility objective 2 regions]; 11 (1,2,3,4) [eligibility of objective 5b areas]; 12 (1,2,3) [available resources] and 12(4) [allocation and appropriations] of Council Regulation 2081/93 (Framework Regulation) [1993] O.J. L193/44.
90. Programming: Article 6 of Council Regulation 2081/93 [period covered and timetable]; Articles 8, 9, 10, 11b of Council Regulation 2081/93 and Articles 5, 6 and 10 of Council Regulation 2081/93 [adjusted procedures]; Article 1 of ERDF Regulation 2083/93; Article 1 of ESF Regulation 2084/93; Articles 2 and 5 of EAGGF-Guidance Fund 2085/93; Article 3 of FIFG Regulation 2080/93 [scope of funds].
91. Partnership: Article 4 of Council Regulation 2081/93.
92. Additionality: Article 9 of Council Regulation 2082/93. Each Member State now has to 'maintain, in the whole of the territory concerned, its public structural or comparable expenditure at least at the same level as in the previous programming period, taking into account the macro-economic circumstances in which the funding takes place, as well as a number of specific economic circumstances, namely privatizations, an unusual level of public structural expenditure undertaken in the previous programming period and business cycles in the national economy'.

the Member States maintain public spending on each objective at no less than the level reached in the preceding period.

Another key principle which is reiterated in the 1993 revised Framework Regulation is co-financing.[93] The Community contribution as a general rule is still not more than 50 per cent of the total costs for Objectives 2, 4 and 5(b) and not more than 75 per cent of the total cost for assistance under Objective 1. However, Article 13(3) of the Framework Regulation specifies that, in exceptional and duly justified cases, the contribution from the Structural Funds in Objective 1 regions in the four Member States concerned by the Cohesion Fund may rise to a maximum of 80 per cent of the total cost, and to a maximum of 85 per cent of the total cost for the outermost regions as well as for the outlying Greek islands which have a handicap as far as distance is concerned.

Objective 1 provides ERD, ESF and EAGGF Guidance Section financial assistance[94] for regions with a per capita GDP of less than 75 per cent of the Union average (almost 70 per cent of total Structural Funds allocation goes to designated Objective 1 regions). Objective 2 covers areas suffering from industrial decline where unemployment rates are higher than the EU average through the ERDF and ESF. Objectives 3 and 4 cover the long-term and young unemployed, and workers whose employment prospects are threatened by industrial change through the ESF. Objectives 5(a) and 5(b) apply to fragile rural areas and farmers and fishermen facing structural changes. Objective 5(a) operations are financed through the EAGGF Guidance Section and FIFG, and 5(b) though the EAGGF Guidance Section, the ESF and ERDF. Finally, Objective 6 was set up to cater for the special needs of the Nordic countries when they joined the European Union in 1995, and aims to promote employment and structural adjustment in areas with an extremely low population density, through all the funds.[95]

Where a form of assistance involves participation under more than one Structural Fund and/or more than one other financial instrument, it may be implemented in the form of an integrated approach.[96]

The revised regulations thus not only made possible the financing of operations in new regions and the co-financing of new operations, but also introduced new procedural rules, as we shall see.

2.2. Fraud and the Structural Funds

Although much has been written about fraud affecting the CAP, and in particular the EAGGF Guarantee Section fraud, there is a dearth of literature on Structural Funds, in spite of the growing number of reported irregularities, which must be at

---

93. Article 13 of Council Regulation 2081/93 O.J. (1993) L 193/5.
94. For correspondence between funds and objectives, *see* Article 2 of Council Regulation 2081/93, *op. cit.*
95. Article 52 of Council Decision 95/1 [1995] O.J. L1 adjusting the instruments concerning the accession of new Member States to the European Union amending Protocol number 6 annexed to the Act of Accession [1994] O.J. 241, in particular page 354.
96. Article 5(5) second subparagraph of Council Regulation 2081/93 ('Framework Regulation').

least partly related to the new requirements placed on Member States by the 1993 reform.

In 1995, 58 per cent of cases of irregularities notified concerned the European Social Fund, 20 per cent the European Regional Fund, 20 per cent the EAGGF-Guidance, 2 per cent FIFG and 1 per cent the Cohesion Fund.[97] The total financial impact was estimated at 44 million ECU,[98] although it is not always possible to quantify the exact financial impact. Broadly, frauds affecting the Structural Funds, whether they affect national or Community initiatives, seem to fall into three categories: (i) cases where 'phantom' activities are involved, (ii) cases where funds are used or a different purpose and (iii) procurement frauds, when the EC competition rules are breached. Frauds usually involve over-invoicing, falsifying documents and/or bribery of officials (*see* Chapter 6 on corruption).

2.2.1. ESF Fraud

Community fraud involving vocational training programmes tends to be of two types: (i) when the project appears to meet all the criteria but its cost has been deliberately inflated, and (ii) when false accounts are submitted in order to get approval for a non-existent or ineligible project or to obtain more than the project actually costs.[99]

Case 1. Between 1989 and 1993 a Belgian institute received the equivalent of 760,000 ECU by way of co-financing for training schemes. The schemes never took place: the instructors mentioned in the files were in fact research workers who had never done any teaching.[100]

Case 2. An Italian firm received 5 million ECU of ESF between 1985 and 1992 to train pilots. The students listed were in fact fictitious. Following an investigation by the Naples Court seven airline officials were prosecuted.[101]

Case 3. The Commission found a number of anomalies in the contract management procedure operated by a recipient company in Sardinia. Apart from anything else, there was no way of distinguishing training costs (if indeed there were any) and salary costs.[102]

---

97. European Commission, *Protecting the Community's financial interests, The fight against fraud*, Annual Report for 1995 (1996) COM(96) 173, table 7 p. 90.
98. *Ibid.*, table 5, p. 88.
99. A. Bassi, 'Community frauds upon the ESF: the Italian experience' (1994) in *The legal protection of the financial interests of the Community – Progress and prospects since the Brussels seminar of 1989*, pp. 225–238.
100. European Commission, *Protecting the Community's financial interests, The fight against fraud*, Annual report for 1994 (1995), p. 51.
101. *Ibid.*, p. 52.
102. *Ibid.*, p. 51.

Case 4. In Lisbon, a trade union federation and some of its leaders and subcontractors have been prosecuted for diverting ESF and national subsidies worth 1.5 million ECU. The organizers had presented artificially inflated expenditure and had failed to organize training courses.[103]

Case 5. More recently (July 1996) a British university has come under scrutiny over 600,000 pounds of ESF, which allegedly had not been used to retrain unemployed people, but rather to finance existing students.[104]

2.2.2. ERF Fraud

The granting of large regional development contracts can involve breaches of the EC procurement rules,[105] when for example public works contracts are granted in exchange for favours.[106]

Case 6. On scrutinizing the administration of the French Departement of Var in 1994–95, the Provence-Alpes Cote d'Azur regional audit body discovered over-invoicing involving more than 5 million ECU in connection with the supply of equipment to encourage technical innovation (ERDF co-financing 38 million ECU under the Renaval programme for the conversion of shipbuilding areas from 1990 to 1993). The judicial inquiries suggest that local councillors received under-the-counter payments totalling at least 0.5 to 1 million ECU in exchange for falsifying public contracts.[107]

2.2.3. Guidance Section Fraud

Case 7. As a result of an investigation by the magistrates at Reggio Calabria (Italy), carried out in conjunction with a Commission on-the-spot investigation in January 1994, it was established that serious irregularities extended to olive oil storage and bottling facilities at the Calabria regional centre at San Lorenz, as well as to the storage centres at Castri and Eboli. The three centres had visibly never actually operated, for at both Castri and Eboli buildings were dilapidated, access roads were impassable and bottling machinery was neither bolted to the floor nor connected to vats. The Commission commenced the procedure for halting assistance and

---

103. *Ibid.*, p. 74.
104. Newspaper article: 'EU fraud squad calls on campus', in *The Guardian*, 23 July 1996, pp. 2 and 3, Education Section.
105. *See* Article 7(1) of Council Regulation 2081/93 and second subparagraph of Article 25(6) of Council Regulation 2082/93.
106. F. D'Aubert, *Main basse sur l'Europe* (1994) pp. 181–186 on the Abruzzo scandal.
107. European Commission, *Protecting the Community's financial interests, The fight against fraud*, Annual report for 1995 (1996) COM(96) 173, p. 75.

recovering sums already paid – approximately 3 million ECU. It joined *partie civile* proceedings to the prosecution at San Lorenzo.[108]

2.2.4. Community Initiative Fraud

Set up in 1990,[109] INTERREG is the largest Community initiative. It is intended to prepare frontier regions for the completion of the internal market and aims to solve the specific economic development programmes of the Community's internal and external border regions. The total Structural Funds contribution to INTERREG during the 1989–1993 period was initially estimated at 800 million ECU. Typical frauds affecting INTERREG[110] involve the use of INTERREG funds for projects which involve little or no inter-regional cooperation.

Case 8. When the Court of Auditors carried out its audit of the INTERREG Community initiative between Ireland and the UK, it found that only 39 out of the 270 projects of which the OP consisted were of a trans-frontier nature and were receiving joint financing from two Member States on the basis of this.[111]

Case 9. In Sardinia, six persons were committed for trial on charges of diverting aid granted by the Commission for the construction of an innovative wind-power plant costing an estimated 1.25 million.

Case 10. In 1994, for the first time, the Commission sent a request to twelve Member States under Article 209a EC[112] in order investigate a network of contractors in the tourism field. The use of fictitious subcontractors and over-invoicing were two of the means used by the networks.[113]

2.3. Structural Funds Control Framework

According to Article 23 of Council Regulation 4253/88,[114] Member States had to inform the Commission of the measures taken to verify that operations had been properly carried out, to prevent and to take action against irregularities, and to

---

108. European Commission, *Protecting the Community's financial interests, The fight against fraud*, Annual report for 1994 (1995) p. 53.
109. Communication C(90) 1562/3 [1990] O.J. C215, Annex 1.
110. *See* Court of Auditors Annual Report for the 1994 financial year [1995] O.J. C303, 4.61 – 4.72.
111. *Ibid.*, at 4.68.
112. The second paragraph of Article 209a reads: 'Without prejudice to the provisions of this Treaty, Member States shall coordinate their action aimed at protecting the financial interests of the Community against fraud. To this end they shall organize, with the help of the Commission, close and regular cooperation between the competent departments of their administrations.' The implementation of more comprehensive cooperation on enforcement to tackle cross-border fraud committed by organized crime rings is thus a particular aim of Article 209a of the EC Treaty.
113. European Commission, *Protecting the Community's financial interests, The fight against fraud*, Annual Report for 1994 (1995) p. 54.
114. [1988] L374/1.

recover any amounts lost. This vague requirement was supplemented by a Code of Conduct[115] requiring Member States, *inter alia*, to report irregularities above 4,000 ECU every four months. This code of conduct was subsequently annulled by the European Court of Justice in 1991,[116] on the grounds that it went beyond the measures intended in Article 23(1) of Council Regulation 4253/88.[117] This, predictably, had a negative impact on Member States' reporting activities. At the end of 1992, for example, only two Member States had reported cases with total financial implications of approximately 1 million ECU.[118] In its Annual Report for the year 1991, the Court of Auditors denounced this state of affairs.[119]

The same Regulation empowered the Commission to carry autonomous[120] or associated checks, which involve Commission officials taking part in on-the-spot checks carried out by the Member States' authorities.[121] However, it seems that, with scarce reporting from the Member States, the Structural Funds remained a low inspection priority for the Commission, since no associated checks were carried out until 1994.[122] But the regulatory landscape was to change dramatically after 1993.

After the second reform, the Structural Funds including the Cohesion Fund still share the same regulatory framework, which can be found in Council Regulation 2082/93[123] (the Coordination Regulation) which amends Council Regulation 4253/88[124] and extends its provisions to the Cohesion Fund and FIFG. The former Regulation 2082/93 lays down rules for financial control (Article 23), the reduction suspension and cancellation of assistance (Article 24) and monitoring, appraisal and evaluation (Articles 25 and 26) within the framework of partnership, as defined above. Articles 23 and 24 in particular herald two significant changes. Firstly, there is a move from the 1989 system of control of individual projects, towards a regime of control based on 'systems audit', which places greater emphasis on controls carried out in the Member States. Secondly, there is also more emphasis on the role of Member States in managing and controlling funds, in line with the recognition that Member States' administrations are responsible for 80 per cent of expenditure, and also with the principle of subsidiarity enshrined in the EEC Treaty by the Treaty on European Union signed at Maastricht. As a result of this new approach, Commission Regulations 1681/94[125] and 1831/94[126] (inspired from Council Reg-

---

115. Code of Conduct [1990] O.J. C200/3 on the implementing provisions for Article 23(1)of Council Regulation 4253/88 relating to irregularities, and the organization of an information system for irregularities.
116. Case C-303/90, *France* v. *Commission*: judgment of the Court of 13 November 1991.
117. [1988] O.J. L374/1.
118. European Commission, *Report and Action Programme for 1993* (1992) COM(93) 141, p. 10; also European Commission, *Protecting the Community's financial interests, The fight against fraud, Annual report 1995* (1995) COM(96) 173, table 23 p. 96.
119. Court of Auditors Annual Report for the 1991 financial year [1992] O.J. C330, 7.43–7.44.
120. Article 23(2) first and second subparagraphs of Council Regulation 4253/88 [1988] O.J. L374/1.
121. Article 23(2) third and fourth subparagraphs of Council Regulation 4253/88, *op. cit.*
122. European Commission, *Protecting the Community's financial interests, The fight against fraud*, Annual Report for 1995 (1996), table 5 p. 88.
123. Council Regulation 2082/93 [1993] O.J. L193/20.
124. [1988] O.J. L374/1.
125. [1994] O.J. L178/47.
126. [1994] O.J. L191/9.

ulation 595/91,[127] already in force in the EAGGF Guarantee Section) were adopted in order to define the duties of Member States with respect to irregularities and recovery in more detail.

2.3.1. Financial Control

According to Article 24 of Council Regulation 2082/93[128] (the Coordination Regulation), the Commission may now reduce or suspend assistance if an irregularity or significant change affecting the nature and conditions for the implementation of the operation or measure are revealed. Sums received unduly or to be recovered must be repaid to the Commission.[129]

2.3.2. Reporting Fraud

Every quarter, Member States have a duty to make a detailed report to the Commission concerning any irregularities involving sums of over 4,000 ECU[130] (unless expressly required by the Commission) which have been the subject of an initial administrative or judicial investigations.[131] In this context Member States must also report, on a quarterly basis, the measures taken to recover sums wrongly paid. This includes the reasons for any abandonment of recovery procedure or any abandonment of criminal prosecutions.[132] By the end of 1993, nine out of twelve Member States had reported a small number of cases, with a financial impact of 5 million ECU.[133] But by the end of 1995, 194 cases of irregularities had been reported in total, with a total financial impact of 44 million ECU.[134]

2.3.3. Recovery

Unlike Council Regulation 591/91,[135] Council Regulations 1681/94[136] and 1831/94[137] make no provisions for a 'reward' for national government departments amounting to 20 per cent of sums recovered, but they do allow the possibility of

---

127. [1991] O.J. L67/11.
128. [1993] O.J. L193/20.
129. Article 24(3) of the Coordinating Regulation.
130. Article 12 of Commission Regulation 1681/94 [1994] O.J. L178/43, concerning irregularities and the recovery of sums wrongly paid in connection with the financing of the structural policies and the organization of an information system in this field.
131. Article 3 of Commission Regulation 1681/94, *op. cit.*
132. Article 5 of Commission Regulation 1681/94, *op. cit.*
133. European Commission (1995), *Protecting the Community's financial interest, The fight against fraud*, Annual Report for 1994, OOPEC, table 3 page 73 and table 4 page 74.
134. European Commission, *Protecting the Community's financial interests, The fight against fraud*, Annual Report for 1995 (1996) COM(96) 173, table 5 p. 88.
135. Article 7 of Council Regulation 595/91 [1991] O.J. L67.
136. [1994] O.J. L178/47.
137. [1994] O.J. L191/9.

amounts recovered being entirely reassigned for the benefit of operations or final beneficiaries other than those involved in the irregularity, subject to the constraints of transparency and budgetary discipline.[138]

2.3.4. Mutual Assistance

When irregularities may have repercussions outside their territories or they show a new malpractice, Member States have a duty to report to the Commission to the other Member States concerned.[139]

2.3.5. Monitoring

Member States are responsible for the monitoring of the assistance. Such monitoring must be carried out by way of jointly agreed reporting procedures, sample checks and the establishment of monitoring committees.[140] Furthermore, monitoring must be done with the help of indicators showing:

– the stage reached in the operation and the goals to be attained within a given time span,
– the progress achieved on the management side and any related problems.[141]

The Commission and EIB may delegate representatives to the monitoring committees, with the agreement of the Member State concerned.[142]

For multi-annual operations, progress reports must be submitted every six months, and a final report must be submitted to the Commission within six months of completion of the operation.[143]

The monitoring committee may adjust the procedure for granting assistance. These amendments have to be notified immediately to the Commission and to the Member States concerned. They become effective as soon as confirmation is received from the Commission, within a period of 20 working days. Other amendments are decided by the Commission, in collaboration with the Member State concerned, after the monitoring committee has delivered its opinion.[144]

The Commission is concerned about transparency, and for this purpose, and within the context of the application of Community rules on the award of public contracts, notices sent to the *Official Journal* for publication must specify those

---

138. Article 11 of Commission Regulation 1681/94 [1994] O.J. L178/43.
139. Article 4 of Commission Regulation 1681/94 [1994] O.J. L178/43.
140. Article 25(1) of Coordinating Regulation.
141. Article 25(2) of Coordinating Regulation.
142. Article 35(3) of Coordinating Regulation.
143. Article 25(4) of Coordinating Regulation.
144. Article 25(5) of Coordinating Regulation.

projects for which Community assistance has been applied for or granted.[145] The Commission publishes implementation details in the *Official Journal*.[146]

2.3.6. Evaluation

In order to ensure the effectiveness of Community assistance, measures taken for structural purposes must be subjected to appraisal monitoring and, after their implementation, evaluation.[147]

2.4. Evaluation of Control Framework

Three main criticisms have been levelled at the present system by the Commission:

   (i) the system is complex and the division of responsibilities between the Commission and the Member States on financial management and control is not clear.
  (ii) The number of initiatives causes confusion.
 (iii) The number of committees also causes confusion.

The Commission has suggested that one way of avoiding confusion would be to cut down the number of committees involved in the process, and to tighten control systems.[148] One way of tightening controls would be to make the continuing financing of a programme more strictly conditional upon agreed terms.

> 'The Commission should be stronger and stop paying out money if it is not satisfied with the programmes. Under the Structural Funds we can say that if something is not changed after the first set of payments, we will not hand over the remaining funds.'[149]

More fundamental criticism has also been put forward.

(a) The highest proportion of reported fraud concerns the ESF. The services subsidized by the ESF tend to be intangible, and it can be difficult to monitor progress or evaluate the impact of a measure. Generally with respect to the ESF and other Structural Funds goals need to be more clearly defined.

---

145. Article 25(6) of Coordinating Regulation.
146. Article 25(7) of Coordinating Regulation.
147. Council Regulation 2052/88 [1988] O.J. L185/9.
148. *See* newspaper article 'Venice to duck regional funding issue', in *European Voice*, 2–8 May 1996, p. 5.
149. *Cf.* extract from *European Voice* newspaper of 9–11 May 1996, 'Gradin demands tougher measures to combat fraud' in *AGON* number 12, June 1996, page 16.

(b) The task of assessing genuine additionality can be complicated – particularly in the case of multiple funding.[150] Occasionally infra-state issues of subsidiarity arise and disputes about the level at which additionality should operate (local, regional or national).[151] This means that the principle of co-financing may not offer the desired safeguard against fraud.

(c) ERDF payments are mainly paid in advance and have had the temporary effect of an advance to national budgets, at least where these advances are not paid out immediately to the final recipient. This situation, the Court of Auditors has suggested, 'does not constitute a guarantee for the best possible use of the resources mobilized'.[152]

The reforms needed in order to fraud-proof Structural Funds therefore go beyond the proposed reinforcement of *ex ante* and *ex post* assessments.

2.5. New Developments

Member States have been holding back matching funds, which means that unclaimed funds have risen from 15 billion ECU in 1993 to 16 billion ECU by July 1996.[153]

A series of cooperation protocols have been signed to cooperate on the control of the use of Structural Funds.

Concern has been expressed over the future of the Structural Funds in an enlarged Union, although decisions on support for regions under the Structural Funds after 1999, including the designation of eligible areas, will not be made before the beginning of 1998.

---

150. *See* for example European Commission, *Report on the audit and management and control systems for Structural Fund measures in the Member States* (1994) SE(94) 1654, p. 20.
151. *See* S. Fothergill, *The struggle over European funding* (1996) Local Government Information Unit, London; also S. White and N. Dorn, 'EC fraud, subsidiarity and prospects for the IGC: a regional dimension?' (1996) 3(3) *European Urban and Regional Studies*, pp. 262–266.
152. Court of Auditors Annual Report for the 1994 financial year [1995] O.J. C303, at 4.93.
153. Newspaper article 'EU states fail to spend £16 billion in regional aid', in *Financial Times*, 29 July 1996, p. 1.

PART III

Recovering Unwarranted Payments

Chapter 5. The Recovery of Unwarranted Payments

1. INTRODUCTION

This chapter deals with the recovery of unwarranted payments in the UK. Firstly it outlines the responsibilities of the Member States in the present budget structure (§ 1). It then goes on to examine the modes of recovery available in English law in some detail (§ 2). A brief comparison of British and Danish systems (§ 3) leads to a concluding discussion on possible improvements (§ 4). It is hoped that this chapter, including its brief, but necessary comparative element, will have the potential to stimulate discussion on ways of improving recovery rates.

At a time when a consensus no longer seems to prevail on the 'European Project', waste and fraud in the budget of the European Communities, more than ever, have the potential to undermine the credibility of the Union.[1] The United Kingdom has been particularly vociferous in demanding improvements in this area, at times even urging the Commission to take more steps to combat waste and fraud. Since the late 1980s the Commission has been highly active in assisting the Member States in the fight against fraud affecting the Community budget, as evidenced by a series of policies and measures.

The recovery of unwarranted payments, however, is the sole responsibility of the Member States. In the words of the Commission:

> '[T]he recovery of all income due to the Community budget and all Community funds which have been acquired fraudulently is a[nother] high priority. Virtually all own resources are collected by the Member States and about 80 per cent of Community funds are paid out to the final beneficiary by the member States. This is why recovery in the first instance is a task for the Member States.'[2]

Such recoveries are effected with varying degrees of speed and success throughout the European Union. In its Annual report for the 1993 financial year, the European

---

1. *See* Report by the European Court of Auditors to the Reflection Group, May 1995, 3.1 p 8; also speech by Anita Gradin, Commissioner with a responsibility for fraud prevention, reported in Reuter textline of 30 March 1995; speech by Diemut Theato, MEP, Chairman of the Committee on Budgetary Control of the European Parliament at the University of Urbino, 9 June 1995 reported in *AGON*, no 10, October 1995.
2. European Commission *Protecting the Community's financial interests The fight against fraud Annual Report 1994* (1995) COM (95) 98.

Court of Auditors deplored the general 'lack of success so far' in that area and stressed the need for urgent attention. This view was also shared by the Commission's Directorate for Financial Control (DG XX), and led to the commissioning of a study in 1995, which focused on each of the Member States' rules governing settlements and similar arrangements and their application to Community expenditure (the 'settlement' study). For the purpose of the study, on which this chapter draws, 'settlement' was broadly defined by the Commission as 'any act whereby the authorities of a Member State exercise a power to negotiate and terminate a dispute or state of uncertainty as to rights and obligations in the context of procedures for the recovery of sums of money or for the imposition of penalties'.[3] The aim of the United Kingdom national study, carried out by the present author, was to throw some light on the way the relevant United Kingdom authorities recover sums which have been wrongly paid by national authorities from EC funds. It paid particular attention to extra-judicial settlements since the Commission was concerned that extra-judicial settlements in particular lead to sub-optimal recoveries.

The first, and probably the most striking feature of the British way of settling such matters, is that the three jurisdictions of the United Kingdom[4] do not display the same type of 'two-phase' system commonly found in most other European Union Member States.[5] Settlements occur *either* judicially (mostly through the civil courts) *or* extra-judicially through long established procedures such as compounding, or setting-off. This 'either-or' system is addressed in more detail in 2.1.–2.3 below. Secondly, although some of the European Union Member States have centralized systems of fraud enforcement and recovery,[6] the United Kingdom operates through a number of agencies. Their roles and recovery policies (when they have been made public) are addressed in 2.4., as well as the particularities of various extra-judicial settlement procedures, such as setting-off, compounding and writing-off. The effectiveness of such procedures is discussed in 2.5. Issues arising from administrative discretion, and of redress against administrative decisions are dealt with in 2.6. A brief comparison between the Danish and British systems is offered in § 3, followed by concluding remarks in § 4.

But first, a brief outline of the EC budget and of the duties of the Member States with regard to the recovery of EC funds may prove useful background.

---

3. European Commission, DG XX (Financial Control), Methodological note to researchers (1995).

4. This chapter refers to England and Wales, unless otherwise stated. The law of Northern Ireland is closely modelled on English law, which applies in England and Wales. Scots law is markedly different: its legal principles, rules and concepts are modelled on both Romanistic and English laws.

5. 'The judicial procedure is usually in two stages, the first corresponding to the ordinary first instance hearing by a judge sitting alone, and the second being an appeal procedure of one kind or another' (p. 16 of the Delmas-Marty Report).

6. For example the Guardia di Finanza in Italy, the Office Général de Lutte contre la Délinquance Economique et Financière Organisée in Belgium, and the Office Central pour la Répression de la Grande Déliquance Financière and the Office Central de Prévention de la Corruption in France.

1.1. Budget Structure

The European budget has been multiplied by a factor of 2.7 in ten years, rising from 28,800 million ECU in 1985 to 79,800 million ECU in 1995.[7] To give an idea of the magnitude of the EC budget, it suffices to add that the European Court of Auditors at present audits revenue and expenditure representing approximately 4–5 per cent of the total budgets of all the Member States.[8] The structure of the budget, however, is relatively simple.

The Union itself has no power to raise taxes, so it is dependent on the Member States' contributions for its budget. In 1977 Council Regulation 2991/77[9] established a system of 'Communities' own resources', which established a basis for the Member States' contributions. Contributions from the Member States now fall into three broad categories. Firstly, over 50 per cent of EC revenue comes from a weighted percentage (usually around 1 to 1.4 per cent) of the Member States' VAT revenues. This amounted to 38 billion ECU in 1993 and 36 billion ECU in 1994.[10] Since 1988 the Member States have also made a contribution based on their national GNP,[11] which constitutes the second largest contribution from the Member States. Lastly 'traditional own resources', made up of Customs duties, sugar and isoglucose levies and agricultural levies, altogether amounted to approximately 20 per cent of total estimated revenue in the 1994 financial year. On the expenditure side, in 1994, over 52 per cent of the budget was spent on EAGGF Guarantee Section Fund, concerned with the support of prices for agricultural products, and over 30 per cent on 'structural operations and fisheries' to help the more disadvantaged regions.

Although media reports have tended to focus on irregularities affecting subventions to the agricultural sector (i.e. on the expenditure side), frauds and irregularities affect all parts of the budget.

1.2. Frauds and Irregularities

In March 1995 the Commission adopted the 1994 Annual Report[12] by its Coordinating Unit for combatting fraud in which it emerges that 4,264 cases of irregularities and fraud were detected by the Member States and the Commission in 1994, an increase of a third on 1993. The amounts involved in these irregularities doubled in relation to the previous year and reached 1,032.7 million ECU, which constitutes 1.2 per cent

7. European Court of Auditors Report to the Reflection Group on the operation of the Treaty on European Union (1995), p. 2.
8. European Court of Auditors, *The European Court of Auditors – Auditing the finances of the European Union* (1995) p. 13.
9. Council Regulation 2891/77 [1977] O.J. L336/1 implementing the Decision of 21 April 1970 on the replacement of financial contributions from Member States by the Communities' own resources.
10. European Court of Auditors Annual Report for the 1993 financial year [1994] O.J. C327, diagram 1: general budget 1995: estimated revenue; also European Court of Auditors, *Statement of Assurance concerning activities financed from the general budget for the financial year 1994* (1995), diagram 1, annex A: general budget 1994: estimated revenue.
11. Article 2 of Council Decision 88/376 [1988] O.J. L185/24.
12. *See* C. Goybert, 'La fraude communautaire: mythes et réalités' (1995) 388, RMC, pp. 281–283.

of the total budget. It is the area of 'traditional own resources', i.e. the area concerned with the collection of import levies, which seems to present a more acute problem. Reported irregularities amounted to 3.4 per cent of revenue in 1993.

Commentators have argued that these figures were only 'the tip of the iceberg'. The extent to which one can rely on official statistics to measure the extent of crime remains one of the classic disputes in criminology.[13] The position taken by UCLAF is typically institutionalist: 'There is no evidence that the level of frauds on the EU budget is increasing. However, there is a steadily increasing trend to discover fraud, ... which can be attributed to initiatives taken by UCLAF to achieve effective enforcement and verification efforts on the part of the Member States.'[14] In this figures and statistics from the Commission data bases are useful in as much as they draw our attention to the level of reporting and enforcement activity. However, there is no doubt that the more irregularities are reported, the more money the Member States have to recover in order to pay it back into the common purse. It is to the specific duties of the Member States that we turn now.

1.3. Duties of Member States

The Member States have a set of duties to fulfil with regard to the sanctioning of irregularities. For instance, sanctions must guarantee real and effective judicial protection[15] and have a real deterrent effect.[16] Furthermore, redress must be available against administrative decisions. The remedies themselves must be effective. They must not be available under less favourable conditions than those applicable to the enforcement of a similar right of a domestic nature.[17] Remedies must be designed in such a way that it is not impossible to exercise the rights the national courts have a duty to protect.[18] Finally, remedies should not be less favourable than those governing the same[19] or similar rights of action in an internal matter.[20] Member States also have particular duties with respect to recovery, both on the revenue and expenditure sides.

On the revenue side, Council Regulation 2891/77[21] requires the Member States to establish, enter in the accounts and recover any amounts due in cases where fraud or irregularity has been established. The Commission's role is to ensure that recovery procedures are indeed initiated and completed by national authorities so

---

13. D. Jupp, *Methods of criminological research* (1989), London, pp. 47–48; also P. Eglin, 'The dispute over the meaning and use of official statistics in the explanation of deviance' (1987) *Classic disputes in sociology*, eds. J. Hughes, J. Anderson and W. Sharrock, London, pp. 108–136.
14. UCLAF, 'Anti-fraud coordination in the EU' (1995) 3:2 *European Journal on Criminal Policy and Research*, pp. 65–74.
15. Case 68/88, *Commission* v. *Greece*, [1989] ECR 2965, para 23.
16. Case 79/83, *Dorit Hartz* v. *Deutsche Tradax GmbH*, [1984] ECR 1921, 1941.
17. *See* for example cases 33/76, *Rewe* v. *Landwirtschaftskammer für das Saarland*, [1976] ECR 1989, 1997–1998; 309/85, *Barra* v. *Belgium and the City of Liege*, [1988] 2 CMLR 409, 418.
18. Case 45/76, *Comet* v. *Produktschap voor Siergewassen*, [1976] ECR 2043.
19. *Ibid.*
20. Case 199/82, *Amministrazione delle Finanze dello Stato* v. *San Giorgio*, [1983] ECR 3595, 3612.
21. Council Regulation 2891/77 [1977] O.J. L336/1.

that Member States can be given a discharge when their management is satisfactory. If sums are not recoverable owing, for example, to bankruptcy or lapse of time, the onus is on the Member State to show that it has done everything possible to recover them if it is to be exempted from making them available to the Community.[22] The Regulation also introduced the possibility of releasing Member States from the obligation to make amounts available for reasons of *force majeure*. Because of the very restrictive interpretation of *force majeure* by the Court of Justice, the Member States have only made use of this possibility in very rare occasions since the Regulation entered into force.

In accordance with Article 6(2)(b) of Regulation 1552/89,[23] Member States must, in the quarterly statements which they send to the Commission, enter established entitlements that have not yet been recovered in a separate 'B' account. These are then incorporated annually into the Commission's balance sheet and revenue and expenditure account. However, in its report on the application of Council Regulation 1552/89[24] produced in 1992, the Commission remarked that few cases had been reported where amounts of more than 10,000 ECU had not been recovered, as required by Article 6(3)(2) of the Regulation. The cases involving more than 10,000 ECU reported by Germany, the Netherlands and the United Kingdom had been the result of bankruptcies where there were no assets, the disappearance of debtors or insufficient guarantees.[25] In its special report accompanying the Statement of Assurance for the financial year 1994,[26] the European Court of Auditors pointed out that 'the separate accounts held by the Member States, which serve as the basis for the Commission's data, contain numerous errors and omissions, the main one being that they are not exhaustive.... The checks carried out in various Member States revealed a variety of shortcomings in the way the separate accounts were kept, particularly in the United Kingdom, where, following the audits carried out, the national authorities called upon the services concerned to make the necessary improvements.' An assurance has now been given by the British government that 'B' accounts would be kept in future. This state of affairs has made it difficult to quantify amounts yet to be recovered in the UK.

The Commission has proposed changes to Regulation 1552/89,[27] in order to help secure an improvement in the follow-up of recoveries. The proposed amendment, yet to be agreed by the Council, seeks to achieve the following:

- more effective penalties for delays in making available amounts due;
- an analysis of the reasons for failure to recover own resources, so that criteria can be drawn up defining the financial liability of the authorities responsible for collection;

---

22. European Commission, *The fight against fraud – Annual Report for 1994* (1995), pp. 70–71.
23. [1989] O.J. L155/1.
24. *Ibid.*
25. *See* European Commission, *Report on the application of Council Regulation 1552/89* (1992) COM (92) 530.
26. European Court of Auditors, *Special Report in support of the Statement of Assurance concerning activities financed from the general budget for the financial year 1994* (1995).
27. *See* second proposal for a Council Regulation amending Council Regulation 1552/89 [1994] O.J. C382/6.

– more uniform and comprehensive information on fraud and irregularities involving more than 10,000 ECU;
– an improvement in the Community's ability to assess the quality and results of the recovery and inspection activities of the national authorities through comprehensive annual reports presented according to a standard model.

On the expenditure side, Council Regulation 729/70,[28] amended by Council Regulation 2048/88,[29] requires the Member States to recover EAGGF sums paid as a result of irregularities or negligence, and to inform the Commission of the measures taken for those purposes and in particular of the state of the administrative and judicial procedures. Read literally, this is sometimes interpreted by officials to mean that full recovery must be pursued in the courts, which would leave little room for administrative discretion.

Similar obligations to recover funds exist with respect to Structural Funds, in accordance with Council Regulations 4253/88[30] and 2082/93.[31] Member States are free, in the absence of a remedy expressly provided by the Community measure in question, to choose between sanctions available under national law.[32] Where the question of sanctions is not dealt with in Community measures, then:

> '[P]eriods of limitation, rights of set off, the extent of rights or reimbursement of improper charges, payment of interest and so on are matters to be regulated by the domestic law of the Member States in whose courts the individual right-holder seeks to proceed.'[33]

1.4. Recoveries

It is also in the area of traditional own resources that Member States seem to have the most difficulties in effecting recoveries. For the period 1991–1994, a total of 94 per cent of the money obtained through irregularities in the traditional own resources sector was still to be recovered, as opposed to 83 per cent on the expenditure side (*see* Tables 5.1 to 5.4).

In the area of traditional own resources, in the period 1991–1994 the Member States recovered between 0 per cent and 53 per cent of amounts outstanding. The United Kingdom notified 22 per cent of cases, but only recovered 2 per cent of sums due (*see* Tables 5.3. and 5.4.).

On the expenditure side, and for the same period, the Member States recovered between 3 per cent and 66 per cent of unwarranted payments. The United Kingdom

28. [1970] O.J. L94/13.
29. [1988] O.J. L185/1.
30. [1988] O.J. L374/1.
31. [1993] O.J. L193/20.
32. Cases 50/76, *Amsterdam Bulb BV* v. *Produktschap voor Siergewassen*, [1977] ECR 137; 265/78, *H Ferweda BV* v. *Produktschap voor Vee en Vlees*, [1980] ECR 617.
33. Case *Bourgoin S A and others* v. *Ministry of Agriculture and Food*, [1986] QB 716, 755, per Oliver LJ (dissenting).

notified 15 per cent of cases and recovered 41 per cent of sums due (*see* Tables 5.1. and 5.2.).

Table 5.1. Communications of Member States on Irregularities, EAGGF Guarantee Section 1991–94

	Cases			Amounts in ECU		
	Notified	Closed	Open	Notified	Recovered	To be recovered
BE	119	58	61	11 450	737 154	10 715 940
DK	221	175	46	10 503 868	4 908 684	5 595 184
DE	546	265	281	66 217 645	12 301 686	53 915 959
EL	327	65	262	86 353 034	58 267 596	28 085 438
ES	519	218	301	82 746 803	2 263 922	80 482 881
FR	389	254	135	54 252 457	17 282 240	36 970 217
IR	65	48	17	5 507 529	2 137 890	3 369 639
IT	955	108	847	560 685 454	35 748 902	524 936 552
NL	428	331	97	22 621 210	11 093 595	11 527 615
PT	270	38	232	14 961 534	1 037 472	13 924 062
UK	670	466	204	26 774 056	11 006 035	14 825 247
ALL	4 509	2 026	2 483	942 073 684	156 785 176	784 348 734

Source: European Commission (1995), *Protecting the Community's financial interests, The fight against fraud*, Annual Report 1994, pp. 82–83.
Luxembourg had no irregularities to report. Belgium and Greece are represented only for the first three quarters of 1994.

Table 5.2. Recovery of EAGGF Guarantee Section, 1991–94 (first two quarters of 1994)

	Cases notified	Amount notified	% of amount notified	
			recovered	to be recovered
BE	3%	1%	6%	94%
DK	5%	1%	47%	53%
DE	12%	7%	19%	81%
EL	7%	9%	66%	33%
ES	12%	9%	3%	97%
FR	9%	6%	32%	68%
IR	1%	1%	39%	61%
IT	21%	60%	6%	94%
NL	9%	2%	49%	51%
PT	6%	2%	7%	93%
UK	15%	3%	41%	55%
ALL	100%	100%	17%	83%

Source: European Commission (1995), *Protecting the Community's financial interests, The fight against fraud*, Annual Report 1994, pp. 82–83.

Table 5.3. Communications of Member States on Irregularities,
Traditional Own Resources, 1991–94 (first two quarters of 1994)

	Cases			Amounts in ECU		
	Notified	Closed	Open	Notified	Recovered	To be recovered
BE	328	203	125	49 205 846	7 267 239	41 938 607
DK	86	41	45	6 848 827	2 799 554	4 049 273
DE	1 548	115	1 433	171 442 258	7 715 408	163 726 850
EL	66	0	66	3 223 998	0	3 223 998
ES	192	15	177	14 051 855	1 025 938	13 025 917
FR	544	9	535	53 500 248	5 093 467	48 406 781
IR	32	13	19	8 001 875	1 183 211	6 818 664
IT	408	41	367	92 474 916	654 257	91 820 659
LU	2	1	1	85 220	45 417	39 803
NL	44	1	43	9 513 448	122 232	9 391 216
PT	84	39	45	2 969 940	579 444	2 390 496
UK	961	224	737	92 167 252	1 844 104	90 323 148
ALL	4 295	702	3 593	503 485 683	28 330 271	475 155 412

Source: European Commission (1995), *Protecting the Community's financial interests, The fight against fraud*, Annual Report 1994, pp. 82–83.

Table 5.4. Recovery of Traditional Own Resources, 1991–94
(first two quarters of 1994)

	Cases notified	Amount notified	% of amount notified	
			recovered	to be recovered
BE	8%	10%	15%	85%
DK	2%	1%	41%	59%
DE	36%	34%	5%	95%
EL	2%	1%	0%	100%
ES	4%	3%	7%	93%
FR	13%	11%	10%	90%
IR	1%	2%	15%	85%
IT	9%	18%	1%	99%
LU	0%	0%	53%	47%
NL	1%	2%	1%	99%
PT	2%	1%	20%	80%
UK	22%	18%	2%	98%
ALL	100%	100%	6%	94%

Source: European Commission (1995), *Protecting the Community's financial interests, The fight against fraud*, Annual Report 1994, pp. 82–83.

The jurisprudence of the Court of Justice offers little guidance on what may be an acceptable delay for the recovery of a sum owed to the EC budget. A recent case

(1992) states that Member States have a duty to take steps to rectify irregularities promptly, whether time-limits are expressly laid down by relevant Community rules or not.[34] Although it is not clear what the Court meant by 'promptly', it found that delays of ten and four years before commencing proceedings constituted negligence under Article 8 of Council Regulation 729/70.[35] At the moment delays of several years in recovering unwarranted payments seem to be the norm rather than the exception throughout the Union.

2. RECOVERING EC FUNDS IN THE UK: BACKGROUND

In the United Kingdom, for some time, there has been concern over the perceived inadequacies of serious fraud trials.[36] This has added momentum to the 'creeping decriminalization' of fraud, including revenue fraud. The result has been that 'many against whom there is a strong *prima facie* case of fraud negotiate their way out of the criminal justice process'.[37] Civil proceedings, on the other hand, tend to be long, complex and costly, so amounts are often settled before the hearing. In contrast, extra-judicial (administrative) recovery has consistently been praised as fast, efficient and inexpensive.[38] This type of recovery is in tune with the present government's pragmatic approach to revenue collecting, and its general concern for cost-effectiveness. This preference in turn raises the issue of the availability and effectiveness of remedies against administrative decisions. The general features of criminal, civil and extra-judicial routes are explored below.

2.1. The Civil Route

Unlike most of its European Union neighbours, the United Kingdom has no administrative finance courts. All courts have full jurisdiction to decide cases in administrative matters and to exercise control over administrative bodies and tribunals. As a rule, only courts can impose fines. Another feature of the British systems is that civil and criminal jurisdictions are separate and distinct.

With some exceptions, the County Court (Sheriff Court in Scotland) usually deals with cases involving a debt up to a certain amount[39] and the High Court (Court of Session in Scotland) with debts above that limit.[40] It is open to the defendant to pay to the court the amount claimed before the hearing. If this is done at any time up to the time of the hearing, the action is stayed. The court and its administration take no part in preparing a case for trial other than to make orders and to grant relief but only upon the application of a party to the proceedings. Another important

---

34. Case C-34/89, *Italy* v. *Commission (olive oil production aid)*, [1992] 2 CMLR 797, 7–14.
35. *Ibid.*
36. *See* for example Fraud Trials Committee Report chaired by Lord Roskill (1986) HMSO, London.
37. M. Levi, *Regulating fraud, white-collar crime and the criminal process* (1987), London, p. 183.
38. *See* for example case *Patel* v. *Spence*, [1976] 1 WLR 1268, 1270 and *A-G* v. *Johnstone* (1926) 10 TC 758.
39. £50,000 in England and Wales.
40. S. 3 of the Courts and Legal Services Act 1990.

feature of civil judgments is that they are usually awarded irrespective of the debtor's ability to pay.

If the action is for a sum not exceeding £1,000 and when both parties agree[41] the matter can go to a Small Claims Tribunal in the County Court (or Sheriff Court in Scotland). The usual rules of procedure do not apply and the waiting time for a hearing is shorter (usually six to eight weeks). The Intervention Board (*see* below), for example, has made increasing use of this procedure since the increase in upper limit. The parties do not have to be represented, and it is possible for the State to send a non-legal member of staff to the hearing as a representative.[42] The award is final although an arbitrator can set it aside if, for example, it was made in the absence of one of the parties, and a reasonable excuse for the absence is provided.

Insolvencies have increased at a vertiginous rate these last few years, and must be mentioned as they increasingly affect the authorities' ability to recover debts.[43] In its first Statement of Assurance (for the financial year 1994) the European Court of Auditors points out that in one case a British company receiving a subsidy in the regional sector had gone out of business; neither a manager nor the company's accounts were available.[44] Generally, in cases of insolvency,[45] the official receiver (attached to the court) appoints a trustee or liquidator when there are assets to be distributed amongst creditors.[46] The trustee is then responsible for the distribution of assets amongst creditors *pari passu*, but in strict order of priority. First, the expenses of bankruptcy must be paid.[47] The costs can consume 40 per cent of assets, about twice as much as an individual voluntary arrangement. The government takes the biggest bite, followed by the insolvency practitioner, with lesser amounts by selling agents and solicitors.[48]

Second, preferential debts to a few Crown bodies take precedence. They are debts due to the Inland Revenue or Customs and Excise, social security contribu-

41. This limit can be raised to £5,000 when both parties agree.
42. Intervention Board for Agricultural Produce (IBAP): authority responsible for the administration of the CAP in the United Kingdom.
43. *See* newspaper article: '4,000 directors thought to be serial failures' in *Financial Times*, 28 October 1996, which reads: 'Out of 952,432 UK company directors, 37% have been associated with one or more [business] failures in the past seven years. The number of directors with 10 or more failures to their names has climbed four-fold in two years [1994–1996] to 4,000. [This is due to] a general increase in criminal and fraudulent behaviour in the corporate world. Many of the 4,000 directors deliberately closed down companies to avoid paying debts and then set up new ones, often in a bid to defraud customers, suppliers or business partners.'
44. European Court of Auditors, *Statement of Assurance for the financial year 1994* (1995) p. 71.
45. This is far from being an uncommon problem in the UK where the number of personal and corporate bankruptcies now number around 60,000 a year. This is due to a system where, broadly speaking, the advantages of bankruptcy or winding-up (getting rid of creditors) far outweigh the disadvantages (temporary disqualification for directorship of a company, for example). The leniency of this system has lead to the 'Phoenix Syndrome' where bankrupts repeatedly 'resurrect' 'new' companies under different names without paying old creditors. Some legal commentators talk about 'the bankruptcy of bankruptcy' and argue for reforms which allow more differentiation between the small domestic debtor and the corporate debtor.
46. S. 324 (1) of the 1986 Insolvency Act.
47. *Ibid.*, s. 324(1) of the 1986 Insolvency Act.
48. Graham Report chaired by David Graham, *QC Insolvency law: an agenda for reform* (1994), Justice, London.

tions, contributions to occupational pension schemes, remuneration of employees, etc.[49]

Third, ordinary debts can be settled and, in this, all unsecured creditors rank equally. This usually means that each of the ordinary creditors receives a dividend expressed as so many pence in the pound upon the debt in question. As a rule the insolvency process produces minimal returns for ordinary unsecured creditors.

Clearly all bodies engaged in the recovery of EC funds are not granted the same status with respect to debt recovery, with Customs and Excise enjoying an advantage with respect to the recovery of VAT. All others are unsecured creditors. One criticism of the system is that creditors are not kept informed of developments.[50]

In its 1985 Report, the Civil Justice Review identified the main deficiencies of civil justice as being 'delays, cost and complexity'. The Heilbron-Hodge Report painted a similar picture in 1993 and called for reforms.[51] Indeed, it is not unusual for recoveries to take over two years, and for costs to exceed monies recovered. A recent study estimated that when the costs of both sides were combined, they amounted to 125 per cent of recoveries in the County Court and between 50 and 75 per cent in the High Court.[52] This has led Lord Woolf to comment that 'the present system provides higher benefits to lawyers than to their clients'.[53] The 'cost-effectiveness threshold' is quite high, whatever the nature of the claim. More recently (June 1995) the Woolf Interim Report on the civil justice system in England and Wales[54] put forward a series of recommendations, which in brief include:

- litigation to be divided into fast-track cases (£3,000 to £10,000) and multi-track cases (more than £10,000);
- fast-track cases to be subject to a streamlined procedure including an abbreviated trial, normally restricted to three hours, within 20 to 30 weeks;
- sanctions to be imposed by judges in cases where lawyers fail to meet strict deadlines;
- lawyers to take a precise pleading in a statement of case;
- judges to be given discretionary powers to allocate the burden of costs at the end of the case by reference to the conduct of the parties.[55]

Some of the proposals relate specifically to 'offers to settle' and aim to encourage reasonable and early settlement of proceedings:

---

49. Preferential debts are listed in Schedule 6 of the Insolvency Act 1986.
50. *Ibid.*
51. *Civil Justice on trial: The case for change.*
52. *See* G. Slapper and D. Kelly, *English Legal System* (1993), London, pp. 123–145.
53. Newspaper article 'The Mackay solution', editorial in the *Financial Times*, 29 July 1996, p. 15.
54. Woolf Enquiry Team / The Right Honourable the Lord Woolf, *Access to Justice: interim report to the Lord Chancellor on the civil justice system in England and Wales* (1995) published on behalf of the Woolf Enquiry Team, London, 266 pages, June.
55. *See* newspaper article 'Woolf report in sheep's clothing', in *Times* of 6 August 1996, p. 35.

(1) The present practice of making payment into court should be replaced by a system which permits the parties to make an offer of settlement.
(2) Offers to settle can be made by a plaintiff as well as a defendant.
(3) Offers to settle can relate to individual issues.
(4) Offers to settle can be made before the commencement of proceedings.
(5) Offers to settle can result in substantially enhanced costs and interest being payable.
(6) The extent of entitlement to costs and interest in respect of an offer should be in the court's discretion and should depend on the extent of disclosure by the parties.

Criticisms of the proposals have been, *inter alia*, that it fails to break the 140-year cycle of making no real inroads on cost and delay, and that it augments judges' undirected discretion.[56]

The situation at present is that most civil disputes are settled out of court: fewer than 10 per cent of cases where a writ is issued actually go to court. Notwithstanding this preference for out of court settlements, by far the largest number of cases dealt with by the County Court still relates to debt recovery. Currently the civil courts in England and Wales deal with over three million such claims each year. Should the Woolf recommendations with respect to settlements be implemented, one can expect that in the future, overall, an even larger proportion of cases will be settled out of court.

The civil fraud regime. There has been a steady move away from criminal prosecution in the fiscal sphere. The 1985 Finance Act decriminalized VAT regulatory offences. As a whole VAT offences remain the most decriminalized, as the great majority are dealt with under the civil fraud regime. This regime, which was brought into being by Section 13 of the 1985 Finance Act on VAT, was extended to excise duties by the 1994 Finance Act, and will also apply to Customs duties shortly. The 'civil fraud' regime is therefore of particular significance in this context.

Under this regime, anyone who evades duty (whether or not his behaviour gives rise to any criminal liability) is liable to a penalty. The degree of proof required is based on the balance of probabilities rather than the criminal standard of beyond reasonable doubt.

In the civil fraud regime the standard of proof of dishonesty is not stated. Evasion is defined as the act of claiming any repayment, rebate or drawback of duty, any relief exemption from or any allowance against duty, or any deferral or other postponement of liability to pay any duty or of the discharge by payment of any such liability, without being entitled to it.[57] Although these acts do not necessarily attract the full range of financial penalties (fixed or proportionate penalty, daily penalty), failure to pay any amount appears to be a decisively

---

56. G. Watson, 'From an adversarial to a managed system of litigation: a comparative critique of Lord Woolf's interim report' (1996) in *Achieving civil justice – Appropriate dispute resolution for the 1990s*, ed. R. Smith, Legal Action Group, London.
57. Article 8 (2) of the 1994 Finance Act.

aggravating factor, and attracts the full range of financial penalties from the court in all cases.[58]

A person convicted of the fraudulent evasion, or the attempted evasion of duty chargeable on goods (this usually involves forgery), or any provision of CEMA applicable to goods is liable to a penalty of the prescribed sum or three times the value of the goods, whichever is the greater, or to imprisonment for a term not exceeding six months.[59]

In VAT cases, Customs and Excise will usually prosecute if a sworn statement (as to true earnings and profits) turns out to be incorrect.

Early cooperation with officials is taken into account when assessing the fine.[60]

Fines in the civil fraud regime. Under the civil fraud regime (soon to be extended to Customs duties, as mentioned earlier), the system of assessing the fine is mixed. It is proportional to the loss sustained, but also has a fixed-sum element (i) and (ii):

(i) for a failure to pay any amount of duty in contravention of subordinate legislation, 5 per cent or £250, whichever is the greater amount;

(ii) for the continuation of the above or failure to send a return, above the initial penalty in (i) to a penalty of £20 for every day, after the first, on which the conduct continues.[61]

There is also a right to mitigation on grounds which exclude insufficiency of funds.[62]

Criminal and civil liability. When irregularities entail both criminal and civil liability, parallel civil proceedings are usually delayed until the criminal prosecution is concluded. A fine or compensation order can be imposed by the criminal court at that stage. It is usually a matter of judicial discretion as to whether concurrent civil proceedings about the same subject-matter as a prosecution are stayed. The court must decide whether justice between the parties requires this. It will have regard, *inter alia*, to the following circumstances:

– the possibility of prejudicial publicity from the civil proceedings,
– whether the criminal trial is imminent and
– whether there is a real danger that the defendant would be prejudiced by being forced to disclose his defence to the criminal charge prematurely.[63]

---

58. Article 9(4) of the 1994 Finance Act.
59. Article 170 of the Customs and Excise Management Act 1979 (CEMA).
60. Article 8(7)(b) and (d) of the 1994 Finance Act 1994.
61. Article 9 of the 1994 Finance Act.
62. *See* F. Lagerberg, 'It's no longer criminal' (1994) *Taxation*, 17 March, pp. 530–531.
63. *Jefferson Ltd* v. *Bhetcha* [1979] I WLR 898. *Cf.* Supreme Court Practice, Vol. 2, para. 3355 (1982 ed.); *but see* Andenaes, M., *Enforcement of financial market regulation – Problems of Parallel proceedings* (1995), PhD thesis, Jesus College, Cambridge.

2.2. The Criminal Route

With regard to Crown prosecutions, the principle of expediency (*opportunité*) prevails.[64] This means that the Crown Prosecution Service (CPS),[65] the Lord Advocate in Scotland or those responsible for prosecution decisions in departments such as HM Customs and Excise decide whether to prosecute or whether to pursue some other course of action (including dropping the case). In this context, Harding has pointed out that:

> '[I]t would be misleading ... to divorce negotiated settlements from the analogy of criminal proceedings when it is clear that at a national level of criminal procedure issues in relation to prosecution, trial and sentence may be decided in an administrative fashion.'[66]

The CPS, for example, processes cases put up for prosecution through a two-stage evidential test. The first test consists in deciding whether there is enough evidence to provide a 'realistic prospect of conviction' against each defendant on each charge. 'Weak evidence' remains the most often quoted reason for not going ahead with prosecution.[67] The second test relates to the public interest. This means that even if the evidential sufficiency test is satisfied, it must still be in the public interest to prosecute. In cases of any seriousness, a prosecution will usually take place unless there are public interest factors tending against prosecution.[68] Two of the public interest factors against prosecution listed in the Code for Crown Prosecutors appear to be particularly relevant:

– the defendant has put right the loss or harm that was caused (but defendants must not avoid prosecution simply because they can pay compensation); or
– details may be made public that could harm sources of information, international relations or national security.

But Crown prosecutors must decide how important each factor is in the circumstances of each case and go on to make an overall assessment.

There is no constitutional interpretation of the public interest. The executive is free to interpret public interest as it wishes. In this context, Levi recently (1995) pointed out that:

---

64. Professor Ashworth identified three groups of countries: (i) Member States where the principle of legality was maintained without significant exceptions like Austria, Greece and Spain, (ii) Member States where the principle of expediency played a limited role like Portugal, Germany and France and (iii) Member States where prosecutors were allowed to make a wide use of the principle of expediency like Luxembourg, Sweden and the systems within the United Kingdom (J. Ashworth, 'Techniques for reducing subjective disparity in sentencing' (1989) in *Disparities in sentencing causes and solutions*, Council of Europe, Strasbourg).
65. The Crown Prosecution Service was set up in 1986 and the prosecution of most criminal offences is now in its hands.
66. C. Harding, *European Community investigations and sanctions* (1993) Leicester University Press, p. 68.
67. *See* Home Office, *Case screening by the Crown Prosecution Service: how and why cases are terminated* (1994) Research Study 137, HMSO.
68. *See* Crown Prosecution Service, *Code for Crown Prosecutors* (1994).

'[W]hat is or is not "in the public interest" is essentially subjective and can be political (with a small or a large p). British examples in which it has been alleged that pressure has been exerted not to prosecute in fraud cases include the House of Fraser case (involving the take-over of Harrods department store by the Fayed brothers, allegedly supported by the Sultan of Brunei); the Peter Cameron-Webb case (involving alleged "baby syndicates" given preferential treatment at Lloyd's of London); and the decision by the Department of Public Prosecution (DPP) in 1978 not to prosecute companies that broke sanctions imposed at the time of Rhodesia's Unilateral Declaration of Independence on the grounds that "no good would be served by raking over these almost dead coals". (The last is the only example in which policy rather than that usually unfalsifiable category "insufficient evidence" was given as the reason for non-prosecution.)'.[69]

In the more recent 'Supergun' affair,[70] Customs and Excise were advised that there were no realistic prospects of a conviction. But in view of the nature of the case, Customs and Excise sought advice from the Attorney-General as to whether there might be exceptional circumstances justifying prosecution in the public interest. The Attorney-General concluded that a prosecution should not be brought without a reasonable prospect of conviction and that public interest considerations should not be introduced as a way to justify prosecutions (without a prospect of conviction). Sir Richard Scott later endorsed this advice in his report, concluding that while there may be wholly exceptional circumstances in which such a prosecution could properly be brought, he could not formulate any practical examples.[71] The CPS has been openly criticized for reducing or even dropping charges to save money.[72]

In his report, Sir Richard Scott took the view that although the CPS and the SFO were independent prosecuting agencies, government departments were not. Government departments' prosecutions could be regarded as a means of enforcing departmental policies in the area in question.[73] This can lead (as in the 'Supergun' affair) to two different prosecuting bodies taking contrary decisions in the same circumstances. At present there are no signs that the various agencies which, in one

---

69. M. Levi, 'Serious fraud in Britain' (1995) in *Corporate crime: Contemporary debates*, eds. F. Pearce and L. Snider, University of Toronto Press, p. 188.

70. The 'Supergun' affair involved the seizing in 1990 by Customs and Excise at Tees Dock, Middlesborough, UK of large tubes which were discovered to be sections of barrel for a huge long-range artillery gun. No export licence had been applied for as they were exported as petrochemical pipes. Customs and Excise prosecuted managers in the British firms who had forged the tubes. Two lines of defence emerged. The first was that the defendants did not know that the tubes were intended to be used as weapons. Secondly, the defendants had expressed concerns to the Ministry of Defence and the DTI in 1988 about a possible military use of the tubes. The government departments had failed to investigate the concerns.

71. 'Scott Report' or *Report of the Inquiry into the Export of Defence Equipment and Dual-Use Goods to Iraq and Related Prosecutions* (1996) HMSO, by Sir Richard Scott, Vice-Chancellor of the Supreme Court, Jl 33, Jl 39.

72. *See* D. Rose, *In the name of the law: the collapse of criminal justice* (1996); also newspaper article 'When justice takes a walk', in *Guardian*, 19 November 1996, pp. 2–3.

73. Scott Report, *op. cit*, K.4.7.

way or another, represent the public interest actually converge in their approach to EC fraud.[74]

Government departments with powers of prosecution have their own guidelines for prosecution, which also adhere to the principle of opportunity. However, policies on prosecutions are rarely set out publicly.[75]

Fines. Financial penalties are, by far, the most frequent penalties imposed by the criminal courts. A financial penalty can be imposed on its own, or in combination with a term of imprisonment, or any other sentence. In England, the magistrate's courts, which exercise jurisdiction over less serious crime, can impose a fine for any offence tried before them, up to a fixed upper limit.[76]

The Crown Court is empowered to impose a fine in lieu of or in addition to imprisonment (provided that the offence does not carry a mandatory sentence such as life imprisonment). It enjoys an unlimited fining jurisdiction, although the prohibition of excessive fines found in the Magna Carta (1215)[77] and the Bill of Rights (1689)[78] still apply. In criminal courts generally, the level of the fine is determined by the gravity of the offence and the offender's financial circumstances.[79] (A 'unit fine' experiment of 1991–1994 has been abandoned by the government.) A fine can be paid in instalments. This is usually granted at the hearing without having to make a special application to the court. Both amount and period of repayment are subject to judicial discretion.

A criminal court can request a financial circumstances report before imposing a fine. A fine can be imposed in addition to a term of imprisonment, or in addition to a probation order. Alternatively, it can be imposed on its own (*see* compensation order below). A request to pay a fine by instalments is usually granted to the offender by the court without special application. Again, the amount and period of repayment are the subject of judicial discretion. In case of default to the terms agreed, a 'means inquiry' is ordered by the court. A means warrant has the effect of producing payment in most cases but, when it fails, the court is empowered to change the sum of the fine imposed or to remit. But generally speaking the Keith Committee (1983) found that, in revenue cases:

> 'compared with the scale of culpable arrears, the fines imposed in the larger cases are modest.... The recovery of fines imposed in the larger cases ... is slow and difficult ... given the circumstances and scale of the larger tax frauds, it is questionable whether such sentences have significant deterrent value.'[80]

---

74. S. White, 'The public interest as represented in English law: relevance for EC fraud', proceeds of Urbino conference held in July 1995.
75. R. Harwood, 'Corruption and public sector fraud Prosecution by government agencies' (1996) 4:1 *Journal of Financial Crime*, pp. 51–54.
76. Where for example an offender has been summarily convicted of an offence triable either way, the maximum fine is £5,000 under s. 17(2)(c) of the 1991 Criminal Justice Act.
77. G. Grebing, *The fine in comparative law – a survey of 21 countries* (1982) Cambridge Institute of Criminology, Occasional Papers number 9, p. 86 and note 479.
78. It forbids 'excessive baile... excessive fines and cruell and unusuall punishments'.
79. S. 19(2) of the 1991 Criminal Justice Act explains that this may have the effect of either reducing or increasing he amount of the fine.
80. Keith Committee (1983) *op. cit.*

Compensation orders. Compensation orders, which seek to compensate the victim for any damage caused, have been described as a method of short-circuiting civil proceedings. It is difficult to gauge, within the remit of this research, what role they have in the protection of the financial interests of the European Community, if any. Although in the past a compensation order could only be made in addition to another sentence for crime, a criminal court can now make one in its own right. A compensation order can also be made even though the precise amount of the loss or damage has not been proved.[81]

Bankruptcies. In cases of criminal bankruptcies the CPS is invariably the petitioner. In deciding whether to apply for a criminal bankruptcy order[82] (which has the effect of making available the machinery of civil bankruptcy administration for the recovery of sums owed), the CPS applies two criteria:

– first, whether the offender has sufficient means to make bankruptcy proceedings worthwhile;
– second, whether it is in the public interest to take proceedings in respect of those assets (because, for example, such action might cause severe hardship to the criminal bankrupt's family).[83]

But generally speaking, as Levi (1989) pointed out '... Civil redress against convicted persons is comparatively rare: it is more common as an alternative to prosecution.'[84]

Finally there is no 'constitution de partie civile' whereby the civil and criminal actions can be joined in one single proceeding.[85] Nor can the victim apply to join the proceedings as a civil party (*plainte de partie civile*).

2.3. Extra-judicial Settlements: UK Agencies and Their Practices

It is also within the discretion of government bodies managing EC funds to recover unwarranted payments without going to court. Such settlements occur when the agencies decide to offset amounts, to compound or to withhold payments. In line with the 'either/or' system in operation, extra-judicial proposals for settlement are not presented to an independent body for approval. In practice, it is up to the aggrieved person to challenge the administrative decision with the administration itself. Most administrations have a formal internal review mechanism, and they will review on request, on the understanding that 'mistakes can occur on either side'. If the dispute persists a judicial remedy has to be sought. In some cases, the treasury can write off unrecoverable debts. These are addressed in more detail under Part 5.

---

81. *Ibid.*
82. S. 39 of the Powers of Criminal Courts Act 1973.
83. *See* Hodgson Report, *Profits of crime and their recovery – Report of a Committee chaired by Sir Derek Hodgson* (1984) Heinemann, London.
84. M. Levi, 'Fraudulent justice? Sentencing the business criminal' (1989) in *Paying for crime*, eds. P. Carlen and D. Cook, Open University Press, Milton Keynes, UK.
85. *See* M. Cappelletti, *The judicial process in comparative perspective* (1989), Clarendon Press, Oxford.

UK agencies. There is no central organizational framework in the United Kingdom for the prevention, detection, investigation and prosecution of EC fraud or irregularities.[86] Instead, a fragmented approach prevails, with each government body with a responsibility for the management of EC funds adopting a different policy with regard to the recovery of funds, as we shall see. MAFF, the Intervention Board for Agricultural Produce (IBAP), HM Customs and Excise, the Department of Employment and the Treasury are the main government departments with responsibilities for EC funds which are examined below.

MAFF. MAFF (the Ministry of Agriculture, Fisheries and Food) administers, with the Agriculture Departments in Scotland, Northern Ireland and Wales, government policies on agriculture, horticulture and fisheries. These departments deal with the recovery of sums relating to the funds they administer. These include funds from the guarantee and from the guidance section of the EAGGF, from FIFG[87] and from some of the Community initiatives.[88]

The Intervention Board for Agricultural Produce (IBAP). IBAP is a separate government department which is accountable to the four Agriculture Ministers and funds all the expenditure in the United Kingdom under the Guarantee Section of the EAGGF.It also administers the trader-based Guarantee Section schemes in the United Kingdom. It is responsible for accounting for the recovery of overpayments and the collection of levies in respect of the schemes which it administers.

From time to time the authorities (MAFF, the Intervention Board) find themselves due to make a payment to a beneficiary of the Common Agricultural Policy who has failed to pay a levy or repay an overpayment within the time limit that has been given. The legal position in the UK is that mutual debts may be set off against each other provided that there are established debts, that the two parties are acting in the same capacity in relation to both debts and they both agree. Set-off is the right to set up a compensating debt against a creditor in extinction or diminution of the claim, so that both obligations are to that extent simultaneously discharged and a net obligation is substituted.[89] Set-off postulates mutual but independent obligations between two parties.[90] It applies regardless of the degree of fault. Indeed 'in the case of an insolvent trader, such set-off may constitute the only practicable way open to the authorities to recover the wrongly paid sums'.[91] Unlike Customs and Excise, the authorities dealing with agricultural subventions do not have any power to seize goods or assets, so when farmers are not agreeable to set-off, they become liable to civil proceedings. Set-off is used mostly when there are repeated payments, for example in the case of subventions to farmers within the context of the EAGGF Guarantee Section funds.

---

86. *See* A. Doig, 'A fragmented organizational approach to fraud in a European context – The case of the United Kingdom public sector' (1995) 3:2 *European Journal on Criminal Policy and Research*, special edition on corruption and corporate crime, pp. 48–64.
87. The Financial Instrument for Fisheries Guidance (FIFG) provides structural assistance in the fisheries and aquaculture sector and for the processing and marketing of its products.
88. For example under LEADER II or PESCA.
89. *Hanak* v. *Green* [1958] ALL ER 141 at 153.
90. D. Southern, 'Set-off revisited', (1994) 6669 *New Law Journal*, pp. 1412–1414.
91. Case 250/78, *Deka Getreideprodukte GmbH* v. *EEC*, [1983] ECR 421.

HM Customs and Excise. Customs and Excise is responsible for the collection and administration of Customs and Excise duties and value added tax, the compilation of overseas trade statistics, the collection of Customs and agricultural levies for the European Union and the enforcement of prohibitions of the importation of certain goods. Most of the work is now organized in executive units. The department is responsible for control of the export of all goods subject to export refunds and gets involved in negotiating extra-judicial settlements with respect to VAT and trade levies. It can prosecute in its own right.

Customs and Excise have the power to compound. This power, to be exercised entirely within their discretion, means that they can drop a case altogether, or reach an agreement with an individual to drop a case, generally in consideration of a payment of money.[92] The Inland Revenue also has the power to compound.[93] The Keith Report found that this power was exercised with respect to 90 per cent of VAT fraud cases.[94] Figures show that, in 1993 and 1994, this power has also been exercised with respect to CAP levies, as well as other duties (*see* Table 5.5.), but not to the degree reported in the Keith Report in respect of VAT.

Table 5.5. Outcomes of court cases and compounded resolutions:
CAP offences, 1992–94

	Court			Settlements under s. 152 CEMA
	No. of people involved	No. of people imprisoned	Fines (in £1,000)	Fines (in £1,000)
From 1/4/92 to 31/3/93:				
Import	5	2	200.9	39.5
Export	11	4	200	88.5
From 1/4/93 to 31/3/94:				
Import	3	N/A	N/A	N/A
Export	8	2	158	41.75

Source: HM Customs and Excise Annual Report for the year ended 31 March 1993, pp. 88–89; HM Customs and Excise Annual Report for the year ended 31 March 1994, pp. 92–93.

Both compounding and civil fraud penalties are used in areas controlled by Customs and Excise, i.e. VAT, excise, duties and levies. There is no difference in treatment between national funds and EC funds.

92. S. 152 (a) of the Customs and Excise Act 1979; *see also* H.M. Customs and Excise, *Customs, compounding, seizure and restoration, customers' booklet* (1992) HMSO.
93. S. 102 of the Taxes Management Act 1970.
94. *Keith Report* on Enforcement Powers of Revenue Departments (1983) para. 16.4.3.

121

The Department of Trade and Industry (DTI). The Department's responsibilities are wide-ranging and include government policy on regional development, inward investment, energy, export services, innovation, environment, deregulation, competition policy, small firms and consumer affairs. The Department's responsibilities cover the UK as a whole, with the exception of some of its duties relating to regional assistance, which are devolved. It is within the Department's discretion to negotiate extra-judicial settlements with respect to the European Regional Fund (ERF) and of Community initiatives such as the SMEs initiative[95] INTERREG II,[96] LEADER II,[97] RECHAR II,[98] RESIDER II,[99] RETEX,[100] KONVER,[101] URBAN,[102] PESCA[103] as well as pilot initiatives in inter-regional cooperation[104] and most activities under the fourth R&D programme[105] when it sees fit. It can also prosecute in its own right, in certain circumstances.

The Department of Employment. The responsibility for the administration of the European Social Fund (ESF) and of various Community initiatives[106] rests with the Department of Employment. It discharges its responsibilities through the ESF Unit based in London. Its Verification and Audit Section (VAS) was established recently in order to meet the responsibilities under Article 23 of Council Regulation 2082/93.[107] In Scotland, the Secretary of State for Scotland now has responsibility for training policy and the administration of Objectives 1, 2 and 5(b) under the ESF now rests with the Scottish Office Industry Department (SOID). The Northern Ireland Office too has similar devolved responsibilities with respect to Northern Ireland. These agencies can be involved in negotiating extra-judicial settlements with respect to the

---

95. The SME initiative is intended to help small and medium-sized enterprises to participate in the economy.
96. INTERREG II supports the development of networks and cross-border, transnational and inter-regional cooperation in areas such as the transfer of skills and technology towards the less-favoured regions.
97. LEADER II supports local initiatives for rural development.
98. RECHAR II assists the economic and social conversion of coal mining areas hardest hit by mine closures.
99. RESIDER II assists the economic and social conversion of steel areas.
100. RETEX aims to promote the diversification of activities in regions which are over-dependent on the textile and clothing industry.
101. KONVER aims to helps to help areas affected by the run-down of defence-related industries and military installations.
102. The URBAN initiative is aimed at supporting schemes in depressed urban areas.
103. PESCA aims to help areas which are heavily dependent on fishing to adapt to economic changes and diversify their activities.
104. For example PACTE, which promotes cooperation at local and regional level in the area of development; OUVERTURE and ECOS, which promote cooperation between the less favoured regions of the European Union and their counterparts in Central and Eastern Europe, and RECITE, which supports 36 inter-regional projects and networks of regional and local authorities across the European Union in fields such as economic development.
105. The fourth framework programme for Community Research and Technological Development (1994–1998) supports research and development activities in key industrial technologies.
106. EMPLOYMENT-NOW, to reduce unemployment amongst women; EMPLOYMENT-HORIZON to improve employment prospects of disabled people; EMPLOYMENT-YOUTHSTART to prevent youth unemployment and several equal opportunities action programmes, etc.
107. [1993] O.J. L193/20.

European Social Fund, but have no power to prosecute in their own right. In the 1994 financial year, the United Kingdom reported no fraud in this area. According to the London office, minor mistakes and irregularities, when they occurred were dealt with, for example, by withholding payments until appropriate targets were met.

HM Treasury: overseeing role and direct involvement. The Treasury is responsible for tax and monetary policy, the control and planning of public expenditure, international financial relations, supervision of the financial system, and a range of Civil Service management issues. The responsibility of the Treasury and its executive agencies[108] extends throughout the United Kingdom. Apart from its general executive role, the Treasury is directly involved in certain decisions, for example those relating to write-offs.

2.4. Particularities of Extra-judicial Recoveries in English Law

2.4.1. Setting-off: Background

The right of set-off exists both under common law and under statute. The statutory right of set-off belongs to the administrative branch of the law and can be found in various forms in banking and consumer rights legislation.[109] It is based on the 1592 Compensation Act in Scotland, and the 1729 and 1735 Statutes of Set-off in the rest of the United Kingdom. In England the Statutes of Set-off were repealed but their effect were preserved in the procedural rules of 1879.[110] Because set-off is procedural in nature, it is *lex fori*[111] – which means that it is classified according to (the many) circumstances in which it can arise. Furthermore set-off can only be invoked as a defence: it is 'a shield, not a sword'. We shall see that in the discretionary British systems, this can create problems because set-off is being used more pro-actively than it was intended to be.

Mutuality and equity are two central pre-requirements to set-off. The doctrine of mutuality (also called reciprocity, privity or the requirement of *concursus debiti et crediti*) requires that one person's claim shall not be used to pay another person's debt.[112] The requirement of equity (i.e. that the demands be held in the same right) would seem to mean no more than each of the parties who is liable to the other, should be the beneficial owner of a cross-demand.[113]

The literature confirms that set-off can be regarded as similar to payment. In setting off his cross-claim, the debtor 'pays' the creditor's primary claim *pro tanto* and obliges the creditor to 'pay' the cross-claim. There is therefore a *pro tanto* redemption, discharge, satisfaction, extinguishment or reduction of the reciprocal debts.[114]

---

108. *See The Civil Service* (1995) HMSO.
109. For example the Sale of Goods Act 1979 s. 53(1)(a) provides for set-off.
110. S. 2 of the Civil Procedure Act Repeal Act R.S.C. ord. 17, r. 18 paragraphs 2–6 *et seq.*
111. *Meyer* v. *Dresser* (1864) 16 CB (NS) 646.
112. *See* P. Wood, *English and international set-off* (1989) Sweet and Maxwell, London, p. 1221.
113. R. Derham, *Set-off* (1987) Clarendon Press, Oxford, p. 155.
114. Wood, *op. cit.*, p. 16.

Set-off is used when there has been an overclaim (deliberate of not) of a subsidy and when the amount over-claimed can be deducted from the next payment. The type of set-off we are mostly concerned with here is of the solvent variety which has some similarities with a banker's right to set-off sums from customers' accounts.

The right to offset is not automatic, with some exceptions.[115] In cases of insolvency, set-off is mandatory. The Insolvency Act 1986, section 323, provides that where before the commencement of a bankruptcy there have been mutual dealings, an account shall be taken to establish the net balance for which the creditor may prove in the bankruptcy. The substance of mandatory set-off in solvency remains the same for companies as for individuals.[116]

Some regulations specifically request that aids should be paid to the beneficiaries in their entirety.[117] In defence of set-off under these circumstances, the UK authorities have argued that:

> '... [S]et-off does not actually decrease the entitlement of the beneficiary to be paid the amount in question ... [t]he setting-off of part or all of the subsidy payment does not affect the entitlement to aid which has been calculated without deduction.'[118]

This has been the subject on an on-going debate between the UK authorities and the Commission, the case law of the European Court of Justice shedding little light on this subject.[119] This state of uncertainty led the Intervention Board to produce a 'non-paper' in 1992 stating that:

---

115. Wood (*op. cit.*) states that in France and many other jurisdictions basing themselves on the Napoleonic Code, set-off is automatic as soon as mutual independent claims are eligible for set-off, i.e. when they both are liquid and have matured due and payable. The set-off occurs without the parties being aware of it. Jurisdictions following automaticity of independent set-off includes (besides France) Belgium, Luxembourg and Spain (...) although it may be that not all these jurisdictions are wholly faithful to the Code.

116. R. 4.90 of the Insolvency Rules 1986, SI 1986 adopts identical wording, *mutatis mutandis*, to s. 323 of the Insolvency Act.

117. For example Council Regulations 1765/92 (arable crops), 2066/92 (beef), 2082/93 (structural aids), 615/92 (oilseeds) and 84/93 (tobacco).

118. Extract from a letter from Robert Lowson, Minister for Agriculture to Guy Legras, Director General of DGVI dated 14 February 1995.

119. In case 118/76, *Balkan-Import-Export* v. *Hauptzollamt Berlin-Packhof*, [1977] ECR 1117 the Court of Justice gave a preliminary ruling to the effect that a national administration could not apply a domestic rule when 'its effect would be to modify the scope of the provisions of Community law'. In the case of *Pigs and Bacon Commission* v. *McCarren and Co, Supreme Court of Ireland*, [1981] 3 CMLR 408, the Court of Justice ruled that a question of set-off was one to be decided according to national law although the obligation to repay the levy and recover the bonus both derived from Community law. Similarly in joined cases 146, 192 and 193/81, *BayWa AG and others* v. *Bundesanstalt für Landwirtschaftliche Marktordnung*, [1982] ECR 1503, the Advocate General pointed out that the application of a national rule is forbidden when it would 'alter the effect of the Community rules'. In case 250/78, *Deka* v. *EEC*, [1983] ECR 421, Advocate General Mancini inferred from this that set-off in relation to sums payable under Community legislation was governed by EC law. This view appears to have been endorsed by the Court itself when it said that Community rules 'may give rise, as between authorities and traders, to reciprocal and even related claims which are an appropriate subject for set-off'.

'... [T]he United Kingdom authorities would welcome a provision of Community law enabling the competent authorities of the Member States to withhold payments under CAP schemes to the extent that they believe the beneficiary to be indebted to them under the CAP.'

The main pre-conditions to set-off are that:

(i) there is no obvious intent to defraud,
(ii) a payment becomes available to set-off,
(iii) the farmer/trader agrees, and
(iv) the conditions for mutuality are present.

With respect to the third requirement, which says for example that an agreement should be sought before amounts are offset, practice varies. When an agreement has not been properly sought by the authorities, this may lead to judicial review.

There is no fixed upper limit of set-off in financial terms. For practical purposes, the maximum that can be offset is the total amount due to the beneficiary by the administration.

The main principle governing set-off is the principle of mutuality, which postulates mutual but independent obligations between two parties. In some circumstances, the mutuality requirement is difficult to satisfy, as we shall see.

Third agency involved in set-off. When a third agency is involved in the management of EC funds, for example of EAGGF Guidance Section Funds, two possibilities have to be envisaged:

(1) the third agency is a Crown body and the principle of mutuality applies (the Crown being indivisible) or
(2) the third agency is not a Crown body, because its agents do not act merely as agents of the Crown in exercising their functions. Without mutuality, there is no (self-help insolvent) set-off, *stricto sensu*.

Although the second possibility was only encountered in Northern Ireland, it cannot be dismissed as an oddity. This is because these last few years have seen a vast programme of privatization, reaching areas hitherto the sole preserve of the Crown. As a result, agencies proliferate which act on behalf of the Crown, but are not necessarily Crown bodies themselves.[120] If this trend is to continue, it may well have an increasing impact on the availability of set off as a defence.

Multiple registrations. Strictly speaking the principle of mutuality does not apply when, for example, claims originate:

– from different members of the same family running the same farm or business,
– from different individuals in the same partnership, or

---

120. J. Davies and J. Willman, *What next? Agencies, departments, and the Civil Service* (1991) Institute for Public Policy Research, London.

– from the same individual(s) but under different or new company names (concurrently or successively).

One of my interviewees was sanguine about this difficulty, and suggested that it could be overcome by extending the system of securities/guarantees, perceived as successful, to more areas of the CAP. This system has the advantage that the security created can be used to settle relevant debts, and also remains valid in the event of the debtor's insolvency.

Setting-off across schemes. There does not appear to be any reason in English or Scots law why set-off should not occur across schemes, as long as the schemes are run by the same Crown body and this does not involve any unauthorized transfer of information.

Setting-off between national and EC funds. Can the authorities set off between national and EC funds? This has been the subject of an on-going debate. Recent correspondence (1994) from the Commission to the British authorities shows that subsidy stops should not apply on Community premia provided for in certain regulations.

> '... Several Community Regulations ... provide that the Community premia are to be paid over to the beneficiaries "in their entirety" (*cf.* Regulation 615/92, oilseeds, Regulation 1765/92, cereals, Regulation 2066/92, beef, Regulation 84/93, tobacco and Regulation 2082/93, structural aids). The Commission services take the view that these provisions exclude the possibility for national authorities to withhold the Community premia concerned in order to recover debts arising from national schemes or provisions.'[121]

In other words:

> '... The use of any such direct aid granted as part of the reform of the CAP to offset a State claim against those entitled to this aid (for example, a national tax liability) is not permitted.'[122]

But more recently (February 1995) the UK authorities have argued that:

> '... [T]here may be cases where purely national debts are recovered from payments under wholly Community funded schemes and, conversely, cases where it will be possible to recover Community debts from payments under wholly UK funded schemes which would be of particular benefit to the Community. It is our understanding of the law handed down from the European Court that a debtor should not be treated more or less favourably in

---

121. Extract from letter originating from G. Legras, Director General of DG VI to Mr Richard Grant, the Scottish Office, Agriculture and Fisheries Department, Edinburgh dated 1 July 1994.
122. Extract from letter originating from René Steichen to The Rt. Hon. William Waldegrave, Minister of Agriculture, dated 27 December 1994.

relation to Community schemes than he would be in relation to national schemes. The rules of set-off under the national law should therefore not be operated in a way which prejudices the operation of Community law. By parity of reasoning, the Community rules should, whenever possible, be interpreted in such a way that there is no discrimination against the operation of national law.... We have a long experience of using "subsidy stops" both in Scotland and elsewhere in the UK and we have found that this is a very useful method of debt recovery. There have rarely been objections from farmers or traders directly affected and their application avoids recourse to alternative protracted and expensive debt recovery procedures.'[123]

2.4.2. Compounding

There is no limit to the amount that can be recouped through a compounded settlement. Each settlement has a reparative element (sum to be recovered) and a punitive element (fine). The amount of the punitive element in the settlement is discretionary. Compounding is part of Customs law. In order to compound, Customs must have enough evidence for a criminal prosecution. Compounding applies both to criminal offence proceedings and to condemnations which are civil proceedings. There is no set rule about when the negotiations for a compound should begin, and section 152 of CEMA does not place any time limit on the matter.

Customs and Excise may also, after a court judgment, mitigate or remit any pecuniary penalty imposed under section 152(c) of CEMA – although this does not apply to VAT and the so-called civil penalties which the Department can assess under the Finance Act 1985.

According to Customs and Excise, the one unequivocal guideline in deciding the suitability of a case for compounding is that the evidence would support a criminal prosecution. Each case is considered on its merits after a careful evaluation of all known mitigating or aggravating factors including relative seriousness. Evidence of guilt (but not admission of guilt) is a prerequisite to compounding. An alleged offender is free to make an offer of settlement, but Customs and Excise can turn it down. A person who is offered a compounded settlement and turns it down is prosecuted in the criminal court. The general policy on compounding can mostly be found in answers to Parliamentary questions, and in the Keith Report.[124] As a rule the Department is reluctant to compound, and will usually prosecute in the following cases:

(a) where a person already has a departmental record;
(b) where he is known to be subject to a suspended prison sentence or on bail, nor when other related offences are being considered, either by Customs themselves, another Government department or the police;
(c) when he is an undischarged bankrupt or in the case of a limited company is in administration or receivership;

123. Extract from letter originating from Robert Lowson, Minister (Agriculture) to Guy Legras, Director General of DG VI, dated 14 February 1995.
124. Keith Report, *op. cit.*

(d) where a person, in virtue of his occupation, is supposed to have been more aware than the general public of the gravity of his offence (judges, lawyers, accountants and civil servants fall into that category);
(e) in obscenity cases involving children;
(f) when illicit distillation is involved, with a risk to public health;
(g) when Customs personnel have been assaulted by members of the public;
(h) when abuse of hydrocarbon oil road fuel is involved;
(i) when firearms are involved.

This list is not exhaustive, and may be added to by Customs.

There is no threshold for compounding, and compounding settlements can reach millions of pounds. As far as civil fraud is concerned, there is a discretionary limit of £100,000 beyond which Customs and Excise prefer to prosecute.

According to Customs, compounded settlements are only available for first offences. Further offences are dealt with by the courts.

With regard to compounding, in 1983 the Keith Committee[125] recommended that although the tax authorities should be able to compound or make settlements, the names of the persons concerned should be publicized, except where there had been full spontaneous voluntary disclosure.[126] This was not taken up.

There is no special provision for the notification of third parties (apart from the provisions to be found in EC law). In case of insolvency, creditors are not usually kept informed of developments.

Fines in compounded settlements. According to Customs and Excise, the punitive element of a compounding settlement (or the 'fine' part of the compounded settlement) rests (informally) on a sliding scale between roughly 25 per cent and 100 per cent of the reparative element, but can occasionally exceed 100 per cent. In deciding on the amount of the punitive element of the compound, Customs broadly follow the guidance issued to the courts in CEMA, although they are not bound by it in this respect and enjoy complete discretion. In the Act a sum of up to three times the value of the goods can be set,[127] although in compounded settlements involving EC funds, the amount of levy is usually taken into account, rather than the value of the goods.

The fine part of the compounded settlement can also be reduced when the alleged offender cooperates with the authorities at an early stage.

There is no hard and fast rule and authorities decide on a case by case basis.

2.4.3. Withdrawal/Request for Repayment

The 1995 Structural Funds Manual contains a draft offer letter which states that the Secretary of State reserves the right to withhold any or all of the payments and/or to require part or all of the grant to be repaid under certain circumstances. There is

---

125. *Ibid.*
126. *Ibid*, paras. 18.5.54 and 20.2.11–12.
127. Article 170 (3)(a) of the Customs and Excise Management Act 1979.

no provision for any contract of this type to be put up for approval to an independent tribunal.

2.4.4. Withholding Payment

Authorities managing the Structural Funds make plain in their offer of contract to beneficiaries that they reserve the right to withhold any or all of the payments in the following circumstances:

(i)   there is a substantial, or material, change in the nature, scale, costs or timing of a project;

(ii)   the future of the project is in jeopardy;

(iii)   there is unsatisfactory progress towards completing the project, or the project is not completed by the agreed date;

(iv)   there is unsatisfactory progress towards meeting the forecast outputs specified;

(v)   any of the information provided in the application for grant or in supporting or subsequent correspondence is found to be substantially incorrect or incomplete;

(vi)   the applicant is in receipt of a grant from other Community institutions towards project costs, unless the grant has already been taken into account;

(vii)   the assistance exceeds European Community aid limits to the extent that any grant paid should not have been paid; or a decision of the European Commission or of the European Court of Justice requires payment to be withheld (or recovered);

(viii) this point applies to the public sector only: any grant or other payment, which is payable towards the project, has been received or is likely to be received from any public authority. Of course, this does not apply to payments whose availability and amount have already been taken into account at the time the offer was made;

(ix)   the project is used for purposes other than those specified in the offer letter during its economic life as specified in the offer letter.

The authorities can withhold payment of certain sums pending the outcome of court proceedings. In the recent case of *Jewers*, DG VI found that the Intervention Board had acted appropriately in doing so.

2.4.5. Exchequer Write-offs

Under Article 8(2) of Council Regulation 729/70, Member States must bear the financial consequences of irregularities and negligence attributable to their administrative authorities or other bodies.

In some cases, therefore, debts are written off and the loss borne by the Exchequer. For the 1993 financial year (March 1993 to April 1994), a comparatively small amount of just over £247,000 was put forward by the Intervention Board to be written off in that way. The Treasury is keen to ensure that write-offs should be kept to a minimum. One of the strategic objectives, stated in the Corporate Plan 1993–94 to 1997–98 of the Intervention Board in relation to disallowance resulting from its actions and falling on the Exchequer following the clearance of the 1991 EAGGF accounts, is to limit such disallowance to within 0.40 per cent of the total of the accounts submitted for that year.

The position at the moment is that for EAGGF write-offs under £10, no prior recovery action is necessary. In the case of overpayment of subsidies and refunds or under collection of co-responsibility levies not exceeding £40, no prior recovery action is necessary except when overpayments to the same payee for the same cause total more than £40 a month. The same applies for own-resources uncollected debits not exceeding £40. The Treasury may withhold their authority to write off, when they are not satisfied that proper steps have been taken to investigate a loss, to impose financial penalties or take adequate disciplinary procedures. A refusal by the Treasury to sanction write-off is reported to the Comptroller and Auditor General, and by the latter to the Public Accounts Committee, who may question the Accounting Officer about the action taken.[128]

Write-off can also occur, on a case by case basis, as a result of consultation with the Commission.[129] In a case where the Intervention Board was owed in excess of £800,000 by a trader on the peas and beans scheme, it was approached by the debtor with the following dilemma. The debtor said he could pay £250,000 and carry on trading and retain his firm's employees – alternatively he could become bankrupt, with a result that very little would be recovered at all. In the circumstances, DG VI agreed that the Intervention Board should accept the £250,000 offered.

2.4.6. Other Arrangements

Repayment of grant. The authorities also reserve the right to require part or all of the grant to be repaid in the circumstances outlined above. When matching funders have acted as guarantors, they are approached for repayment before civil proceedings are instituted.

Informal arrangement in case of insolvency. An 'informal moratorium' can sometimes be reached with creditors, such as a re-scheduling of debt payment. A breakdown of the arrangement leads to civil court proceedings.

---

128. Finance Manual of the Intervention Board for Agricultural Produce (1995) London.
129. Article 4(2) of Council Regulation 595/91 [1991] O.J. L67.

2.5. Discussion: The Effectiveness of Extra-judicial Settlements, from an English Point of View

Three main claims have been made in relation to extra-judicial settlements, namely that they are fast, quick and cost-effective. These claims are briefly examined below.

2.5.1. Effectiveness

Non-court recoveries are perceived as highly effective, although a certain amount of institutionalized 'cherry picking' goes on: for example the person concerned must be solvent and/or in receipt of regular sums.

There are areas of uncertainty, particularly with regard to set-off. For example, it is not clear to what extent set-off can occur when a third party is involved, either between schemes, or between national and EC schemes. Nor are time-limits clear.

At the moment, furthermore, there is no specific appeal procedure which deals with disputes over amounts to be offset. Although agreement is meant to be a *sine qua non* of set-off, it is occasionally used more aggressively.

2.5.2. Quickness

Administrative recoveries have been speedier than those effected by the courts. But it is not known how long administrative procedures can retain their reputation for dispatch now that new appeal procedures are being set up. The policy of the Customs and Duties Tribunal is to hear an appeal within three months of it being ready for listing, and to issue the decision, which will usually have been reserved, within two months of the date of hearing. Currently the waiting time for a hearing is around ten weeks throughout the United Kingdom. It is obviously too early to speculate on how long Customs duty cases will take to go through the system once the new appeal procedures (*see* below) get in full swing. On the other hand, the review procedure may work well and not produce many tribunal cases. But it must be remembered that the inferior courts in the UK are not always fast.[130]

2.5.3. Cost-effectiveness

Unlike court recovery, administrative recoveries are regarded as cost-effective. The importance of cost-effectiveness leads some civil servants to argue that when the defendant is on income support, or when he is drawing legal aid (both are means-tested in the UK), then this is a fair indication that recovery through the courts will

---

130. For example in the recent case of *Darnell* (case of *Darnell* v. *the United Kingdom*, judgment of 26 October 1993, series A, Vol. 272) the European Court of Human Rights found unanimously that the United Kingdom had breached Article 6(2) of the Convention by letting Mr Darnell wait nearly nine years for an Industrial Tribunal hearing.

not be successful, and will cost the tax payer a disproportionate amount to pursue. This is particularly true, they argue, when the defendant is drawing on legal aid funds, in which case the cost to the tax payer will be even greater.[131] The cost-effectiveness argument can thus be carried *ad absurdum* by the executive.

No doubt that when the debtor is solvent, administrative recovery is more cost-effective, and quicker than the courts can be, although it remains to be seen whether the introduction of new procedural safeguards will affect this performance. When the debtor has been declared bankrupt (a relatively easy process in the UK), it may be that little can be done to recover funds. The determination of whether funds are available for recovery or not – i.e., the thoroughness of the financial investigation – therefore remains of crucial importance.

2.6. The Question of Administrative Discretion

Government agencies with a responsibility for the managing of EC funds and the recovery thereof may set-off, compound, withhold funds, or simply request repayment. Small amounts may also be written off. Special arrangements may also apply in cases of insolvency. These settlement modes are addressed in some detail below. On the whole, administrations prefer extra-judicial settlements, because of increasing staff and costs constraints. This state of affairs raises question about the powers of discretion these agencies have. For example, how is that same discretion circumscribed?

The issue of the extent and limitation of administrative power can partly be discussed within the framework of the polarity legality versus expediency. The principle of legality usually refers to the doctrine of mandatory prosecution but also, more generally, to the strict subordination of all administrative or other actions to legal rules. The principle of expediency, by contrast, refers to the ability to act with discretion and deal with matters on a case by case basis.

If one imagines a legalistic expediency-prone continuum, the United Kingdom could perhaps be placed towards the 'expediency' end. We have seen that when cases are put up for Crown prosecution, they are carefully 'filtered' in a two-stage process (*see* 2.2. above), which involves an assessment of the likely outcome. In fact the likely outcome is a consideration very much at the forefront throughout the system.

In reality, however, approaches are never purely 'legalistic' or 'discretionary'. Discretion is always circumscribed: 'authorities vested with discretionary powers by an Act of Parliament can only exercise such powers within the limits of the particular statute'.[132] Sometimes discretion is embedded in the legislation itself with expressions such as 'as they see fit' (*see* CEMA 1979 mentioned earlier) and therefore is statutory. So,

---

131. The case of *Saunders* show that, because of the way the legal aid fund is administered, even relatively wealthy defendants on fraud charges can benefit from legal aid.
132. LJ Kerr in *R* v. *London transport Executive ex parte GLC* [1983] 2 WLR 702.

'Même au sein de l'univers de la règle et du règlement, le jeu avec la règle fait partie de la règle du jeu.'[133]

The opportunity versus expediency debate does not necessarily help to clarify matters in the British context. It is a moot point as to whether any discussion as to the limits of discretion in the UK could more usefully focus on the procedures available to resolve the disputes which unavoidably arise from its use.

2.6.1. Two Types of Discretion

What is the nature of this discretion? Theories of administrative discretion suggest that it arises in two main forms:

- discretionary non-performance or moderated performance of duties, as it seems when viewed from the perspective of strict legalism;[134]
- pro-active discretion, meaning a very active doing of things, possibly going well beyond what explicitly has been provided for in legislation. Yet it is not illegal, since it is not judged illegal by the judiciary, indeed commonly it is not even reviewed by the judiciary.

Discretion as non-action or moderated action. Traditionally, Customs and Excise has been entrusted with a great deal of discretion. Section 152(a) of the CEMA provides that the Customs Commissioners may, as they see fit,

'stay, sist[135] ... any proceedings for an offence or for the condemnation of any thing as being forfeited under the Customs and Excise Act.'

In other words, Commissioners are free to decide not to prosecute. This provision being statutory, it does not require the permission of any member of the judiciary. In this process, an alleged offender may make an offer of compound, but Customs and Excise are quite free to turn it down. Commissioners may also, after judgment, mitigate or remit any pecuniary penalty imposed under section 152(c) of CEMA. But this exercise of discretion does not end there.

Pro-active discretion. It would be wrong to assume, as some legalist commentators have done, that discretion is exercised mostly by deciding not to do things: 'not to prosecute, not to initiate, not to investigate, not to deal or not to publicize'.[136]

---

133. P. Bourdieu, 'Droit et passe-droit, le champ des pouvoirs territoriaux et la mise en oeuvre des règlements' (1990) 81/82 *Actes de la Recherche en Sciences Sociales*, p. 89.
134. Summarized in A. Makridimitris, *Reasoning and legality in administration* (1984), PhD thesis, University College, London; also C. Pérez-Diaz, 'L'indulgence, pratique discrétionnaire et arrangement administratif' (1994) Vol. XVIII No. 4, *Déviance et Société*, pp. 397–430.
135. To 'sist' is the equivalent of staying proceedings in the terminology of the Scottish jurisdiction.
136. K. Davis, *Discretionary justice: a preliminary enquiry* (1979) University of Illinois Press.

Discretion can also mean being highly pro-active – in ways other than prosecution. Such actions cannot be understood as 'doing nothing' or 'indulgence'.[137]

For example, although Customs may decide not to prosecute, they are highly active in achieving compounded settlements. Authorities managing the Structural Funds, for example, spell out very clearly, in their offer letter, conditions which can lead to the withdrawal or suspension of the benefit. In that way, the beneficiary is forewarned and bound by contract. Such pragmatic pro-active agenda takes into account not only the need to deter and prevent, but also the need to recover funds quickly at the lowest cost to the State, whilst enabling traders and farmers to carry on with their commercial activities.

Except in cases of complex and serious frauds, when cases are put up for criminal prosecution, agencies are usually at liberty to take social and other factors into consideration when deciding upon their course of action. In using their discretion, the authorities follow internal guidelines and/or have an internal procedure to decide how a case should be dealt with. These guidelines are not usually in the public domain. A notable exception is the customers' leaflet on compounding from Customs and Excise which makes clear in what circumstances compounding will not be considered.

The use of statutory discretion raises questions of due process, some of which have recently been addressed. But its use must be put in the wider context of the administration of justice. The justice system is overburdened and extra-judicial settlements are increasingly seen as helping to relieve the situation.

2.6.2. Redress Against Administrative Decisions

Redress can be sought through internal reviews and tribunals. New procedures include the Customs' duties tribunal, the Customs' adjudicator and the Intervention Board adjudicator. It can also be sought through the ombudsman, or through the process of judicial review in the courts.

The Customs' duties tribunal. Article 253 of the Customs Code contained in Regulation 2913/92[138] states that Title VIII of the Code, relating to appeals, shall apply to the UK on 1 January 1995.[139]

As a result, in order to 'replace a very limited area of appeal to the High Court on duty matters, which inevitably was lengthy and expensive',[140] the jurisdiction of the VAT Tribunal has now been extended to cover Customs duties. The appeal process provided for in the 1994 Finance Act has two stages: the review stage and the tribunal hearing *per se*, unlike the VAT appeal process which has no intermediary stage.

---

137. This is the French word used in some instances of extra-legal discretion, which clearly describes the practice of 'letting people off'.
138. [1992] O.J. L302.
139. The United Kingdom obtained a delay of one year before implementing the requirement for an appeal system contained in the Customs Code.
140. *See* G. Mc Farlane, 'Customs Tribunals' (1994) *Importing Today*, May/June, pp. 16–17.

The review stage. An administrative (internal) review must be requested before a matter can be referred on appeal.[141] Furthermore a request to review must be made

- by those who are liable to pay duty or penalties or upon whom conditions, restrictions or prohibitions are imposed,
- within 45 days of the written notification of a decision by Customs and Excise.[142]

Under Section 14(1) a request can be made for an internal review of an assessment or a decision in respect of:

- whether Customs duty or an agricultural levy of the EU should be charged;
- the rate and duty of levy, or the amount charged;
- the identity of the person liable to pay the amount charged, or the amount for which he is liable;
- whether and to that extent a person is entitled to relief or repayment, remission or drawback of an amount of duty or levy;
- an assessment for a penalty, as well as duty;
- or any decision of a description specified in Schedule 5 of the Act.

A second request for a review is barred,[143] unless there are new facts. There is no provision for extending the time limit (45 days), though it is expected that Customs will accept genuine requests up to 90 days after the decision.

It is only possible to offer comments made on the review stage with respect to VAT cases. Despite assurances that the review is undertaken by officers not involved in the case,[144] the procedure itself has previously been described as lacking independence and not creating any opportunity for the evidence to be properly heard on both sides. In a report[145] Lord Mishcon described the process as one

> '... of a colleague walking over to another colleague in the same room saying "You have been asked to review this matter. I shall explain to you briefly why I made this decision. Do you mind initialling this paper to say you approve of what I did and said?".'

As a result some observers feel that an external reviewer should be involved. Other commentators also feel that the review:

> 'inserts an extra stage in the appeal process causing further delay and increased costs. It is particularly bad where a universally binding decision is

---

141. Section 14 (2) of the 1994 Finance Act.
142. Section 14(2) and 15 of the 1994 Finance Act.
143. Section 14(2) of the 1994 Finance Act.
144. Section 15 of the 1994 Finance Act.
145. House of Lords Official Report, 29 April 1991, col. 548.

required by an industry on Customs. Customs frequently regard tribunal decisions as not universally applicable, so it is necessary to go the High Court which takes at present 18 months to two years from the date of the tribunal decision.'[146]

The review can confirm, vary or withdraw the original decision. If Customs do not respond within 45 days, they are deemed to have confirmed their original decision. On the other hand, the review procedure is a way of augmenting the level of non-court resolutions.

The tribunal stage. An appeal to the tribunal is only allowed once the internal review has been carried out. It must be lodged by the person who requested the internal review within thirty days of the decision in dispute. An appeal is struck out if all the duty has been paid or satisfactory security provided.[147]

In all cases (VAT, excise, Customs duties) tribunals do not usually hear appeals unless the disputed amount has already been paid. A waiver can be applied for, either from Customs or from the tribunal. In cases of hardship, a 'hardship application' has to be made. If Customs and Excise oppose the hardship application, then the tribunal arranges a hearing to decide whether or not to grant the certificate. Generally speaking third parties do not get involved in this review procedure, unless their property is in danger of forfeiture, confiscation or restitution.

There are two types of appeal: full appeals and appeals on ancillary matters. Fully appealable matters are usually 'money matters'[148] and include liability to excise, Customs duties and agricultural levies, rate of duty or levy or excise, liability of a particular person, any entitlement to repayment and amounts of the new penalties.

Appeals on ancillary matters (non-money matters, authorizations, etc.)[149] are in form of quasi-judicial review. Ancillary matters include decisions relating to the release of goods, unloading, transhipment, etc. With respect to ancillary matters, the tribunal has limited powers. That is to say that it can only overturn a decision by Customs if it is satisfied that Customs could not have reasonably arrived at it. The test of reasonableness was laid down by Lord Greene in the *Wednesbury* case mentioned earlier.

Export refunds remain outside the extended jurisdiction of the VAT and Duties Tribunal. The exporter who is aggrieved by the application of this new penalty regime is obliged either to seek judicial review of a decision adverse to him, or to commence an action for recovery of sums statutorily due to him[150] and to argue the penalty issues in that context. However, 'administrative penalties recently introduced into the export refund regime may be appealed by reference to a higher

---

146. R. Cockfield and M. Mulholland, 'Tribunals, reviews and appeals: Sections 7 and 14–16' (1994) *British Tax Review*, p. 283.
147. Section 16 of the 1994 Finance Act.
148. *See* editorial: 'An appealing trader' (1994) in *Customs News*, p. 3.
149. *Ibid.*
150. *Roy* v. *Kensington and Chelsea FPC* [1992] 1 AC 624.

authority within the Intervention Board. A full appeal mechanism including an independent assessment is currently being set up.'[151]

The tribunal route: remaining problems. Although the extension of the jurisdiction of the VAT tribunal to Customs duties must be applauded, some issues still need to be addressed.

(a) A single importation could involve VAT, Customs, excise and/or agricultural levies. Thus, there could be friction between the various jurisdictions.
(b) The 45 day rule may cause hardship to some importers.
(c) There is no provision for compensation after a successful appeal following judicial review by the tribunal.[152]
(d) There is some concern that the restriction on right of direct access to the tribunal, and the cutting back on full appellate powers for some matters, may actually breach the Customs Code (Article 243 of the Customs Code suggests that there should be the option either of an administrative appeal or of an appeal to an independent tribunal, or both against [all] decisions taken by the Customs authorities which relate to the application of Customs legislation).
(e) The seizure of goods as liable to forfeiture has not been included in the list of appealable matters under CEMA.
(f) Tribunals' decisions are not binding, and can be appealed against in the High Court (which adds on average another two years' delay to the proceedings). At present, in London, approximately 10 per cent of cases heard in the tribunal are appealed against in that way.
(g) Finally, as mentioned earlier, export refunds remain outside the extended jurisdiction of the VAT and Duties Tribunal. Commission Regulations 2945/94[153] and 1829/94[154] amend the base legislation on export refund machinery[155] by inserting a scheme of administrative penalties for overclaims. In practice this may mean less compounding in the future, but it does not resolve the problem of lack of redress to an independent tribunal.

The Customs adjudicator. The role of the Revenue Adjudicator has just been extended to deal with complaints related to Customs. The office had been investigating complaints against the Inland Revenue for two years, and since 1 April 1995 it can now also investigate complaints regarding Customs and Excise. The adjudicator does not deal with appeals on matters where independent tribunals – such as VAT and duties tribunals – already exist for settling disagreements. She deals with cases when people complain, for example, that they have been harassed during an investigation, or when they have been improperly refused information under the Open Government provisions.[156] Her decisions are binding on the Inland Revenue

---

151. Communication from Intervention Board, 26.7.95.
152. Section 7 (5) of the 1994 Finance Act.
153. [1994] O.J. L130/57.
154. [1994] O.J. L191/5.
155. [1987] O.J. L351/1.
156. *See Open Government: Code of practice on access to government information* (1994), HMSO.

and Customs and Excise. Redress can take the form of an apology, putting matters right, or 'consolatory payments', but usually only from the private sector.[157] A person's right to ask their Member of Parliament (MP) to refer complaints to the Parliamentary Commissioner for Administration[158] (also called Parliamentary Ombudsman) is unaffected by the adjudicator's office. The obverse is not true.

The Intervention Board's adjudicator. Another new development is the appointment of an adjudicator by the Intervention Board, whose role it is to examine cases of complaint against maladministration by Intervention Board officials.

The Parliamentary Commissioner for Administration (ombudsman). The ombudsman only deals with certain matters[159] where a member of the public has sustained injustice in consequence of maladministration and where no right of appeal or review exists. The Parliamentary Commissioner Act[160] lays down the rules for access to the ombudsman. A written request must be made to a Member of Parliament[161] who may decide to pass on the complaint to the ombudsman. The investigation is conducted in private[162] and usually within twelve months from the day on which the person aggrieved first had notice of the matters alleged in the complaint.[163]

The main criticism of the Parliamentary ombudsman's system relates to the lack of direct access.[164] A complainant may find it difficult, in some cases, to convince his MP to take his complaint to the ombudsman. Following the 1993 Select Committee's review of the UK ombudsman system, the MP 'filter' is to be retained, although in the interest of speed, once an MP has referred a complaint to the ombudsman, the latter will deal with the complainant directly whilst keeping the referring MP in touch. A nine months target for investigations was also set.

Judicial review. When there is no right of appeal against administrative action or where all rights of appeal have been exhausted, an application can be lodged for judicial review but only on the grounds of procedural impropriety, unreasonableness, irrationality or incompatibility with Community law. It is difficult to underestimate the procedural hurdles this involves. Notwithstanding this deterrent, there has been a spectacular increase in the use and scope of the public law remedy of judicial review of administrative action. In 1974 there were 160 applications for judicial review, in 1984 1,230 applications were lodged and in 1993, 3,335.[165]

---

157. E. Filkin, 'Complaint and redress mechanisms in the public sector', paper given at 1994 OECD Paris Symposium.
158. The office was set up by the Parliamentary Commissioner Act 1967.
159. Parliamentary Commissioner Act 1967 amended in 1967, 1987 and 1994. Section 5 of the Act lists matters subject to investigation.
160. *Ibid.*
161. As per Article 5(2)(a) of the Act. The Member of Parliament, by convention, must usually be the constituent's MP, otherwise the request may be referred back to the said MP.
162. Article 7(2) of the Parliamentary Commissioner Act 1994.
163. Article 6(3) of the Parliamentary Commissioner Act 1994.
164. F. Stacey, *Ombudsmen compared* (1978) Clarendon Press, Oxford.
165. Lord Chancellor's Department, *Judicial Statistics for the year 1993* (1994) HMSO.

The appeal involves a reconsideration of the application *de novo* (an application to set aside a judgment which has been given in default of appearance is not regarded as a form of appeal). The application has to be lodged by the person aggrieved, i.e. a person with a specific legal interest in the issue. The nature of relief offered under judicial review generally is of a narrow and limited dimension.

There is no liability in English law for *ultra vires* activity *per se*, unless a public body or official acts negligently or maliciously or knowingly outside his powers or jurisdiction. Furthermore, when a challenge is made upon the legality of action or decision-making of public bodies, the presumption is always *omnia praesumuntur rite esse acta*, which the plaintiff must displace on a balance of probabilities.[166] Generally speaking, the courts are reluctant to enforce statutory obligations upon public bodies where to do so would cause significant public expenditure.

Damages, interim relief. Claims under *Francovich*[167] have usually been decided within the context of national law on liability, which means that reviews have not usually resulted in an award for damages. But following the House of Lords decision in *Factortame II*[168] injunctive relief, including interim relief, became available against the Crown. The House of Lords has decided that, contrary to its original view in *Factortame II*, interim injunctions, interlocutory injunctions and proceedings for contempt of court were available against ministers as a matter of English law.[169]

> 'The preceding may show that, although there is no explicit requirement of national law to preserve the homogeneity of national law failing within and outside the sphere of Community law, such homogeneity is perceived as desirable. As shown by the decision of the House of Lords in *M* v. *Home Office* it can be achieved, in the field and for the sake of legal protection of the rights of individuals, through means of "homogeneity friendly" judicial interpretation.'[170]

In *Factortame III*[171] the ECJ confirmed that in the event of a breach of Community law attributable to a Member State, in a situation where the same State has a wide discretion to make legislative choices, individuals suffering loss or injury are entitled to reparation, where the rule of Community law breached is intended to confer rights upon them, and when the breach is sufficiently serious and there is a direct causal link between the breach and the damage sustained by the individuals. Such reparation cannot be conditional upon fault on the part of the organ of the State responsible for the breach. Furthermore national legislation which generally

---

166. *Cannock Chase DC* v. *Kelly* [1978] 1 WLR 1 CA n29.
167. Case C-6 and 9/90, *Francovich* v. *Italy*, [1992] ECR I 5357.
168. *Factortame* v. *Secretary of State for Transport* [1990] 2 AC 85.
169. *M* v. *Home Office* [1993] 3 All ER 537.
170. W. Van Gerven, 'Bridging the gap between Community and national laws: towards a principle of homogeneity in the field of legal remedies?' (1995) 325, CMLR, pp. 679–702.
171. Joined cases C-46/93 and C-48/93, *Brasserie du Pêcheur* v. *Germany* and *R* v. *Secretary of State for transport, ex parte Factortame*, judgment of 5 March 1996, nyr.

limits the damage done to certain, specifically protected individuals not including loss of profit by individuals is not compatible with EC law.

In the circumstances, one would expect administrations to exercise a great deal of caution, for example, before imposing any sanctions on economic operators. In this, *Factortame III* may indirectly circumscribe administrative discretion. Only time will tell whether this, in turn, has a negative impact on the recovery rate in the UK. Meanwhile, it may be useful to turn to another Member State in order to glean ideas on how recovery rates could be improved.

3. A COMPARATIVE DIMENSION: DENMARK

We have seen that in the United Kingdom there is no centralized agency responsible for the management and recovery of EC funds. The overall picture is one of flexibility and fragmentation, with the various government agencies concerned evolving different approaches to the recovery of EC funds, as practical circumstances dictate. In the absence of obvious criminal intent, there is overall a preference for extra-judicial settlements, because they are thought to be cost-effective and speedier than court settlements. A possible exception to this rule can be made for small claims court settlements which, because of the informality of proceedings, can be less costly and speedier. Court proceedings usually mean that recoveries will be either protracted, or unsuccessful because of the level of insolvency generally.

At first glance, there are striking similarities between the British and Danish systems. For example, Denmark has no system of administrative courts. The decision whether to instigate criminal proceedings is subject to the principle of opportunity, as it is in the United Kingdom. Denmark has not incorporated the European Convention of Human Rights into its national legislation, although it does have a written constitution. Furthermore the Danes also favour the practice of setting-off whenever possible.

However, the Danish system is characterized by a high level of integration. Firstly, the Inland Revenue and Customs and Excise have fused into one government department. One implication of this fusion is that it widens the possibilities for set-off, and therefore the chances of recovery. Secondly, Denmark has a centralized EU-directorate to manage EC funds. Thirdly, Denmark has a 'fast-track' system of fines and recovery, as we shall see. It is difficult to compare recovery rates within the Union, as so many factors impinge. The Danes, for example, are fond of reminding us that they are a small country, and that this may somehow make recovery easier. The United Kingdom, in comparison, still imports a great deal from outside the European Union, hence the very high number of irregularities in the 'traditional own resources' area. Nevertheless, there is no doubt that Denmark is comparatively successful in recovering funds. For the period 1991–1994, it managed to recover 41 per cent of unwarranted payments in traditional own resources (*see* Tables 5.3. and 5.4.), having reported 86 irregularities during that period. It recovered 47 per cent of unwarranted payments in the EAGGF Guarantee Section Fund, having reported 221 irregularities during that period. In view of this comparative success, which can be gauged by looking at the tables above, it may be interesting to examine the main features of the system for the recovery of EC funds in Denmark.

3.1. General Features of the Danish System

In Denmark the police usually prosecute cases where the statutory penalty for the violation does not exceed a fine (with some exceptions which need not concern us here). Cases under police prosecution are always tried without lay judges. In court a fine may be agreed upon with the consent of the accused and the police, provided the judge sees no reason to doubt the guilt of the accused and considers the fine an equitable one. The judge may also decide the case by issuing a warning to the accused.[172]

In practice the system works as follows. The EU Directorate in Denmark sends a letter with a brief description of the offence and a reference to the provisions which allegedly have been violated. A postal cheque form is enclosed. If the amount is paid the case is closed.[173] The police or the administrations managing EC funds can suggest a fine. The accused can, by not paying the fine, cause the case to be brought before the judge. The police only enter the scene as auxiliaries to the specialized agency, and, most importantly, to prosecute the case immediately before the judge.

Recoveries are expedited:

'... [P]enalties are still comparatively rare, but settlements on recovery of funds unlawfully paid and received are common. When alleged offenders are solvent, recovery may be smooth and expedite, especially when such debtors receive amounts periodically as a set-off is then the solution. Set-off is not unknown in other fields; also in fiscal cases surplus payments in some respects may be set-off against other taxes due. But in no field is set-off such a spectacularly practical and efficient solution as in the EU cases.'[174]

The last sentence is a strong echo of the British position on set-off.

3.2. Particularities of Danish Extra-judicial Recoveries

In Denmark, the police have a general competence to settle a case by an agreed fine, in accordance with Article 931 of the Administration of Justice Act which provides:

---

172. H-G Toft-Hansen, 'The law of procedure' (1982) in *Constitutional and administrative law – Danish law: A general survey*, Bianco Lunos BogTrykkeri A/S, Copenhagen.
173. V. Greve and C. Gulmann, 'Denmark: The system of administrative and penal sanctions' (1994) in *The system of administrative and penal sanctions in the Member States of the European Communities*, OOPEC.
174. P. Garde, *Settlement in Danish law* (1995) p. 9.

'Where it is assumed that a violation will not result in a penalty of more than a fine the police chief may, instead of submitting an indictment to the court, indicate to the accused party that the case may be concluded without any legal action if he pleads guilty and is prepared to pay a fine of an amount stated to him within a stipulated term which, upon his request, may be extended.'

A similar rule applies to confiscation.

Identical rules apply in relation to the Ministry of Agriculture's administration of the EC market organization (Article 29 of the Act) and to the Customs/tax authorities, within their respective fields.

In Denmark, there exists a system of administratively imposed fines. This takes the shape of a letter in the form of an indictment. If the relevant official, typically a senior policeman, opines that the prosecution ought not to ask for a higher punishment than a fine, a postscript will be added to the text of the indictment as follows: 'if you admit your guilt and pay a fine of ... kroner, the case if closed; otherwise the case will be referred to the court' – much like the Dutch *transactie* system.[175]

Section 63 of the Danish Constitution endows the courts with a right to review the legality of administrative decisions. It refers to the right of the courts to 'decide any question relating to the scope of the administration's authority'. This review is placed in the hands of the ordinary courts. However, it is a principle of Danish law that there shall normally be a possibility of having a case tried at two – and only two – levels.[176] The ombudsman, whose powers go beyond that of his British counterparts, is also entitled to review the decisions of an administration.

4. CONCLUSION: IMPROVING RECOVERY RATES

Focusing first of all on set-off, it is clear from the Danish and British examples that setting off is an efficient way of recovering EC funds. The situation in the UK is that set-off between tax and Customs claims is not possible,[177] and that there are uncertainties regarding the application of set-off in particular circumstances. Civil court proceedings in the UK remain slow and costly. The Woolf Report has suggested a number of reforms to speed up procedures in the civil courts, and increase the scope for extra-judicial settlements in England and Wales.

On the basis of a very brief comparison of recovery in the UK and Denmark, it is fair to say that three conditions maximize the recovery of funds: firstly the integration of tax and Customs authorities, secondly an ambitious and robust

---

175. P. Garde, 'The suppression of fraud against the European Communities in Danish law and practice' (1989) in *The legal protection of the financial interests of the Community: progress and prospects since the Brussels seminar of 1989*, pp. 212–217, Oak Tree Press, Dublin.

176. G. Nielsen, 'Constitutional and administrative law' (1982) in *Danish law: A general survey*, Copenhagen, pp. 49–60.

177. Martyn Bridges' cry that '[H]istorically, one of the problems in dealing with tax evasion [in the UK] is that different government departments have not cooperated with, or even spoken to each other' must be echoed. (M. Bridges, 'Tax evasion – A crime in itself: the relationship with money laundering' (1996) 4:2 *Journal of Financial Crime*, p. 165).

approach to set-off with clear ground rules, and finally a fast-track court system to back up extra-judicial recovery. These are reforms which would benefit the UK generally.

One means of speeding up the recovery procedure would be the adoption of the Commission's proposal on amending the Regulation on Own Resources 1589/89. Another means is the more systematic use of the 'clearance of accounts' procedure, where agricultural expenditure is affected by irregularities and deficiencies of control. Here again, the Commission has proposed an amendment to the existing rules.

But the international aspects of recovery should not be overlooked. A recent report stressed the need for mutual assistance legislation to be updated to the realities of the internal market. The Commission has also asked to be automatically associated to requests for assistance when Community interests are involved.[178]

For some time the Commission has been concerned that settlements may not be effective as a mode of recovery. The conclusions of the Edinburgh Council of December 1992 stated that '[O]n agriculture, with particular reference to the clearance of accounts, the Commission intends to give the national authorities more responsibility for applying Community legislation by allowing them, under certain conditions, to negotiate settlements with individuals'. As a result the Commission put forward a proposal for a directive authorizing the Member States, on a case by case basis, to derogate from certain provisions contained in the CAP (i.e. the duty of Member States to recover amounts due in full).[179]

It seems therefore that the Commission has used the word 'settlement' in two different ways. The first way, contained in the proposed directive, denotes 'settling for less', whereas the later Commission definition, used in the settlement (*transaction*) study of 1995 refers to the practice of settling extra-judicially. Indeed, in systems where recovery is effected only through the courts (e.g. Spain, Greece), extra-judicial settlements are often equated to settlements for less than the sum due. However, this is not true of settlements in other systems (for example in the Netherlands, Denmark or the United Kingdom) where recovering full amounts extra-judicially is a normal and legal expression of administrative discretion.

One wonders therefore what intervention (if any) can be taken in this area by a Commission respectful of subsidiarity. As the Labayle Report[180] has confirmed, there is a bewildering diversity of practice in the Union concerning the recovery of EC funds. The proposal puts forward the idea that settlements constituting less than the amount owed should be approved by the Commission. This would not affect the UK, since its agencies already consult with the Commission on such matters when they arise. Perhaps the instances when no recovery can be made at all should be of more concern to a Commission eager to protect EC finance. In this research on insolvency regimes in the Member States and the way they affect the recovery of EC funds could throw a great deal of light on the present state of affairs.

---

178. *See* S. White, 'Recovering EC funds: The extra-judicial route' (1996) in *Fraud on the European budget*, vol. 4 number 3, Hume Papers on Public Policy, Edinburgh University Press, p. 68.

179. Commission minute VI/025658 dated 26.07.93 from G. Legras, Director General of DG VI.

180. H. Labayle, 'La transaction dans l'Union Européenne' (1996) *Rapport de synthèse* ('Labayle Report').

PART IV

Widening the Enforcement Agenda

Chapter 6. Procurement, International Trade and Corruption

1. INTRODUCTION

There is now a recognition that the CAP is not the only area in which fraud is taking place, and of the dangers posed by transit and procurement fraud. In the last area in particular, EC fraud cases continue to throw up a variety of corrupt or 'grey' practices engaged in by officials, economic operators and/or various intermediaries.

However, there is no agreed definition throughout the Union of what constitutes a corrupt practice. This means that some Member States criminalize conduct which others do not. For example, one Member State may define a certain conduct as 'trading in influence' (a criminal offence) whilst another accepts it as 'lobbying'. Furthermore, provisions in the criminal laws of the Member States relating to the corruption of officials are often restricted to nationals.[1] Most national criminal laws punish the bribery of national public officials but at the same time do not make it a specific criminal offence for companies to bribe foreign officials. Bribes to foreign officials are tax-deductible in some of the Member States.[2] This situation creates a 'legal vacuum' as far as certain officials are concerned, whether they be EC officials or officials from another Member State, but also in relation to some economic operators.

Because of the international dimensions of both transit and procurement, the concern over protection of the EC budget has been 'spilling over' – from the Member States and the Union, to international trade and international relations. It is now more difficult to 'detach' EC fraud and corruption conceptually from other types of international and organized financial crime, as we shall see.

This chapter examines these issues. Firstly, the problem with respect to EC funds is discussed, in particular the award of public contracts financed by the Structural Funds, and the prospects for improvement are explored. Secondly, the Union's specific response in the shape of two third pillar proposals is examined in some detail (§ 3.). Thirdly some of the difficulties in evolving a successful anti-corruption strategy are discussed with regard to EC officials (§ 4.). Fourthly the impact of corruption on the terms of international trade – an issue fore-fronted by the United States – is discussed, together with the Union's response. Corruption undeniably has an international dimension, and calls for an international strategy, which is discussed in closing.

---

1. It is not the case in the UK, where the Prevention of Corruption Act criminalizes corrupt acts by 'any member, officer or servant of a public body'.
2. *See* Transparency International, *The fight against corruption: What the European Union can do* (1995); also newspaper article: 'Anger over bribes ruling' in *European*, 18 April 1996, p. 17.

It is argued that the Union must define the problem in its own way, by articulating a strategy which is capable of both protecting the financial interests of the European Communities, but also of dealing with the international ramifications of corruption. Many of these issues recur within the context of enlargement of the Union which, for reasons of space, is dealt with in Chapter 7.

2. PROCUREMENT AND EC FUNDS: THE IMPACT OF CORRUPTION

In 1991, Woolcock found that 'total public procurement in the EC accounts for about 15% of GDP'.[3] However, government contracting has in certain countries been a byword for corruption in many forms: financial, political, social or legal.[4] According to a European Parliament report, in most Member States bribes would amount to between 2 and 10 per cent of the value of transactions.[5] The Council of Europe estimates that in some countries between 10 and 15 per cent of the price the consumer pays for a product goes into corruption.[6] In Germany, for example, the amount involved would reach between 5 and 10 billion DM a year.[7] *Der Spiegel* newspaper reported in July 1996 that 50 employees of private companies and 10 of the Frankfurt airport were being investigated for alleged corruption in the construction of their airport's Terminal 2. Millions of DM were used for bribing airport officials in bids amounting to a total value of 2.5 billion DM. The bribes resulted amongst other things in increased prices for the projects. The public prosecutor estimated an increase of prices by about 20 to 30 per cent.[8] Indeed the main area in which corrupt practices have been highlighted is that related to public work contracts and services.

Within the context of the EC budget, procurement financed out of the Structural Funds, which in the 1994 financial year accounted to approximately 40 per cent of the 68 446 million ECU budget, is naturally also affected. Public works and supplies contracts were the first areas to be regulated at Community level in the 1970s,[9] with an initial emphasis on four specific aspects:

(i) compulsory advertising any tender notices in the *Official Journal* for tenders above certain thresholds,
(ii) the prohibition of discriminatory standards,
(iii) the harmonization of technical requirements and
(iv) transparency in selection and award procedure.

---

3. S. Woolcock, 'Public procurement' (1991) in *The state of the European Community – Policies, institutions and debates in the transition years*, eds. L. Hurwitz and C. Lequesne, Lynne Rienner Publishers, Longman.
4. L. Gormley, 'Public Procurement 1993' (1994) in *The European market – Myth or reality?*, eds. D. Campbell and C. Flint, Kluwer, p. 151.
5. European Parliament, *Report of the Committee on Civil Liberties and Internal Affairs on combatting corruption in Europe*, rapporteur: Mrs Heinke Salish (1995).
6. Council of Europe, *Administrative, civil and penal aspects, including the role of the judiciary, of the fight against corruption* (1995).
7. *Ibid.*, pp. 39–41.
8. *See* Transparency International *Newsletter*, September 1996, p. 13.
9. Council Directives: 71/305 [1971] O.J. L185/5 (coordinating of procedures for the award of public work contracts); 77/62 [1977] O.J. L13/1 (coordinating procedures for the award of public supply contracts). The former was repealed by Council Directive 93/37 and the latter by 93/36.

In anticipation of the internal market and of the related opening up of public procurement, substantial problems were highlighted. A report from the Commission noted that in particular the transposition of the 1970s procurement directives was unsatisfactory and that there were numerous and varied breaches of every Community procurement rule by public purchasers. The report however acknowledged that public procurement was both a complex and politically sensitive area.[10] This lead to a re-casting of the 1970s directives (*see* below) to tighten existing rules, and to a closer monitoring of transposition.

In the mid 1990s procurement cases involving EC funds, corrupt practices often come to light, predictably, in relation to the tendering process itself, but also in the use of intermediaries. There are also a number of 'grey' practices which, more controversially perhaps, need to be examined for their ability to give good value for money and to foster fair practices generally. A few cases are outlined below, followed by discussion of the EC control framework, and the prospects for its improvement.

2.1. Procurement Fraud

2.1.1. The Tendering Process

Case 1: No tendering procedure. A total absence of tendering procedures was found in the majority of projects administered by the regional government of Cantabria (Spain). The contracts, with an estimated worth of 20 million ECU were awarded to the enterprises directly and by word of mouth. The contracts were only formalized subsequently, sometimes not until after the work had been completed.[11]

Case 2: Exclusion of low bids. Low bids were excluded with respect to the Gomeira airport project, worth 13 million ECU and the Almendralejo highway project (Spain) worth 5 million ECU.[12]

2.1.2. Intermediary Bodies

Case 3: Conflicts of interest. In Italy 8 million ECU of Community funds were transferred to a private company acting as an intermediary body. The audit revealed an apparent conflict of interest concerning the management of this 8 million ECU operation by a high-ranking Commission official.

In Andalucia (Spain) the President of a vocational training centre which had received Community assistance was also on the staff of the intermediary body responsible for allocating the funds.[13]

---

10. European Commission, *The opening up of public procurement* (1993) OOPEC; *see also* S. Arrowsmith, *An assessment of the legal techniques for implementing the procurement directives* (1996) W G Hart Legal Workshop, London, July.
11. *Ibid.*, 4.29 (a).
12. *Ibid.*, at 4.29 (g) and (h).
13. *Ibid.*, at 4.54.

Case 4: Insolvency. In Spain the administration of a global subsidy amounting to 46 million ECU was entrusted to an intermediary body which, on the basis of the 1991–92 financial data, did not present the solvency guarantees required.[14]

Case 5: Double charging. In Italy, two suppliers of services had supplied two enterprises with an identical service, which consisted of setting up a quality control manual and an automated management system, and had invoiced both for the same amount, namely 18.6 million ECU.[15]

Case 6: Amendment to project. In the case of the Lucas Estate in Birmingham (UK), the project implemented and costing 5.5 million ECU was found to differ substantially from the project for which the contract was awarded.[16]

2.1.3. Some Grey Areas

Structural Funds are also affected by practices which hardly offer value for money, even if, arguably, they are not illegal. For example, the ERDF was used to co-finance a one-day seminar in Mecklenburg-West Pomerania organized by an association of local businessmen. The ERDF contributed three quarters of the total cost of 165,000 ECU. The main feature of this meeting was a one-hour speech by a Member of the European Commission, who was hired through a private agency at a cost of approximately 20,000 ECU (excluding VAT) for the service. The Court of Auditor's checks established that the cost of this event was quite out of proportion to the result obtained.[17]

The low rate of officials' remuneration in Central and Eastern Europe has been flagged in the evidence given to the Committee of Inquiry on transit fraud as one factor which encourages corrupt practices. The Committee's observation would be in line with a Mertonian reading of corruption, seeing disparities in wealth or income (i.e. extremes) as creating incentives to deviant behaviour. There is little or nothing the European Union can do about low remuneration of officials in Central and Eastern Europe, but PHARE consultancy fees, by contrast, are within its remit. In 1995, average fees paid to western consultants in the PHARE programme ranged from 300 ECU to 1,000 ECU per day (such fees totalled 20 million ECU in Hungary alone). But the range was only 50 to 200 ECU per day for local consultants working in PHARE beneficiary countries.[18] Although it is understandable that standards of living vary from one country to the next, the Commission could perhaps look into ways of not exacerbating already existing and serious disparities.

14. *Ibid.*, at 4.52.
15. *Ibid.*, at 4.59.
16. *Ibid.*, at 4.28(f).
17. *Ibid.*, at 4.82.
18. Euro-East Information Service, *PHARE consultants' fees*, 19 December 1995.

2.2. Procurement Control Framework

Article 7 of Council Regulation 2052/88[19] stipulates that measures financed by the Structural Funds or receiving assistance from the EIB or from another existing financial instrument must be in keeping with the provisions of the Treaties and with Community policies, including those concerning the rules on competition and the award of public work contracts. Compliance with Article 7 therefore requires the full and correct transposition of Community directives on competition. Judging by the number of proceedings under way, the Member States are experiencing the same difficulties in transposing as they did in the 1970s, and/or are as ambivalent, depending on one's preferred reading of the situation.

The group of directives now regulating public work contracts and supplies (89/665, 92/13, 92/50, 93/36, 93/37 and 93/38)[20] are particularly relevant to ERDF interventions, which relate mainly to infrastructure investments involving the award of public work contracts. The aim of the directives is to ensure transparency and competitive tendering for public contracts above 5 million ECU and supplies above 130,000 ECU, so as to avoid discrimination at the time they are awarded. However, all too often their transposition into national law has been either protracted, or inaccurate, as illustrated in Table 6.1. below.

In order to check whether the rules concerning public works contracts were respected in the award of Structural Funds, in 1988 the Commission imposed a system of reporting on the Member States,[21] which included a declaration that those contracts which had not been published (i.e. under the special procedures exempting from publication) had been awarded in accordance with the directives and a questionnaire on public works which has to be sent to the Commission at the latest when the request for payment of the balance of the Structural Funds subsidy is made. However, in its report for the 1994 financial year, the European Court of Auditors found that this system had not been implemented.[22] Usually, the regional and local authorities were poorly informed about the existence, content and purpose of the 'public procurement questionnaire' thus introduced'.[23]

As a result, the Commission abandoned this instrument in favour of a new supervisory system, to take effect in 1994. For all operations exceeding 25 million ECU, decisions to grant Community finance automatically entail the transmission to the Commission of the main details concerning awards of the contracts con-

---

19. [1988] O.J. L185/9.
20. Council Directives: 89/665 [1989] O.J. L395/33 (coordination of the laws, regulations and administrative provisions relating to the application of review procedures to the award of public supply and public work contracts); 92/50 [1992] O.J. L209/1 (coordination of procedures on the award of public service contracts; 92/13 [1992] O.J. L76 (review procedures for contracts in the water, energy, transport and telecommunications sectors); 93/36 [1993] O.J. L199/1 (coordinating procedures for the award of public supply contracts); 93/37 [1993] O.J. L199/54 (coordinating procedures for the award of public works contracts); 93/38 [1993] L199/84 (coordinating the procurement procedures of entities in the water, energy, transport and telecommunications sectors).
21. Communication C(88) 2510, [1989] O.J. C22/3, from the Commission to the Member States concerning checks that the rules relating to public works contracts are being respected in the projects and programmes financed by the Structural Funds and the financial instruments.
22. Court of Auditors Annual Report for the financial year 1994 [1995] O.J. C303/1, at 4.23.
23. *See* European Commission, *The Structural Funds in 1994* (1996) OOPEC, p. 117.

cerned, including the record of the award of tenders, the aim being to ensure systematic and more thorough checks. As a result of those checks, the Commission can (i) agree without reservation the proposed contract awards, (ii) agree in principle subject to retrospective check, or (iii) suspend finance. Smaller projects are monitored on the basis of on-the-spot checks. But in view of the growing number of public work contracts awarded in the Member States, and subject to the rules of subsidiarity, the Commission is now considering a system of certifying that the internal procedures for awarding contracts employed by each awarding authority comply with Community law.[24] It would, however, still be up to the Member States to ensure that the certification is meaningful on a day-to-day basis.

Table 6.1. Transposition of procurement directives as of 30.6.96

	89/440 (Works)	88/295* (Supplies)	89/66 (Remedies)	90/531 (Supplies)	92/13 (Remedies)	92/50 (Services)	93/36 (Supplies)	93/38 (Services)
BE	!	~	~	!	~	N	N	!
DK	~	~	~	~	~	~	~	D
E	~	~	!	!	!	N	N	N
EL	~	~	!	D	D	N	~	D
ES	~	~	!	N	N	~	~	D
FR	~	~	~	~	!	N	N	N
IRL	~	~	~	~	!	~	~	~
IT	!	~	~	~	!	~	N	~
LU	~	~	~	~	~	~	~	~
NL	~	~	~	~	~	~	~	~
PT	!	!	!	D	D	~	!	D
UK	~	~	~	!	!	~	~	N
AUT	~	~	~	~	N	N	N	N
SE	~	~	~	~	~	~	~	~
SU	~	~	~	~	~	~	~	~

Key: N = Full transposition not yet communicated to the Commission
! = Transposition communicated, infringement proceedings taken
~ = Transposition communicated to the Commission
D = Derogation

* Now superseded by Directive 93/38
Source: Communication from DG XV dated 13 August 1996, translated from French by author.

24. *Ibid.*

In its Annual Report for the 1994 financial year, the ECA commented that 'the lack of transparency in awarding public work contracts is not without consequence as regards the risk of fraud and irregularity'.[25] There are two aspects in particular where transparency seems to be lacking. Firstly, Member States seem to prefer to make maximum use of the exceptions[26] provided for under the procurement rules, and secondly it is unclear how intermediaries are selected.

Exemptions to procurement rules. Under Article 7(2) of Council Directive 93/37, contracting authorities may, under certain circumstances, waive the requirements for prior publication of a contract notice and select their own candidates. One criticism which is often levelled at the Member States is that too much use is made of such exceptions: negotiated procedures (with chosen suppliers), restricted procedures (with a list of qualified suppliers) and preference schemes[27] 'where an appeal to local preference permits direct negotiations'.[28] There is still therefore ample opportunity to circumvent basic procurement rules such as advertising, competitive tendering and non-discrimination. This is not aided by the lack of clarity in defining exceptions. What might, for example, constitute an 'urgency brought about by events unforeseen'? Such an emergency has the effect of waiving basic procurement rules [Article 7(3)(c)]. Once transcribed into national law, this exemption could lead to wildly different approaches in the Member States. The abuse of any such exemptions leads to the possibility of contracts (for our purpose, involving EC funds) being awarded on the basis of personal preference and gain.

The selection of intermediaries. The use of intermediary bodies, agencies or other private bodies continues to raise problems, and the system need tightening up. Intermediaries can be designated by the Member States in order to manage global grants. The intermediary then allocates individual grants to final beneficiaries.[29] Intermediaries must have the necessary administrative capability,[30] be present and represented in the regions concerned, operate in the public interest, and represent the socio-economic interests directly concerned by the implementation of the measures planned.[31] Although intermediary bodies must provide adequate solvency guarantees and have the administrative capacity necessary for the administration of the subsidies,[32] there are at present no formal procedures for selecting such bodies. At Commission level, an inter-departmental consultation is provided for, but the authorizing officer retains the option of ignoring opinions given.

25. *Ibid.*, at 4.28.
26. European Commission, *An EC programme for public procurement in the Community* (1987) COM(86) 375.
27. European Commission, *National regional preference schemes in the placing of public contracts* (1989) COM(89) 400.
28. European Commission, *The Structural Funds in 1994* (1996) OOPEC, pp. 116–117.
29. Article 5(1)(c) of Council Regulation 2052/88 [1988] O.J. L185/9.
30. Article 16(1) of Council Regulation 4253/88 [1988] O.J. L374/1.
31. Article 6(1) of Council Regulation 2083/93 (ERDF) [1993] O.J. L193/34.
32. Article 16 of Council Regulation 4253/88 [1988] O.J. L374.

2.3. Prospects for Improvement

There is, according to Draetta,[33] Transparency International[34] and a recent report from the European Parliament,[35] more that the European Union can do to combat corruption within the confines of the first pillar. In particular procurement rules could be tightened up. Exemptions need to be narrowed further, and the selection of intermediaries in particular needs regulating. But bearing in mind that some of the Member States have been slow in transposing the procurement directives, it is clear that such a move could only be a small part of a wider strategy to prevent and control corrupt practices (and recover monies laundered as a result). Such a strategy is at present emerging inter-governmentally.

3. THE EMERGENCE OF A EUROPEAN STRATEGY

The so-called third pillar of the Treaty on European Union is host to two relevant instruments which address this situation: a Protocol focused tightly upon the financial interests of the Community – dealt with at this point in the work – and a broader 'Anti-Corruption' Convention which will be discussed later.

3.1. The Anti-Corruption Protocol to the 'PIF' Convention

The purpose of the Protocol to the Convention on the Protection of the Financial Interests of the European Communities is to combat corruption that damages or is likely to damage the European Communities' financial interests and which involves European or national officials or members of the Commission, the European Parliament, the Court of Auditors and the Court of Justice and corruption of the type referred to in the Convention, committed by the same officials and members.[36] It takes into account the immunities conferred by the Protocol on the Privileges and Immunities of the Communities.[37] The 'PIF' Convention has been agreed and its adoption by Council is anticipated. It was drawn up on the basis of Article K.3(2c), which gives the Council of Ministers a framework within which to draw up conventions in areas of common interest, such as combatting fraud on an international scale.

---

33. U. Draetta, 'The European Union and the fight against corruption in international trade' (1995) 6, *Revue de Droit des Affaires Internationales*, pp. 701–711.
34. Transparency International (1995) and D. Frisch (1996) *op. cit.*
35. European Parliament, *Report of the Committee on Civil Liberties and Internal Affairs on combatting corruption in Europe*, rapporteur Heinke Salish (1995).
36. Council of the European Union (1995) introduction, draft protocol to the Convention on the Protection of the European Communities' financial interests, document 11723/95, November, p. 1.
37. On this point *see* European Commission, *Protecting the Community's financial interests, the fight against fraud – annual report 1995* (1996) COM(96) 173, p. 17; also S. White, 'Proposed measures against corruption of officials in the EU' (1996) 21:6, *European Law Review*, pp. 465–476.

As a necessary first step, the Protocol defines 'European Official' and 'National Official'.[38] A European Official means any employee within the meaning of the Staff Regulations of the European Communities or seconded person carrying out corresponding functions. National Official is to be understood, for the purposes of application of criminal law, by reference to the definition of 'official' and 'public officer' in the national law of the Member State in which the person in question performs that function.

The Protocol also gives a definition of 'passive' and 'active' corruption, where the former refers to the official who is corrupted and the latter to the person who induces corruption.[39] More precisely, passive corruption is defined as the deliberate action of an official who requests, accepts or receives, directly or through a third party, for himself or for a third party, offers, promises or advantages of any kind whatsoever to act or refrain from acting in accordance with his functions or in the exercise thereof in breach of his official duties in a way which damages or is likely to damage the European Communities' financial interests. Active corruption is defined as the deliberate action of whosoever promises or gives, directly or through an intermediary, an advantage of any kind whatsoever to an official for himself or for a third party for him to act or refrain from acting in accordance with his duty or in the exercise of his functions in breach of his official duties in a way which damages or is likely to damage the European Communities' financial interests.

The Protocol also proposes that the two categories of officials, European and national, are to be assimilated for the purpose of national anti-corruption legislation.[40] This means that each Member State would ensure that measures in its respective criminal laws relating to the corruption of officials apply equally to all officials with responsibilities for EC funds. This is not the first time that the principle of assimilation has been used in the protection of the financial interests of the European Communities. The principle was first applied in this area in the *Greek Maize* case,[41] when the Court of Justice ruled that infringements of Community law were to be penalized under conditions analogous to those applicable to infringements of national law. The principle was then enshrined in Article 209a of the EC Treaty, which was added by the TEU, and which requires Member States to take the same measures to counter fraud affecting the financial interests of the Community as they take to counter fraud affecting their own financial interests. The requirement can thus be seen as an extension of already established practice in the Member States.

As well as assimilating Union officials to national officials under criminal law, the protocol requires Member States have established their jurisdiction in a number of circumstances. They must prosecute in any of the following conditions:

(i) if the offence is committed in whole or part in their territory,
(ii) if the offender is a national or an official of the State concerned,

---

38. Article 1 of proposed 'anti-corruption' Protocol.
39. Articles 2 and 3 of proposed 'anti-corruption' Protocol.
40. Article 4 of proposed 'anti-corruption' Protocol.
41. Case 68/88, *Commission* v. *Greece*, [1989] ECR 2965.

(iii) if the offence is committed by or against a European or national official, Government Minister, elected Member of Parliament, member of the Member State's highest courts, member of its Court of Auditors, or a member of the Commission, European Parliament, European Court of Auditors or Court of Justice who is a national of the Member State concerned, and

(iv) if the offender is a European official working for the Community institution or a body set up under the Treaties establishing the Communities and with its headquarters in the Member State concerned.

A Member State which does not extradite its own nationals would have to establish its jurisdiction over corruption offences committed by officials outside the national territory. A Member State also has to prosecute whenever extradition is not appropriate. Files, information and exhibits would be transmitted in accordance with the procedures laid down in Article 6 of the European Convention on Extradition. Bilateral and multilateral agreements concluded between Member States and relevant declarations would remain unaffected.

The measure therefore provides for 'limited extra-territoriality' (in as much as it only applies within the territory of the EU), for EU and national officials and in the context of the protection of the financial interests of the European Communities.

Member States would have to ensure that active and passive corruption are punishable by effective, proportionate and dissuasive criminal penalties, including penalties involving deprivation of liberty which can give rise to extradition. Penalties would apply without prejudice to the exercise of disciplinary powers.[42]

Each Member State would have to take the necessary measures for heads of businesses to be declared criminally liable in cases of corruption involving officials.

A sizeable obstacle to the prosecution of allegedly corrupt officials is the failure of cooperation mechanisms, which lag behind the realities of international criminality. As corruption takes the form of an international crime, its suppression is still regulated by national legal instruments inherently territorial in nature and, therefore, largely inadequate to confront it.[43] When and if the proposed measures come into effect, Member States would acquire duties to cooperate effectively, when the corruption constitutes a criminal offence, in the investigation, the prosecution and in carrying out the punishment imposed, by means, for example, of mutual legal assistance, extradition, transfer of proceedings or enforcement of sentences passed in another Member State. They would also have to cooperate in deciding which Member State should prosecute, in order to 'centralize' prosecutions in a single Member State.

The provisions on *ne bis in idem* contained in the 'PIF' Convention would also be extended to cases of corruption by officials. This means that an official whose trial has been finally disposed of in a Member State may not be prosecuted in another Member State, save in exceptional circumstances. Member States would be able to launch a second prosecution if, for example, the facts which were the subject of the judgment rendered abroad constituted an offence directly against the security

---

42. Article 5 of proposed 'anti-corruption' Protocol.
43. U. Draetta, *op. cit.*, p. 703.

or other equally essential interests of that Member State.[44] However, exceptions would not apply if the Member State in question had requested, in respect of the same facts, prosecution by the other Member State, or granted extradition of the person concerned.

No provision in the Protocol would prevent Member States from adopting internal legal provisions which go beyond the obligations deriving from the 'PIF' Convention. Lastly, Member States would acquire a duty to transmit to the Commission the text of their domestic law into which the provisions of the Protocol are transposed.

The European Court of Justice would have jurisdiction to rule on disputes between Member States on the interpretation or application of the Protocol if no solution is found within six months. This 'compromise' was also adopted in the 'PIF' Convention. In addition, certain disputes (for example, relating to the definitions of corruption, the principle of assimilation, *ne bis in idem*, internal provisions and transmission) between the Commission and the Member States which have not been resolved by negotiation would be submitted to the European Court of Justice. Excluded from this dispute-resolution mechanism are disputes regarding the interpretation of 'National Official' contained in Article 1, second indent of paragraph 1, where presumably the national view would prevail.

The Protocol would not enter into force until the Convention for the Protection of the Financial Interests of the European Communities has entered into force. In any new Member State, it would enter into force ninety days after accession.[45]

As far as the relationship with the 'PIF' Convention is concerned, Article 7 of the 'anti-corruption' Protocol would ensure that the provisions already contained in the 'PIF' Convention with regard to the criminal liability of heads of businesses,[46] extradition,[47] cooperation,[48] *ne bis in idem* (save reservations),[49] internal provisions and transmission[50] would be extended to cases involving corrupt officials.[51]

3.2. Extension of Third Pillar Strategy: The Anti-Corruption Convention

More recently, a more ambitious project has been agreed by the Council of Ministers: a Convention on the fight against corruption of officials of the European Communities or officials of Member States of the European Union.[52]

The contents of this Convention duplicate that of the Protocol, except for one important consideration: its action is not restricted to the protection of the financial interests of the European Communities. According to the Convention, the principle of 'limited extra-territoriality' outlined above is extended to any act of passive or

---

44. This would only be possible if the Member State in question had already made a declaration notifying adoption of the Convention.
45. Articles 9 and 10 of the proposed 'anti-corruption' Protocol.
46. Article 3 of the 'PIF' Convention.
47. Article 5(1), (2) and (4) of the 'PIF' Convention.
48. Article 6 of the 'PIF' Convention.
49. Article 7 of the 'PIF' Convention.
50. Articles 9 and 10 of the 'PIF' Convention.
51. Article 7 of the 'anti-corruption' Protocol.
52. Document 4265/96 JUSTPEN of 12 January 1996, Council Act drawing up the Convention.

active corruption by an EU or national official. The question of the fight against political corruption, however, remains a sensitive issue.[53]

The Convention was drawn up on the same legal basis as the Protocol, with the aim of improving judicial cooperation. Its contents duplicate the provisions (examined above) extracted from a conjoint reading of the 'PIF' Convention and its first Protocol. In its first six articles, the Convention reiterates the Protocol's definitional provisions on National and European Officials, passive and active corruption, with one difference: in the definitions of passive and active corruption, the words 'or is likely to damage the European Communities' financial interests' have been omitted. This means that the 'Anti-Corruption' Convention seeks to establish common rules for dealing with corruption, leaving aside the question of the impact it may have on the EC budget.

The provisions on assimilation, penalties and jurisdiction are reproduced word for word. The provisions found in the 'Anti-Corruption' Convention concerning criminal liabilities of heads of businesses, extradition, cooperation, *ne bis in idem* rules and provisions of national laws can also be extracted from a joint reading of the 'PIF' Convention and its protocol.

Again, the European Court of Justice would have jurisdiction over disputes if no solution were found within six months. The present text suggests that its entry into force would not differ substantially from that of the 'PIF' Convention. The 'Anti-Corruption' Convention would have to be ratified by all the Member States and apply ninety days thereafter. Until then, the Member States could choose to apply the Convention either bilaterally, or through the means of a declaration. This process has been referred to as one of 'rolling ratification'.[54] It would be open to accession by any State that becomes a member of the European Union.

There is only one respect in which the 'Anti-Corruption' Convention differs from the earlier proposal for a Protocol, and it is in the area of cooperation. A conjoint reading of the Protocol and the 'PIF' Convention establishes that, when the corruption of officials concerns at least two Member States and constitutes a criminal offence, then those States would have a duty to cooperate effectively in relation to investigation, prosecution and punishment. This could be achieved by way of mutual legal assistance, extradition, transfer of proceedings, enforcement of sentences passed in another Member State, and/or other means of cooperation.[55] This has the effect of limiting cooperation to criminal proceedings.

The 'Anti-Corruption' Convention, by contrast, states that if officials are involved in passive or active corrupt behaviour (defined above) which concerns at least two Member States, then the States would have to cooperate effectively in the investigation, in judicial proceedings and in enforcing the penalty imposed, for instance by means of mutual legal assistance, extradition, transfer of proceedings or enforcement of judgments rendered abroad.[56] This could be interpreted to mean that administrations have a duty to cooperate in cases of suspected corruption, even if the behaviour in question was not the object of criminal sanctions. This reflects the

---

53. *See* Parliamentary question E-2106/94, [1995] O.J. C36/39.
54. *See Statewatch bulletin*, 6:4, July-August 1996, p. 6.
55. *See* Article 7 of the Protocol read in conjunction with Article 6 of the 'PIF' Convention.
56. *See* Article 8.

opinion, expressed by the Council of Europe Multidisciplinary Group on Corruption, that a comprehensive anti-corruption strategy should not be confined to the criminal sphere alone.[57]

Thus, apparently, the proposed 'Anti-Corruption Convention' would go beyond the proposed Protocol in one important respect, by mandating for cooperation in control of conduct, regardless of whether the diverse legal and other traditions of Member States have led them to regulate such conduct within their administrative, civil and/or criminal law systems.[58] In this way, the proposed Convention builds up and extends existing forms of cooperation in the administrative and civil spheres.

For example, in the administrative sphere, instruments exist to promote cooperation in Customs and tax matters. It is now being recognized that cooperation is equally important in cases of corruption involving officials. Administrative authorities may be in a position to cooperate more speedily than judicial authorities.

Cooperation in the civil sphere is also of primary importance. The need for authorities to cooperate in attempting to recover advantages illegally obtained, of actions for damages, or for breach of contract which may involve more than one Member State, must not be overlooked.

3.3. Discussion on Protocol and Convention

It must be asked whether the proposed measures described above sufficiently address the weakness in the ways in which the European Communities presently respond to the challenge of corruption. For this author, the answer must be that they have potential, which can only be assessed once they come into force. It seems important that these instruments be in place before the next enlargement, which promises to be a difficult one. However, the implementation of conventions in general,[59] and third pillar instruments in particular, tends to be protracted. Once implemented, the usual difficulties associated with judicial cooperation often apply.

At present inter-governmental acts, such as the Protocol and Convention outlined above, require unanimity and escape the scrutiny of the European Parliament. Instruments do not become effective until they are ratified by the fifteen Member States. Disputes over the jurisdiction of the European Court of Justice can be protracted, as in the case of the Europol Convention. In the case of the 'Anti-Corruption' Convention it is hoped that a similar compromise can be reached concerning the role of the European Court of Justice. The Europol Convention stipulates that whenever a dispute cannot be settled within six months, the matter may be referred to the Court of Justice by a party to the same dispute.

This conditionality has lead some commentators to argue that matters related to the protection of the financial interests of the Community, in particular, should be brought under Community competence (first pillar), where these problems do not

---

57. Council of Europe, *Draft Programme of Action Against Corruption by the Multidisciplinary Group on Corruption* (1995) p. 21.
58. *See* Council of Europe (1995) *op. cit.*
59. For example the Dublin Convention, signed in June 1990, still awaited full ratification in 1996.

arise. A similar argument has been made in relation with the fight against corruption (*see* § 5.).

The Protocol to the 'PIF' Convention will not enter into force until the 'PIF' Convention itself has entered into force, that is to say after all the Member States have ratified it. Nevertheless, some aspects of this Convention and its protocols raise considerations that may be delicate for Member States, and interact with broader issues regarding the 'third pillar' and the IGC. One problem for cooperation in criminal investigation of cases of possible corruption is that many different administrations may have to cooperate, which in some cases may cause difficulty. Another is that transfers of criminal proceedings, even within the European Union, are slow.[60] Diplomatic channels have often proved an unsatisfactory conduit for rogatory letters. In addition, the enthusiasm for the use of rogatory letters can vary greatly from one Member State to the next, with for example Italy making the most use of the medium in the European Union, and the United Kingdom seldom doing so.[61] This has prompted some commentators to put forward the 'free movement of judges' as a remedy to this unsatisfactory state of affairs.[62] Indeed the proposed second Protocol to the 'PIF' Convention provides for a network of 'liaison judges' in order to facilitate judicial cooperation.[63] This step in the direction of a common European legal space may however cause pause for thought in some justice ministries.

Meanwhile, should the 'Anti-Corruption' Convention be adopted, any ensuing improvement in cooperation in the administrative and civil spheres could bring considerable benefits. The potential value of the proposed extension of cooperation from the criminal to the civil and administrative spheres will be appreciated by those who acknowledge present difficulties facing cooperation in criminal matters. In some circumstances, evidence may be more readily available within an administrative context than a criminal one. Another potential limitation of relying too much upon criminal proceedings is that in some Member States, the discretion not to prosecute may be used by the prosecuting authorities, perhaps occasionally for political reasons, or sometimes the judiciary itself is 'penetrated by the world of corruption'.[64] For all these reasons, it seems important that future improvements in cooperation not be confined to the criminal sphere alone, and both the Protocol and the proposed Convention are to be welcomed on this score.

Taken together, the proposals go a considerable way towards enhancing cooperation in criminal law for the prosecution of corruption, leaving administrative and civil cooperation as useful back-ups. The problem of corruption is being addressed in an unprecedented climate of transparency and this can only bear witness to the renewed vigour of the European project.

---

60. *See* newspaper article 'Greeks in EU fraud case', *The European*, 15 February 1996, p. 18.
61. G. Leguet, *La confusion dans la répartition des compétences dans le domaine des poursuites* (1996), paper given at the Conference on the protection of the financial interests of the European Communities, held in Lille, 25–26 January.
62. F. De Angelis, *Les problèmes liés à la décentralisation* (1996), paper given at the conference on the protection of the financial interests of the European Communities, held in Lille, 25–26 January.
63. Article 9(2) of the proposed second Protocol to the Convention on the Protection of the European Communities' Financial Interests sees proposal for a Council Act, COM(95) 693, December 1995.
64. *See* Council of Europe (1995) *op. cit.*, report presented by the Italian Minister of Justice.

3.4. International Agreements and American Proposals

The global situation has been considerably altered by the opening-up of markets, culminating in the conclusion of the Uruguay Round and the establishment of the WTO. The impact of these developments has been heightened by the association agreements and the setting-up of the EEA, the accession of the new Member States and the Association Agreements with countries of central and Eastern Europe.[65] Unfortunately, in our 'post-national'[66] economies of increasingly freer trade, where commerce and procurement are international, relevant national rules all too easily fail to address the more negative consequences of the internal market and of the broader internationalization of trade.

Internationally, there are a number of recommendations and codes of practices which have been agreed to in various fora.[67] The 1994 OECD recommendation on bribery in international business transactions,[68] for example, spells out part of the control agenda, but it is not binding. The recommendation suggests, *inter alia*, that bribes should no longer be tax-deductible (as they presently are in some of the Member States), and that the bribery of foreign officials should be sanctioned on par with the bribery of national officials. But the problem with non-binding instruments is basically that no one State wants to be first at making them binding, lest they lose out economically. This perception means that some comprehensive non-binding instruments have remained non-binding to date. Following an OECD pact signed in Paris in April 1996, however, there have been some moves in the direction of abolishing the tax deductibility of bribes in some of the Member States, with iatrogenic consequences, such as the resurgence of legal phone tapping in Germany for the first time since the end of the second world war.[69] The non-deductibility of bribes may, in any case, have little impact if it turns out that most bribes are paid out of laundered money.[70] In this case '*chercher l'argent*' may well emerge as the central anti-corruption task for the international community in the near future.

There has been a robust challenge from the United States. The Foreign Corrupt Practices Act 1977 (FCPA) extends the jurisdiction of US courts to all American citizens and companies, wherever the offence of bribery is committed, attempted or contemplated. US companies maintain that they lose contracts as a result of bribes

---

65. [1994] O.J. C397.

66. *See* for example newspaper article: 'Let's make the global playing field level', in *The Independent*, 5 June 1996; also D. McShane, *Global business: global rights* (1996) Fabian Pamphlet 575.

67. *See* for example International Chamber of Commerce, *Extortion and bribery in international business transactions, Revisions to the 1977 Report and rules of conduct to combat extortion and bribery* (1996). This report covers recommendations to governments and international organizations and rules of conduct to combat extortion and bribery.

68. OECD, *Council Recommendation on bribery in international business transactions* (1994) C(94)/75.

69. *See* newspapers articles: 'Frankfurt fights corruption war on two fronts', in *Financial Times*, 14 August 1995; 'Anger over bribes ruling',in *European*, 18 April 1996, p. 17; 'Germany acts to combat corruption', *Financial Times*, 20 June 1996 p. 2.

70. J. Robinson, *The laundrymen* (1995) Pocket Books, London, p. 24: 'Corporations do it [launder money] to avoid or evade tax, to defraud their shareholders, to get around currency control regulations and/or to bribe prospective clients.'

offered by European competitors in particular,[71] hence American lobbying to see a US-style system operating in Europe. In September 1996 the US Department of Commerce indicated its intention to establish a hot line for US companies to report suspected bribery of foreign officials by non-US companies. The confidential hot line is to be monitored and followed up by the Trade Promotion Co-ordinating Committee (TPCC).[72]

The European response to this pressure has been one of caution, and of reluctance to adopt the American agenda and 'import' ready-made solutions. There are, the author suggests, at least two reasons for this reluctance. The first is historical. For the United States, extra-territoriality has long been understood as a way of influencing conditions of trade beyond the US territory; European powers developed this idea to a much lesser extent. The second reason for caution relates to concern about the effectiveness of the FCPA in particular, and extra-territoriality in particular.

At best, the success of the FCPA can be described as mixed. Extra-territoriality as applied to corruption offences has inherent weaknesses, as the American experience has shown, and in any case the effects of the FCPA have on occasion been circumvented by engaging an intermediary to make illicit payments.[73] Closer to the European Union, in Switzerland, where the prosecution of Swiss nationals for corrupt offences abroad is (in theory at least) possible, this power does not seem to have been used in practice.[74]

Given the European Union's structure, powers and competencies, it has developed its own characteristic responses, based in its first pillar and third pillar competencies, rather than adopting either a purely intergovernmental or an extraterritorial approach. US pressure recently may have influenced the pace of the European response rather than its form. Nevertheless, the approach of the Union is still developing, not without difficulty, unproven and no doubt open to improvement. In the closing pages of this chapter some possible improvements will be noted.

71. *See* newspaper articles: (i) 'US companies lost $20bn in deals after rivals offered bribes – Kantor calls for bribery action' by N. Dunne in *Financial Times*, 26 July 1996, p. 3; (ii) 'US will demand "no-bribe" pledges' by A. Counsell in *Financial Times*, 25 September 1996, p. 7. The latter reads: 'The TPCC report said that bribery was one of the most difficult and persistent barriers to working abroad. US companies had lost 36 out of 139 international commercial contracts which had come under scrutiny for allegations of bribery, at an estimated cost of $11bn.'
72. *Ibid.*
73. *See* newspaper article: 'Greasing wheels: How US concerns compete in countries where bribes flourish, foreign travel, donations and use of middlemen help them win business, paying for reporters' cabs' in *The Wall Street Journal* of 29 September 1995; R. Levy, 'The antibribery provisions of the Foreign Corrupt Practices Act of 1977: are they really as valuable as we think they are?' (1985) *Delaware Journal of Corporate Law*, pp. 71–95; J. Bliss, 'The Foreign Corrupt Practices Act of 1988: clarification or evisceration?' (1989) *Law and Policy in International Business*, pp. 441–469.
74. A. Lachat-Héritier, 'Commercial bribes – The Swiss answer' (1983) 5 *Journal of Comparative Business and Capital Market Law*, pp. 79–96.

4. AN ISSUE NOT YET SQUARELY CONFRONTED: IMMUNITIES

The European budget has increased by a factor of 2.7 in ten years, rising from 28,800 million ECU in 1985 to 79,800 million ECU in 1995.[75] As a result, the financial officers of the European Communities have been called upon to exercise more responsibility on behalf of the European tax payer, in an increasingly complex regulatory environment. The case law of the European Court of Justice shows that occasionally Community funds have been misappropriated through the allegedly corrupt behaviour of EC officials.[76]

4.1. EC Officials: Disciplinary Framework

Under Article 260 EC, if a Member of the Commission no longer fulfils the conditions required for the performance of his duties or if he has been guilty of serious misconduct, the Court of Justice may, on application by the Council or the Commission, compulsorily retire him. The Staff disciplinary framework also provides for a wide range of sanctions to be applied by the appointing authority, irrespective of the immunities officials may enjoy. But these disciplinary sanctions, typically, do not extend to custodial penalties or even fines, and are not made public. They can never be seen as a suitable alternative to sanctions imposed by the courts.

Any failure by an EC official to comply with his duties under the Staff Regulations, whether intentionally or through negligence, renders him liable to disciplinary action and penalties which range from a written warning, a reprimand, a deferment of advancement, a relegation in step to downgrading or removal from post and entitlement to retirement pension according to the severity of the misconduct or negligence. Sanctions with regard to post-employment duties such as confidentiality can also be applied after the official has left the service.[77] Furthermore, where an allegation of serious misconduct is made against an official by the appointing authority, whether this amounts to failure to carry out his official duties or a breach of law, the authority may order that he be suspended forthwith.[78] Indeed, for the fight against corruption, the possibility of post-employment sanctions is important so that a more subtle form of corruption where the official is granted employment, consultancy contracts or other advantages after (or rather as a result of) his employment with the administration can be dealt with. This practice is usually referred to in the continental literature as 'pantouflage'.[79]

---

75. European Court of Auditors, *Report to the Reflection Group on the Operation of the Treaty on European Union* (1995) p. 2.

76. *See* for example cases 46/72, *De Greef* v. *Commission*, [1973] ECR 543; 49/72, *Drescig* v. *Commission*, [1973] ECR 567; 326/91, *De Compte* v. *European Parliament*, [1994] ECR I 2091; and more recently 12/94, *Daffix* v. *Commission*: 28 March 1995, nyr.

77. Article 86 of Regulation No. 31 O.J. Spec. Ed. 59–62, pages 135–200, 1385/62 (Staff Regulations).

78. Article 88 of Staff Regulations.

79. From the French 'pantoufle', which means slipper.

Article 22 of the Staff Regulations also states that an official may be required to make good, in whole or in part, any damage suffered by the Communities as a result of serious misconduct in the course of, or in connection with the performance of his duties. Echoing Article 179 EC, Article 22 also stipulates that the European Court of Justice has unlimited jurisdiction in disputes arising under this provision. The technical and legal difficulties associated with making compensation part of disciplinary procedure have never been put to the test.[80]

There has been some scathing criticism of the Staff Regulations. For example, the House of Lords, in its 1996 IGC Minutes of Evidence, pointed out that the Staff Regulations were overdue for reform so as to 'make it easier for staff to be reviewed, moved, promoted and sacked'.[81] The European Court of Auditors, which is also critical of the present arrangements, has argued for an investigative role in disciplinary hearings, since it is within its powers to perform controls by examining records.[82]

Serious misconduct can include an alleged misappropriation of funds. Such misconduct, however, according to the Disciplinary Board in one case 'justifies a sanction going beyond that recommended by the Disciplinary Board'.[83] This is in line with Commission sentiment. In response to a Parliamentary question, Jacques Delors replied on behalf of the Commission that as far as Commission officials were concerned, if there were any case of corruption, criminal proceedings would normally be launched.[84]

Yet in relation to the protection of the financial interests of the European Communities, such prosecutions under the criminal laws of the Member States are rare. This is because provisions sanctioning corruption and bribery in the Member States' criminal laws tend to be addressed to their own nationals, on their own territory. Notwithstanding this discrimination, the prosecution of national officials is also rare. At present only France, the United Kingdom and Ireland have a less restrictive approach, which does not exclude EC officials.[85] One complicating factor in this already very uneven control space is that EC officials enjoy immunities, which, as we shall see, have to be lifted if a prosecution is to take place.

---

80. *See* M.P. Russo, 'La responsabilité pécuniaire des fonctionnaires communautaires', Seminar held at San Sebastian, Spain, 16–17 April 1997.
81. House of Lords Select Committee on the European Communities, *Inter-Governmental Conference – Minutes of Evidence* (1995) 18th report, p. 386.
82. *See* S. White, 'Reflections on the IGC and the protection of the financial interests of the European Communities' (1995) *AGON* October, p. 10; European Commission, *Préparation CIG 1996 – Contribution de la cour des comptes* (1995) info-note 31/95.
83. Case 12/94, *Daffix* v. *Commission*, 28.3.1995, nyr.
84. Written question E-2478/94 by Fausto Bertinotti to the Commission (30 November 1994) [1995] O.J. C55/58.
85. *See* P. De Koster, *Obstacles causés par le régime d'immunités des fonctionnaires publics* (1995), paper given at a conference on the protection of the financial interests of the European Communities held at Sirmione, Italy.

4.2. Privileges and Immunities

EC officials enjoy privileges and immunities set out in the Protocol on the Privileges and Immunities of the European Communities.[86]

In particular, the premises and buildings of the Communities are inviolable. The property and assets of the Communities cannot be the subject of any administrative or legal measure of constraint without the authorization of the Court of Justice. EC officials are immune from legal proceedings in respect of acts performed by them in their official capacity. This immunity extends even after they have ceased to hold office. Each institution is required to waive the immunity wherever it considers that the waiver of such immunity is not contrary to the interests of the Communities.[87]

4.2.1. Test of Functional Necessity

One important issue is whether these immunities in any way hinder the investigation or prosecution of allegedly corrupt behaviour. The rationale for an official's privileges and immunities is that they must be necessary to enable him to perform his functions. Accordingly, the immunity referred to under Article 1 of the Protocol on Privileges and Immunities of the European Communities cannot be invoked to prevent EC officials' earnings from being docked. Similarly, Article 23 of the Staff Regulations states:

> 'The privileges and immunities enjoyed by officials are accorded solely in the interests of the communities. Subject to the Protocol on Privileges and Immunities, officials shall not be exempt from fulfilling their private obligations or from complying with the laws and police regulations in force.'

In these matters, the institutions and the European Court of Justice have applied the test of functional necessity. The Court of Justice has held constantly that, with respect to administrative or legal measures of constraint, the principle of functional necessity has to prevail. For example, an attachment of earnings affecting the salary of an EC official does not, according to the Court of Justice, constitute an obstacle in the way of the functioning and independence of the Communities, particularly when the serving of such an order was not opposed by the appointing authority itself.[88]

---

86. Protocol signed in Brussels in 1965, superseding the Protocols on the Privileges and Immunities of the European Atomic Energy Community, of the European Coal and Steel Community and of the European Economic Community.

87. Articles 1, 12(a) and 18, second subparagraph of the Protocol on Privileges and Immunities of the European Communities.

88. For example cases 4/62, *Application for authorization to enforce a garnishee order against the High Authority of the European Coal and Steel Community*, [1962] ECR 41; 64/63, *Potvin* v. *Van de Velde*, [1963] ECR 47; 85/63, *Application for authorization to notify the EEC of an assignment of salary*, [1963] ECR 195; 1/71, *Application for authorization to serve an attachment order on the Commission of the European Communities*, [1971] ECR 363; 1/87, *Universe Tankship Incorporated* v. *Commission*, [1987] ECR 2807; 1/88, *SA Générale de Banque* v. *Commission*, [1988] ECR 857.

4.2.2. Immunity from Prosecution

Likewise, the immunity from prosecution under Article 12(a) of the Protocol on Privileges and Immunities cannot be invoked outside the sphere of the official's duties. The European Court of Justice ruled that the immunity against prosecution should be waived in the case of an official prosecuted in a Belgian court following a car accident, since his official duties did not require the use of a car.[89] Crimes unconnected with the performance of officials' duties do not fall within the scope of the immunity against prosecution.

> 'The Commission considers that it is its right and duty to cooperate with the police and the judicial authorities of the Member States and to comply with any legitimate request for information in so far as its own interests, immunities and privileges are not jeopardized. They are in principle not affected in the case of crimes committed by the Commission's staff unconnected with the performance of their duties.'[90]

With respect to crimes connected with the performance of officials' duties, the appointing authority waives the immunity *if it is not contrary to the interests of the Communities*, which remains disturbingly vague. A positive duty to lift immunities immediately when the protection of the financial interests of the European Communities are at stake would go a long way towards clarifying this state of affairs.

Official secrecy. Under Article 19 of the Staff Regulations officials have a duty of discretion. They must not disclose in any legal proceedings information of which they have knowledge by reason of their duties. Permission must be sought, and will be refused only when the interests of the Communities so require. An official continues to be bound by this obligation after leaving the service. However, this provision does not apply to an official or former official giving evidence before the Court of Justice or before the Disciplinary Board of an institution on a matter concerning a serving or former serving staff member.[91]

Duty of assistance. When misconduct is alleged, the appointing authority must give official assistance. Each Community has a right to assist an official in its service, in particular in proceedings against a person perpetrating threats, insulting or defamatory acts or utterances, or any attack to person or property to which he or a member of his family is subjected by reason of his position and duties. It must also compensate the official for damage suffered in such cases, in so far as the official did not either intentionally or through grave negligence cause damage and has been unable to obtain compensation from the person who did cause it.[92] An official may therefore sue for violation of this guarantee if an unproven allegation of fraud has

---

89. Case 9/69, *Sayag and Another* v. *Leduc and others (Reference for a preliminary ruling by the Belgian Cour de Cassation)*, [1969] ECR 329.
90. Case 180/87, *Hamill* v. *Commission*, [1988] ECR 6141.
91. *See* C. Schmidt, 'Le Protocole sur les Privilèges et Immunités des Communautés Européennes' (1991) *Cahier de Droit Européen*, pp. 81–82 in particular.
92. Article 24 of the Staff Regulations.

been made against him and the appointing authority has failed to protect his reputation. This leaves the institution open to a claim for damages, if for example disciplinary proceedings are taken and allegations turn out to be unfounded, or the official is arrested and prosecuted as a result of information communicated by the appointed authority, and is subsequently acquitted.[93] One can see that whilst it might be possible for the appointing authority to investigate in-house and protect the reputation of an official in the meanwhile, this might prove more difficult when cooperating with the judicial authorities of the Member States. There is a potential tension between the duty of the appointing authorities to assist officials and the duty to cooperate with the judicial authorities of the Member States.

4.3. Immunities and Delays

To some commentators, the existence of privileges and immunities in itself does not in fact present a significant obstacle to prosecution.[94] Indeed immunities are relative[95] or functional, so their significance must not be overstated. Immunities were never intended to prevent the investigation of serious crimes against the tax payer. But corruption thrives on secrecy and silence[96] and is by nature difficult to detect.[97] There may be a sense in which the presence of immunities may make the detection of such crimes even more difficult. As was pointed out in the context of diplomatic immunity:

> 'What limits the scope of a diplomat to perform criminal acts? Like any other person guilty of a crime, he must first be detected. Moreover, because of the inviolability of his person and premises, detection is especially difficult.'[98]

Police investigations may be delayed by the administrative processes involved in waiving immunities. In the 'Tourism Unit' case, which hit the headlines in 1995, there seems to have been a long delay before the immunities of several officials were lifted,[99] in what turned out to be 'the first inquiry to involve outside investigators (i.e. the police) in the 40–year history of the Commission', leading to the early retirement of the Director-General of the DG for tourism (DG XXIII).[100]

---

93. Cases 158/79, *Roumengous* v. *Council*, [1982] ECR 4379; 145/83, *Adams* v. *Commission*, [1985] ECR 3539; 59/92, *Caronna* v. *Commission*, [1993] ECR II 1129; 180/87, *Hamill* v. *Commission*, [1988] ECR 6141.

94. P. De Koster, *op. cit.*

95. *See* case 2/88, *Zwartveld and others* v. *Commission*, [1990] ECR 5(1) 3365, p. 3372, points 19–20.

96. Council of Europe (1995) *op. cit.*, p. 21.

97. *See* for example R. Merlin-Calzia, 'Le service central de prévention de la corruption comme possible instrument au service de la défense des intérêts financiers de la Communauté' (1995) *AGON* July, pp. 8–9.

98. G. McClanahan, *Diplomatic immunity, principles, practices, problems* (1989) Hurst, London, p. 128.

99. *See* newspaper articles: 'Audit damns EC tourism unit', *European*, 10 February 1995; 'Immunity lifted on EC suspects', *European*, 24 February 1995; 'EC anti-fraud chief pledges "no cover-ups"', *European*, 10 March 1995, pp. 1 and 19.

100. *See* newspaper article 'Police anger as tourism chief goes', in *The European*, 24–30 October 1996, p. 26.

Indeed the lifting of immunities is the gift of the appointing authority, who has to base its decision on the evidence available. Evidence-gathering may be a difficult exercise in such cases.

To conclude, the privileges and immunities of EC officials, respected by recent third pillar measures, pose problems in the investigation of possible corruption. This issue has also been raised in the context of the European Parliament, and of national parliaments too.[101]

5. TOWARDS A CREDIBLE ANTI-CORRUPTION STRATEGY

Clearly, an anti-corruption strategy needs both increased prevention *and* repression, with respect to both economic operators *and* officials. Transparency must be increased in order to defeat the secrecy which naturally surrounds corrupt practices. But increased transparency must be backed up by a credible system of prosecution. The problem has hitherto only partly been addressed within the European Union, and much remains to be done.

5.1. Immunities: Need for Assimilation

With regard to EC officials, a positive duty could and should be placed upon the institutions to lift immunities promptly when an internal investigation shows that EC funds are be involved. More generally, on the subject of immunities and of elite corruption, DG XX could consider a study on the regimes of immunities politicians and officials enjoy in the Member States with a view to assimilation, as far as the protection of the financial interests of the European Communities is concerned. Without this, the anti-corruption protocol and the convention could prove to be of little value since most officials and politicians handling EC funds seem to enjoy either nationally or internationally determined immunities.

5.2. Third Pillar Action: Conditions for Effectiveness

With regard to the two proposed third pillar instruments outlined above, it is hoped that a permanent compromise can be reached with regard to the jurisdiction of the European Court of Justice, and that a swift ratification will follow. If the instruments are to work well, mutual assistance should be stepped up. This may be difficult at the moment, since mutual assistance still rests on instruments unsuited to a internal market. In this the exchange of magistrates could go some way towards ameliorating the situation. One cannot help but feel, however, that much more drastic reform is needed in order to try and attain a system which functions with the requisite despatch, and which could easily be extended to new Member States upon accession.

---

101. *See* for example newspaper article: 'Who should judge corrupt Mps?' in *Times*, 12 November 1996 p. 39.

The question remains whether the seriousness with which these issues have been addressed by the Council of Ministers will find echoes in the legislatures of every Member State, or whether procrastination once again will emerge as the villain, as was the case when such issues were first debated in the 1970s. There may be good reason for pessimism on this score. Because corruption refers to several distinct but related problems,[102] its 'definition' in a particular historical context is far from value-free. Corruption may be likened to a political 'projective test': each political group highlights particular aspects which it sees as ripe for enforcement, and de-emphasizes other aspects, according to its own preoccupations, interests and position in the world. In many or perhaps all Member States, political agenda may be the result of political compromise, which may make it difficult to get quick and vigorous implementation of third pillar measures.

The question thus arises – can more also be done within the first pillar?

5.3. First Pillar Action

There is scope within Community law to protect the integrity of the internal market by seeking to eradicate commercial behaviour, such as corrupt practices, which grant an unfair advantage and distort competition. This could be put in the context of the already existing, and largely successful Community crime prevention space which has evolved mostly since the Single European Act,[103] with the aim of protecting the internal market.

It has been argued in particular that Article 92 EC could be used to ban the tax-deductibility of certain payments, the provision of export credit guarantees concerning illicit payments and the public financing of exports which includes illicit payments[104] by treating bribes as state aids, which have the effect of distorting competition and impacting on intra-Community trade. As part of this strategy, and in view of the growing number of corruption cases involving public procurement, it has been suggested that procurement rules would be tightened up. However, the problem of speedy and accurate implementation remains.

Such an approach, once part of the *acquis communautaire*, would in turn become part of the pre-accession strategy for Central and Eastern Europe through the existing Europe agreements under Article 113 and 228(a).[105] By contrast, Partner-

---

102. J. Gardiner, 'Defining Corruption' (1993) 7 *Corruption and Reform*, pp. 111–124.
103. G. Vernimmen and A. Missir di Lusignano, Editorial (1995) *AGON* number 9; N. Dorn and S. White, 'Beyond "pillars" and "passerelle" debates – The European Union's emerging crime prevention space' (1997) *Legal Issues of European Integration*, forthcoming.
104. Transparency International (1995) *op. cit.*
105. The EU now has Europe Agreements with Bulgaria (entered into force 1.2.95), the Czech Republic (1.2.95), Estonia (not yet entered into force), Hungary (1.2.94), Latvia (not yet entered into force), Lithuania (not yet entered into force), Poland (1.2.94), Romania (1.2.95), the Slovak Republic (1.2.95) and Slovenia (not yet entered into force). Each of these agreements stipulate that (i) all agreements between undertakings, decisions by associations of undertakings and concerted practices which have as their project or effect the prevention, restriction or distortion of competition must be progressively abolished; (ii) any practices will be assessed on the basis of Articles 85, 86 and 92 EC and the relevant secondary legislation. The necessary rules for implementation must be adopted by 31 December 1997.

ship and Cooperation Agreements, taken under the same legal basis, impose less constraining duties on the signatory States, such as the duty not to enact or maintain any measure distorting trade between the Community and the signatory State.[106] Trade and Economic Cooperation Agreements, meanwhile, with Articles 113 and 235 as a legal basis, only impose a duty not to impose counter-trade requirements.[107]

There has been no direct case law as to whether competition is within Article 113. In 1992[108] the Court opined that the Community's power to enter into international agreements in the competition field arose from the competition rules in the EC Treaty.[109] This power remains uncontested to date. More recently, in 1996[110] the Court opined that Article 235 EC could not be used as a legal basis to justify the Community's accession to the Convention of Human Rights as such accession would entail substantial changes of a constitutional nature which go beyond the scope of Article 235 EC. This could potentially limit the field of action of the Community to enter into international agreements only in areas where it has explicit competence, and whilst emphasizing downwards subsidiarity, may well limit the potential for Community-based action to fight corruption.

Procurement. There may be a sense in which, as far as the Structural Funds are concerned, neither co-financing nor programming have delivered the expected protection. Firstly, not all operational programmes are co-financed in any case. Community initiatives, for example, are financed 100 per cent from Community funds and other initiatives only require a small participation from the Member States. In other cases, costs have sometimes been inflated in order to lessen the impact on the local purse. Secondly, the Commission has argued that it is in the nature of the system of contributing to the financing of programmes, rather than projects, under the Structural Funds that monitoring of compliance with public tendering rules must take place essentially at the level of national authorities. This probably indicates that the Commission is thinking about having shorter-term, better defined projects in the future, whilst subjecting them to rigorous on-the-spot checks.

Procurement rules could be tightened up, as suggested earlier, if it becomes clear that the desired effect can only be achieved by legislative action in the first pillar. This means, in particular, regulating the selection of intermediaries and monitoring the use of 'emergency' procedures, which allow normal procurement rules to be circumvented when contracts involving EC funds (and others) are involved. Without this tightening of rules, the problem could reach dramatic proportions after the next enlargement.

---

106. PCAs have partially entered into force in Belarus, Kazakhstan, Kyrgystan, Moldova, Russia and Ukraine where interim agreements on trade aspects are awaiting ratification.
107. The TECA with Albania entered into force on 1.12.92. TECAs also apply when the full PCAs have not been ratified yet (*see* previous note).
108. Opinion 1/92 [1992] ECR 2821 at para. 40.
109. *See* I. McLeod, I. Hendry and S. Hyett, *The External Relations of the European Communities* (1996) Clarendon Press, Oxford, pp. 271–273.
110. Opinion 2/94 re the accession of the Community to the European Human Rights Convention [1996] 2 CMLR 265.

International trade: the CCEEs. Outside the Union, it is through the Europe Agreements that there is the most scope to prevent economic crime through procurement rules, although in some cases these rules will not be effective until 1998. Procurement rules, which as we have seen take their place in instruments regulating the (economic) external relations of the European Union, have the potential to be of strategic importance in the fight against procurement fraud in an enlarged Union. More is said on enlargement in the following chapter.

With regard to the grey area which concerns projects which offer disastrously low value for money, or which let certain consultants 'cream off' funds destined to help Central and Eastern Europe, there seems to be a need for the Commission itself to look at the way it awards contracts.

5.4. Conclusion

The potential of first pillar instruments to bring about changes in Member States' criminal laws should not be underestimated. Cadoppi stressed that harmonization of criminal law had already come largely through the European Court of Human Rights, but also through economic regulation.[111] Economic matters being dealt with under the first pillar, measures preventing economic criminality and indeed putting an obligation on the Member States to harmonize their criminal laws have also arisen therefrom. This is the 'Trojan Horse' quality of the first pillar, which is so often overlooked.

Nevertheless there would remain practical and administrative issues requiring attention in order to give effect to first pillar measures against corruption. Such measures would entail cross-directorate cooperation which, unfortunately, does not seem to be forthcoming at the time of writing. But it is not beyond the realm of possibilities that this situation could improve rapidly. If so, then first pillar action might be demonstrated to have potential lacking in third pillar action. It would be both an irony and tragedy if an impediment to that demonstration were to be found not in the Member States but in the guardian of the first pillar.

---

111. A. Cadoppi, 'Towards a European Criminal Code?' (1996) 4:1 *European Journal of Crime, Criminal Law and Criminal Justice*, pp. 2–17.

Chapter 7. Enlargement of the European Union

1. WHITHER THE CAP?

We are now moving towards a Union where in the future a 'core' may forge ahead by fulfilling EU policy goals, whilst others may well accede only to part of the *acquis communautaire*. In view of the proposed proportional increase in expenditure on structural measures, what might this mean for the future of fraud prevention and enforcement?

1.1. Background: Anticipated Enlargement

The Community has been subjected to a regime of rapid enlargements and its budget has increased exponentially, as well as CAP expenditure. Hungary, Poland, the Czech Republic, Slovenia, Estonia and Cyprus are first in line for accession, and accession talks are scheduled for early 1998.

Clearly a Union of 20 Member States, or even as many as 27 by next century, cannot be run on the same lines as a Union of twelve of fifteen. Back in 1972 Spinelli had already predicted that the enlargement of the Community would not automatically bring a better balance to agriculture, but that it might, on the contrary, increase the desequilibria.[1] At the Essen summit (1994) the then president of the Commission, Jacques Delors, made it clear that the European Union would have to reform its own policies to cope with eastern enlargement, including reform of the CAP and the Structural Funds.

1.2. CAP: Major Obstacle

Notwithstanding attempts at trimming the CAP, its size is still such that it has been described as the major obstacle to further enlargement.[2] Estimates as to how much the budget would have to increase if the four Visegrad countries joined the Union and the present level of CAP intervention was extended to them vary between an

---

1. A. Spinelli, *The European adventure – Tasks for an enlarged Community* (1972) London, Charles Knight & Co, p. 69.
2. R. Baldwin, *Towards an integrated Europe* (1994), London Council for European Policy Studies; also M. Sutton, 'Transition to the European Union?' (1994) in *Economies in transition Eastern Europe and the former Soviet Union*, London, Economist Intelligence Unit.

increase of 40 to 70 billion ECU.[3] That is to say, some commentators estimate that a doubling of the budget would be needed in order to extend the present system at the next accession. In realpolitik, this is impossible. Yet a radical reform of the CAP promises to be a political minefield. It has been pointed out that the agricultural lobby is an 'insider' in the policy community and has been the most consistently powerful economic interest in the EC.[4] It is therefore to be expected that the lobbies would oppose preferential treatment being given to Central and Eastern European agricultural products.

As far as Structural Funds are concerned, it has been acknowledged that they still have an important role to play in the completion of the internal market and in promoting economic and social cohesion, but that they need to be deployed to underpin this force for convergence more effectively. It has been suggested that in an enlarged Union they should be better geared to local development needs and that they should give more support to programmes which involve more than one country, particularly in financing trans-European networks in the areas of transport, telecommunications and energy. This would strengthen their role in stimulating investments in which there is a shared interest, and would also provide crucial support for the creation of new infrastructure in the internal market by supplementing other sources of financing, including loans floated on the capital markets.[5]

Unfortunately, programmes which involve more than one country have hitherto offered particularly poor value for money, and have attracted fraud. From the ascendent position of Structural Funds will not necessarily follow a movement downwards (in subsidiarity terms) of control to the Member States. In fact, one can safely predict a substantial enlargement in UCLAF's personnel, whose task it is to deal with complex trans-national investigations.

2. PREVENTION/ENFORCEMENT IN AN ENLARGED UNION

As we have seen, extending present agricultural policies to the CCEEs could lead to a considerable increase of the present EC budget. This would not be acceptable to the main contributors (Germany, France and Italy). Although Germany and the UK see scope for reductions in regional and CAP funding, this is likely to be resisted by the main contributors as well as the mediterranean countries and compromises will have to be sought.[6] There seem to be three possible 'ideal type' scenarios for future enforcement, which are mooted below. The first possibility

---

3. The following reports were commissioned by Directorate-General I of the European Commission: A. Buckwell, *Report on the feasibility of an agricultural strategy to prepare the countries of central and eastern Europe for EU accession* (1994); S. Tangermann and T. Josling, *Pre-accession agricultural policies for central Europe and the European Union* (1994); S. Tarditi and S. Senior-Nello, *Agricultural strategies for the enlargement of the European Union to central and east European countries* (1994); L-P. Mahé, *Agriculture and enlargement of the European Union to include the central and eastern European countries – Transition with a view to integration or integration with a view to transition?* (1995).
4. N. Collins, 'The European Community's farm lobby' (1995) 5 *Corruption and Reform*, pp. 235–257.
5. Opinion on the Single Market in 1994 [1996] O.J. C39/70.
6. *See European Parliament News*, 13–17 February 1995.

illustrates a situation where 'classical enlargement'[7] takes place, with the CCEEs taking on the full *acquis communautaire*, after transition periods of varying lengths. The second possibility is that connected with 'partial membership', where new entrants only take on part of the *acquis*, namely the second and third pillars of the present Treaty establishing the European Union. A mixed scenario is also possible, with parallel systems (CAP, Structural Funds) in operation. All these scenarios have different implications for anti-fraud enforcement, as we shall see.

2.1. Classical Enlargement

Such a scenario could involve the (reformed) CAP and Structural Funds being extended to the new entrants, and the Customs Union extended to include them. The whole *acquis communautaire* is taken on gradually, which means that all measures relating to the protection of the financial interests of the European Communities apply after an agreed period of time.

2.2. Partial Membership

By contrast, partial membership through accession to only the second and third pillars would theoretically entail exclusion from first pillar re-distribution policies, such as the CAP and Structural Funds, until the full *acquis* is taken on at a later stage. This would be an enlargement firstly looking to the free movement of goods (already greatly encouraged by the extension of the Community transit system to the Visegrad countries), but without free movement of persons. The Customs Union would not at first be extended to some or all of the new entrants. In an ideal type partial membership scenario, the new entrants do not at first benefit from the redistributive policies of the Union any more than they do at present, so enforcement problems remain qualitatively unchanged.

In such a scenario, it seems important that, in the eventual move from partial to full membership, both redistributive policies and first pillar anti-fraud measures be taken on simultaneously. The 'decoupling' of the two could prove financially disastrous for the Union.

2.3. Mixed Membership

A mixed scenario is also likely, where parallel systems develop. A 'compromise' may involve a complex re-organization of funds to fit in with the various levels of integration. This is, for example what Buckwell envisaged, with regard to the CAP:

'A separate CAP could be designed for the countries of eastern and central Europe which would operate *alongside*[8] the existing CAP for the EU.'

7. F. De La Serre, 'L'élargissement aux PECO: Quelle différenciation?' (1996) 402 *Revue du Marché Commun*, pp. 42–655.
8. Emphasis added.

175

Parallel Structural Funds may also be put in place, to deal with the specific problems experienced by the new entrants. Enforcement, as a result, may become highly contingent and may include more integrated areas with mature control systems, and others where parallel control systems have yet to be put in place, leading to (more) uneven enforcement and a degree of unpredictability throughout the Union. Unless the Treaty of Amsterdam manages to provide for both consistency and flexibility.

Chapter 8. Current Proposals for Development of the Legal Space

In this chapter, the author looks at the latest proposal to protect the financial interests of the European Communities, a *Corpus Juris*. The description of this proposal – which is reproduced in full in an appendix – is preceded by a very brief overview of the existing legal space, in so far as it relevant to EC fraud. Unfortunately, from the point of view of the author, the *Corpus Juris* does not look like a very likely prospect in the very short term, and so, having noted its most interesting features, the author concludes on the basis of institutional and legal arrangements in existence in 1997.

1. THE EXISTING LEGAL SPACE

The evolution of control bears witness to the increased heterogeneity of the legal space. Measures to prevent and combat fraud affecting the EC budget, either directly or indirectly, can now be found not only in sectorial economic regulations under the first pillar, under Article 235 EC, under various K articles, but also in international conventions.

1.1. A Diversity of Approaches

The role of Community law in preventing criminal activities generally was outlined in detail by the Commission at the ninth United Nations Conference in May 1995.[1] It is in this wider context of Community crime prevention that the numerous sectorial rules for the protection of the financial interests of the European Communities, and procurement rules can also be located.[2]

Additionally, Article 209a EC creates an obligation on the Member States to treat fraud affecting the EC budget in the same way as fraud affecting national interests, but it has yet to be used as a legal basis, the more ambiguous Article 235 having hitherto been preferred.[3]

---

1. *See* G. Vernimmen and A. Missir di Lusignano (1995), *op. cit.*
2. N. Dorn and S. White (1997) *op. cit.*
3. J. Vervaele, 'L' Application du droit communautaire: la séparation des biens entre le premier et le troisième pillier?' (1996) *Revue de Droit Pénal et de Criminologie*, pp.5–22; also J. Vervaele, 'Criminal law in the European Community: about myth and taboos' (1995) *AGON* No. 7.

'If action by the Community shall prove necessary to attain, in the course of action of the operation of the common market, one of the objectives of the Community and this Treaty has not provided the necessary powers, the Council shall, acting unanimously on a proposal from the Commission and after consulting the European Parliament, take the appropriate measures.' (Article 235 EC)

Article 235 EC retains some of the distinctive characteristics of the first pillar: the Commission has a right of initiative and the Court of Justice has jurisdiction to rule on disputes.[4] But the advantage of the article is that, given political consensus in the Council, it offers the possibility of inter-governmental action under the first pillar, in furtherance of one of the objectives of the Community. Both the 'PIF' Regulation and the Regulation[5] concerning on-the-spot checks and inspections by the Commission (*see* Chapter 1) have Article 235 EC as a legal basis. It has been argued that Article 235 EC provides the legislator with the necessary flexibility to meet some of the challenges of integration. It has also been suggested that Article 235 EC should be used more widely, and in particular that it could be used as a legal basis to establish penal sanctions.[6] Generally, learned commentators[7] have opined that the time had come for the 'penal landscape to be re-constituted'[8] and for the Community to have a '*compétence dans le domaine répressif*' – which would enable it to establish uniform sanctions for breaches of Community regulations.

However, in matters relating to the repression of fraud and corruption the Member States have chosen, since 1995, to take action within the inter-governmental framework.

One reason for such action being preferred within an intergovernmental framework has been the absence in the Treaty of Rome of any explicit basis for action strictly compensatory to the establishment of the internal market. Another, perhaps, is the Member States' reluctance to prejudice their control of policing or criminal law.[9]

In general, the entry into force of conventions relating to the European Union space has been protracted, with few improvements since 1993.[10] This is one of the arguments often used in an attempt to 'move' law-making to the first pillar. A number of conventions also have been concluded under the aegis of the Council of Europe in order to further cooperation in judicial matters. However, as a rule, entry into force has been protracted. The money laundering convention, for example, has only been ratified by 5 Member States within the European Union.

---

4. Article 169 EC.
5. Council Regulation 2185/96 [1996] O.J. L292/2.
6. A. Missir di Lusignano, 'La protection des intérêts financiers de la Communauté' (1996) *Journal des Tribunaux Droit Européen*, 18 April, p. 78.
7. *See* F. Schockweiler, 'La répréssion des infractions au droit communautaire dans la jurisprudence de la Cour' (1995) *Proceeds of seminar on judicial cooperation in criminal matters in the European Community*, Luxembourg; H. Labayle, 'La protection des intérêts financiers de la Communauté' (1995) *Revue Europe*, March.
8. M. Delmas-Marty, *Pour un droit commun* (1994), Seuil, Paris, *see* chapter on 'La recomposition d'un paysage'.
9. M. Anderson et al., *Policing the European Union* (1995) Clarendon Press, Oxford, p. 198.
10. M. Delmas-Marty, *Vers un espace judiciaire Européen, Corpus Juris portant dispositions pénales pour la protection des intérêts financiers de l'Union Européenne* (1996) pp. 4–9.

1.2. Creative Cross-overs or Uncertainty?

A certain amount of 'cross-over', or 'enchevêtrement'[11] has occurred between legal bases. This has not escaped the notice of the Committee on Civil Liberties and Internal Affairs which, on the subject of the choice of legal bases for the two 'PIF' instruments, opined that because of their parallel contents, both should have been submitted in the same institutional context:

> 'The ["PIF"] Convention and the proposal for a ["PIF"] Regulation on the materialities of the penalties are both operative at the level of criminal/administrative law and no clear distinction can be drawn in terms of content and legal nature justifying their being assigned to two different institutional frameworks (EC Treaty and Title VI of the Treaty on European Union).'[12]

As a result of this 'cross-over', and looking at precedents in the fight against fraud affecting the EC budget, it is difficult to predict, for example, under which legal basis the protection of the Community's VAT-based income would take place. The protection of VAT revenue is a more difficult issue at the level of the institutions, since the EC only receives a small percentage of national VATs, which nevertheless constitute over 50 per cent of the total EC budget. However, since fiscal frontiers were abolished in 1993, and the transitional system established, VAT collection can no longer be described as a 'national' revenue collecting system. VAT evasion affects the EC budget and there is scope for creative fraud prevention of an international nature in that area too.

Looking at what has happened since the adoption of the Treaty on European Union, one finds increasing interpenetration between the legal bases (for example between Articles 100a, 235 and K.3). Yet the frontiers of this increasingly diversified legal space are being tested by a proposal, explored below, which has the effect of putting the relationship between Community law and national criminal laws back very firmly on the agenda.

2. THE *CORPUS JURIS* PROPOSAL

The difficulties of dealing with fraud within the Union, the breakdown of the transit system, and projects for expansion of the Union to the CCEEs, make clear the need for the Community to devise more effective action not only at local level and nationally, but also internationally. In 1995, the Commission began to argue that assimilation, cooperation and harmonization (the three goals hitherto pursued) could provide but an incomplete and thus unsatisfactory answer to the protection of the financial interests of the European Community. The *'Espace Judiciaire Européen'* project was launched, and in the autumn of 1996 a draft for a unified body of rules

---

11. F. Tulkens, 'Les fraudes communautaires – Un observateur pénal Européen' (1994) 18:2 *Déviance et Société*, pp. 215–226.
12. European Parliament, *Report on the joint guideline of the Council on the proposal for a Council regulation on protection of the Communities' financial interests* (1995).

to deal with criminal offences affecting the budget, or *Corpus Juris* (CJ henceforth) was produced by a team of experts.

It is easy to see why the Commission came to the conclusion that assimilation, cooperation and harmonization were insufficient. Firstly, assimilation on its own does not guarantee effective sanctions (*see* above). In addition, for economic operators, assimilation means that treatment continues to differ from Member State to Member State. Secondly cooperation, too, remains marred with difficulties. Conventions dealing with cooperation matters are dependent upon the ratification of all the Member States, which means that a number remain un-implemented to date. This applies equally to Council of Europe Conventions, Conventions relating to the Schengen area as well as third pillar conventions specific to the protection of the financial interests of the European Community. It is widely acknowledged that cooperation still relies on outdated, less than speedy mechanisms, such as the delivery of rogatory letters through diplomatic channels (*see* Chapter 6). Furthermore, incompatibilities between national legislations, and 'asymmetries'[13] between national investigating and prosecuting agencies make cooperation highly complex in practice. Van den Wyngaert[14] has argued that even if all the above texts were duly ratified by all and implemented, the resulting situation would still be one which falls short of establishing the recommended[15] extra-territoriality and universal competence in criminal matters. With respect to harmonization (much of which still depends upon the ratification of 'PIF' third pillar instruments), matters relating to procedure and evidence, as well as matters relating to the determination of criminal liability, for instance, remain un-harmonized. The Commission believes that this leads to slow, and inefficient enforcement.[16]

Bearing in mind the above, the Commission has asked whether it is satisfactory just to pursue these three objectives (assimilation, cooperation and harmonization), and to wait for incremental improvements, through the slow convergence of national systems. This concern is voiced by Delmas-Marty in her introduction to the CJ.

> 'A cette étape de la contruction européenne, se pose la question de savoir si l'on peut encore se contenter de ces trois voies, et se résigner à attendre des années pour observer quelque amélioration du système répressif.'[17]

It is on this basis that the CJ was drafted, as a synthesis of several reports written between November 1995 and May 1996. The draft CJ is in response to the bold

---

13. This term was first coined by Van den Wyngaert in 1995, and refers to the lack of correspondence between national agencies performing similar tasks. For example, a French investigating magistrate carrying out an investigation may have to liaise not with an English magistrate, but with any of several British agencies endowed with investigative powers.
14. C. Van den Wyngaert, *Etude espace judiciaire européen – Groupe thématique no 2, Règles de compétence et extra-territorialité* (1996).
15. M. Delmas-Marty, *Rapport Final – Etude comparative des dispositions législatives, réglementaires des états membres relatives aux agissements frauduleux commis au préjudice du budget communautaire – un rapport de synthèse, étude sur les systèmes de sanctions communautaires* (1994), SEC 1994(93), OOPEC.
16. M. Delmas-Marty, *Vers un espace judiciaire Européen, Corpus Juris portant dispositions pénales pour la protection des intérêts financiers de l'Union Européenne* (1996) pp. 1–18.
17. *Ibid.*, p. 17.

suggestion that the only way to combine justice, clarity and effectiveness is to pursue 'unification' through a common body of rules. Such unification of criminal justice systems, in areas concerned with the protection of the financial interests of the Community, was felt to be only a 'step away from harmonization'.[18] A brief summary of the CJ's contents follows (2.1.), followed by a discussion on its chances of becoming law (§ 3).

2.1. *Corpus Juris*

The CJ is a set of penal rules, set out under two titles. Title I of the CJ deals with principles of criminal law (Articles 1–17). Title II, more controversially, deals with criminal procedure (Articles 18–35) by proposing a discrete European Prosecuting Service for offences damaging the financial interests of the European Community. The English version of the CJ, which only became available in April 1997, can be found reproduced in full in appendix C.

2.1.1. Title I: Principles of Criminal Law

Title I, which is in three parts, deals with the principle of the legality of crimes and penalties (Part 1, Articles 1 to 9); the principle of fault, basis of criminal liability (Part 2, Articles 10 to 14); the principle of proportionality of penalties (Part 3, Articles 15 to 17).

At present, Part 1 of Title I lays down common definitions for various offences: fraud affecting the Community budget (Article 1); market-rigging (Article 2); corruption (Article 3, which duplicates definitions found in the Protocol to the 'PIF' Convention); abuse of office (Article 4); misappropriation of funds (Article 5); breach of confidentiality (Article 6); money laundering and receiving (Article 7); conspiracy (Article 8). Finally a range of penalties is set out in Article 9. The tariff for offences described in Articles 1 to 8 and committed by natural persons includes prison sentences of up to five years and/or a fine of up to one million ECU, which may be raised to five times the amount in the offence. For bodies corporate, parallel penalties are prescribed: legal supervision for a maximum of five years and/or a fine of up to one million ECU, which may be raised to five times the amount involved in the offence. A range of additional penalties also apply to the same offences. They include the exclusion from future subsidies, the exclusion from future contracts and a ban from Community and national public office. These additional penalties can only be imposed for a maximum of five years (Article 9).

Part 2 defines criminal liability of individuals and businesses (Articles 10 to 14). All offences set out in Articles 1 to 8 require intention or fraud, with the exception of Community fraud (Article 1) for which recklessness or gross negligence is sufficient. This is because it was felt that in some cases an offender might entrust important tasks to collaborators who have no experience in the area and thus

---

18. *See* M. Delmas-Marty, 'La criminalité économique internationale – Pour une politique criminelle à stratégie diversifiée' (1995) *Le Trimestre du Monde*, pp. 83–90.

negligently or recklessly endanger EC funds. In cases involving errors, liability is excluded if the error could not have been avoided by a careful, sensible person. If the mistake was avoidable, the judge may not impose the maximum penalty. Finally Article 12 of the CJ differentiates between principal offender, inciter and accomplice. This distinction, meant to reflect a tradition common to most of the current legal systems, is not new and already appears in Article 2 of the 'PIF' Convention of 1995. The definitions chosen for the different categories of offenders are drawn mainly from the German and French Criminal Codes.

Part 3 of Title I (Articles 15 to 17) lays down rules to ensure the proportionality of penalties in cases involving aggravating circumstances and concurrent offences. Penalties are to be imposed in accordance with the seriousness of the act, the fault of the offender and the extent of his participation in the offence (Article 15). Circumstances are aggravated when (a) the fraudulent result sought is achieved or (b) the amount of the fraud or profit sought through the offence exceeds 200,000 ECU or (c) the offence is carried out in the context of a conspiracy (Article 8(2) of the CJ describes a conspiracy as 'when two or more persons work together, setting up the necessary organization, with a view to carrying out one or more of the offences set out in Articles 1 to 7'). In cases involving concurrent offences (defined under Articles 1 to 8 of the CJ), the penalty for the most serious offence can be increased by up to three times that amount. Interestingly, Article 17 foresees that 'when a single act constitutes a criminal offence under both Community regulations and national laws, only Community regulations are to be applied', thus invoking the primacy of Community law. In all other cases, the principle of *ne bis in idem* applies, and the competent authorities are required to take into account penalties already imposed for the same act.

2.1.2. Title II: Criminal Procedure

Title II, which deals with procedure, is in four parts, which respectively deal with the principle of European territoriality (Part 4, Articles 18 to 24); the principle of judicial control (Part 5, Articles 25 to 28); the principle of proceedings which are *contradictoire* (Part 6, Articles 29 to 34) and finally the subsidiary application of national law (Part 7, Article 35).

Part 4 (Articles 18–24) lays down rules for the establishment of a European Public Prosecutor (EPP) to investigate and prosecute in matters defined in Articles 1 to 8 of the CJ. The EPP is independent from the Community institutions and the national institutions. It consists of a European Director of Public Prosecution (EDPP) based in Brussels and European delegated Public Prosecutors (E.Del.P.P.) based in the capital of each Member State. The EPP is informed of any offences under Articles 1 to 8 by the national authorities. The decision to open an investigation may be taken by the EPP whatever the sum of the fraud involved. The EPP may also decide to drop a case, or to grant an authorization for settlement to a national authority (Article 19). The CJ tries to strike a balance between an inquisitorial system, where investigation is carried out by the *juge d'instruction*, and an accusatorial system, which entrusts most powers of investigation to the police. Yet as far as investigative activities are concerned, the system proposed in the CJ seems basically inquisitorial in nature. This means that in Member States with an accusatorial system, the interface between accusatorial and inquisitorial styles of investigations would have to be managed. Such difficulties may not be unsurmountable. The CJ commentary expresses the hope that by transferring the decision to prosecute from national to European level, the problem of disparity in prosecution between legalistic systems and systems based on the principle of opportunity would thus disappear. But since national courts would still be responsible for determining convictions, it is not altogether clear how disparities in sentencing would be erased.

The EPP's office is granted vast investigative powers in order to fulfil its role (Article 20). The EDPP oversees and coordinates investigations undertaken by the E.Del.P.P. as well as by national police forces and competent national administrations. When investigating offences set out in Articles 1 to 8, the E.Del.P.P. may question suspects, collect documents, visit the scene of the offence, request expert witnesses from a national judge, order searches, seizures and telephone tapping, hear witnesses and notify the accused of charges, and make request for a person's remand in custody. With a particularly circular sort of logic, powers delegated to the E.Del.P.P. may be partly subdelegated to a national authority who will be bound to respect all the rules contained in the CJ. One would expect that an overburdened E.Del.P.P. may indeed wish to subdelegate a great deal of investigations – which may mean, more often than not, referring cases back whence they came! This may, in some cases, involve considerable delays.

Article 21 describes the closure of the preparatory stage. When investigations are completed, the E.Del.P.P., under the authority of the EDPP, decides whether to prosecute. If the case is dropped, this decision is communicated to the Commission. Otherwise it is passed to the competent national legal authority for action. The EPP remains the prosecutor, with the national authority as joined party when national interests are also under threat. A prosecution is extinguished on the death of the defendant, or the dissolution of a group, or by the expiry of a limitation period of five years or by settlement. Settlement is ruled out in certain circumstances. In the case of repeated offences, where arms or forgery were used, or if the sum involved is 50,000 ECU or more, prosecutions rather than settlements are expected. With regard to the execution of sentences (Article 23), the EPP is responsible for the communication of sentences to the authorities of the Member States and oversees the execution of the sentence. Execution of the penalty is governed by the laws of the Member States. Article 24 lays down rules for the exercise of competence *ratione loci*. The EPP has competence to bring prosecutions and conduct investigations throughout the European Union. A European warrant for arrest issued on the instructions of a EPP is valid across the whole territory of the Union. Judgments are also valid across the whole territory of the Union. In cases where legal cooperation is required from third countries, the EPP requests the national authorities of the principal country where investigations are taking place to apply to the third State concerned, following the procedure laid down by the national and international instruments in force.

Part 5 (Articles 25 to 28) lays down procedural guarantees. Article 25 makes provision for a 'judge of freedoms' appointed by each Member State from the court of the E.Del.P.P. to exercise judicial control over the proceedings throughout the preparatory stage. Any measure restricting rights and freedoms recognized by the European Convention of Human Rights must first be authorized by the judge of freedoms. At the end of the preparatory stage, if the EPP decides to commit the case to trial, he must first submit this decision to the judge of freedoms who checks the lawfulness of proceedings and seizes the court of trial. Article 26 requires trials to take place in courts where the E.Del.P.P. is based, and staffed by professional judges, wherever possible specializing in economic and financial matters. Such expertise may be rare in Member States without a system of financial courts. In cases which involve more than one Member State, the trial takes place in the Member State which seems appropriate in the interests of efficient administration of justice. In practice this means the Member State where the greater part of the evidence is found, or the State of residence or of nationality of the accused or the State where the economic impact of the offence is the greatest.

Appeals can be heard in a higher court of the Member State, which is duty bound to apply the rules contained in the CJ. Appeal is also open to the EPP. In the case of appeal by a convicted person, the court seized may not pronounce a stiffer penalty. Article 28 governs appeals to the European Court of Justice. The ECJ can rule on preliminary questions of the CJ and any of its application measures. Upon the request of a Member State or the Commission it can also rule on any dispute concerning the application of the CJ. Lastly it can rule on conflicts of jurisdiction if the EPP or a national authority requests it.

Part 6 (Articles 29 to 33) lays down the rights of the accused, and rules for the admissibility of evidence. The accused enjoys the rights of the defence guaranteed under Article 6 ECHR, including the right to remain silent (Article 29). The Commission (in this instance 'the victim') may constitute itself '*partie civile*' before the competent judge. As such, it entitled to the rights and prerogatives of a party to the proceedings (Article 30). No person is obliged to actively contribute, directly or indirectly, in establishing his own guilt (Article 31). Admissible evidence is defined as: (a) direct testimony, or testimony presented through an audiovisual link, (b) a European interrogation report, (c) statements made by the accused, (d) accounts, (e) documents produced during the investigation. These forms of evidence do not exclude the validity of other forms of evidence considered as admissible under the national law in force in the State of the court of judgment (Article 32). This, admittedly, constitutes a comprehensive definition of evidence, which should allow for any national idiosyncrasy. Finally Article 33 lays down rules for the exclusion of evidence, and Article 34 for publicity and secrecy. Investigations carried out under the authority of the EPP are secret; a hearing before the judge of freedoms may be published if all parties consent to it; the judgment must be given publicly, although access to the court may be denied to the press and the public under the conditions stipulated in Article 6(1) ECHR.

Part 7 (Article 35) defines the subsidiary role of national law in relation to the CJ: the *lex fori* would apply whenever the CJ fails to provide rules. Clearly the implementation of the CJ would require a major adjustment in the Member States. Can it be more than an idea?

3. CAN THE *CORPUS JURIS* BE MORE THAN AN IDEA?

The CJ has been welcomed by some key European *pénalistes* whose main concern is of course, efficient repression of crimes affecting the EC budget. Such a body of rules is meant to supplement, and not replace, existing provisions. Further diversification, or creative use of the legal space can therefore be envisaged.

3.1. Legal Basis: Discussion

The CJ aims to establish a centralized repressive system, with prescribed penalties (including prison sentences) applying throughout the Union. Thus it appears that the CJ would be a major break with the approach hitherto adopted, rather than a small step away from harmonization, as Delmas-Marty has argued.[19]

Furthermore, it is difficult to see how it might fit into the present legal architecture.

In a video-linked conference between ALPFIEC and the European Commission, which took place on 16 January 1997, the author had the opportunity to ask the Commission representative what legal basis was envisaged for the CJ, and whether the Commission had hitherto received any reaction for the CJ from any the Member States' executives. The response was that the Commission felt that the CJ could be adopted under Articles 100a/189b, which together allow for the adoption of measures for the approximation of laws, and with the aim of establishing the internal market, by a qualified majority and with the fullest available participation of the European Parliament. It was too early for detailed responses from the Member States' executives.

The suggestion that any instrument to protect the financial interests of the Communities should be placed under the first pillar should not unduly surprise. The Commission is only reiterating its well-rehearsed argument that matters relating to Community finances should be taken under the Community pillar. The argument that such a measure should be taken by qualified majority is a recognition that it is controversial, and therefore likely to be blocked should unanimity be required, for example under Article 235 EC.

Council Directives which aim to harmonize rules in order to prevent financial and other crimes in the internal market environment have already been adopted under Article 100a. For example Council Directives 91/308[20] on money laundering, 92/109[21] on precursors, 89/595[22] on insider dealing all have Article 100a either as a sole legal basis, or as a conjoint legal basis with another article. What these directives have in common is that, although penal measures may be mentioned in their preambles, they do not figure in the texts of the directives proper, which however refer to 'prohibitions', 'penalties' requiring Member States to 'take appropriate measures' in order to prevent criminal opportunities from being created

---

19. *See* introduction to the CJ.
20. [1991] O.J. L166/77 (Money Laundering Directive).
21. [1989] O.J. L370/76 (Precursors Directive).
22. [1989] O.J. L334/30 (Insider Dealing Directive).

through the internal market. However, the word 'penal' seems to have been banished from qualified majority first pillar instruments so far, so the ambition to introduce a veritable *tranche* of penal measures, as represented by the CJ, is a very considerable ambition.

3.2. Specificity of the *Corpus Juris*

An issue arises in relation to the specificity of the CJ. The CJ is aimed specifically at the protection of the financial interests of the European Community. But it is suggested, in the introduction of the CJ itself, that its innovatory character makes it a suitable prototype for exploring the possibilities of centralizing prosecutions in areas other than those concerned with the protection of the financial interests of the European Communities. For example, the argument that harmonization of criminal law has failed to protect the interests of European Union economic interests could, in the view of the author, be extended to several other areas, such as the smuggling of radio-active waste, drugs, trans-national environmental crimes, all of which damage EU economic and wider interests. So far, there has been little discussion of the possibilities of creating supranational jurisdiction in order to deal with 'pan-EU' crimes more efficiently. In fact, hitherto, supranational jurisdictions have been restricted to the 'big issues' of war crimes and human rights. From this perspective, the CJ would, if implemented, represent a major cultural shift in legal thinking.

Chapter 9. The Treaty of Amsterdam: Post-IGC Considerations

In this penultimate chapter, the author gives an overview of the amendments to the Treaties agreed in Amsterdam in June 1997 and discusses their impact on the EU legal environment, in as much as they are relevant. Some 'grand themes' of the Treaty (flexibility, transparency, subsidiarity) are considered first, followed by changes in the Community and in the Justice and Internal Affairs spheres. This is followed by an account of the changes affecting the institutions more directly. A discussion follows on implications of the above changes for the construction of the European Legal Space in anticipation of the next enlargement. Whenever possible, the new numbering found in the consolidated version of the Treaty is given.

1. FLEXIBILITY, TRANSPARENCY, SUBSIDIARITY

Progress has been made in relation to three of the 'grand themes' of the IGC. The Amsterdam amendments to the Treaties anticipate enlargement and introduce flexibility, in areas where both the Member States and the Community have competence to act.[1] Measures on transparency have been included in the amendments, and the principle of subsidiarity has been tightened in a protocol.

1.1. Flexibility

In the draft Treaty of Amsterdam, an article on closer cooperation or 'flexibility' amends the general clauses of the Treaty. Member States intending to establish closer cooperation between them may make use of the institutions, procedures and mechanisms laid down by the Treaties, provided that the intended cooperation:

(a) is aimed at furthering the objectives of the Union and protecting and serving its interests;
(b) respects the principles of the Treaties and the single institutional framework of the Union;
(c) is only used as a last resort, where the objectives of the Treaties could not be attained by applying the relevant procedures laid down therein;
(d) concerns at least a majority of Member States;

---

1. Article 11 of the consolidated Treaty of Amsterdam, signed on 2 October 1997.

(e) does not affect the *acquis communautaire* and the measures adopted under the other provisions of the Treaties;

(f) does not affect the competencies, rights, obligations and interests of those Member States which do not participate in the arrangement;

(g) is open to all Member States and allows them to become parties to the cooperation at any time, provided that they comply with the basic decision and with decisions within that framework;

(h) firstly complies with the specific additional criteria laid down in Article 11 (previously Article 5a) of the TEC and Article 40 (previously Article K.12) of the Treaty, depending on the area concerned and secondly is authorized by the Council (in accordance with a prescribed procedure laid down in the Treaties).

These basic flexibility requirements would appear to apply both to the Community, and the Justice and Internal Affairs spheres, where measures for the protection of the financial interests of the European Communities can be found.

1.2. Transparency

The second protocol of Article A has been amended and now states that decisions must be taken as openly as possible. A new Article 255 (previously Article 191a) has been inserted, requiring the EP, Council and Commission to elaborate, in their own rules of procedure, specific provisions regarding access to documents. Public access to documents has in the past been hindered, and the Ombudsman has dealt with many complaints in relation to the Council and its third pillar activities. Article 207(3) (previously Article 151(3)) has been amended in order to apply Article 255(3). The Article now requires the Council to elaborate, in its Rules of Procedure, the conditions under which the public can have access to Council documents. Greater public access to documents is envisaged, particularly in cases when the Council is acting in its legislative capacity. Article 207(3) states that in any event, when the Council acts in its legislative capacity, the results of votes and minutes must be made public.

1.3. Subsidiarity

A protocol on the application of the principle of subsidiarity and proportionality has been added to the Treaty. It states that for any proposed legislation, the reasons on which it is based must be stated with a view to ensuring that it complies with principles of subsidiarity and proportionality. The reasons for concluding that a Community objective can be better achieved by the Community must be substantiated by qualitative, or wherever possible, by quantitative indicators.

For Community action to be justified, both aspects of the subsidiarity principle must be met:

(a) the objectives of the proposed action is such that they cannot be sufficiently achieved by Member States' action in the framework of the national constitutional

system (for example if the issue under consideration has transnational aspects which cannot be satisfactorily regulated by action by Member States); and
(b) the objectives can be better achieved by action on the part of the Community.

The protocol also states that directives should be preferred to regulations, and framework decisions (the new third pillar 'directives') preferred to detailed measures. It goes on to say that the Community must legislate only to the extent necessary and as much scope as possible should be left to national authorities. Whilst respecting Community law, care should be taken to respect established national arrangements and the organization and working of Member States' legal systems.

2. THE COMMUNITY SPHERE

Noteworthy changes in the Community sphere have included the rewording of Article 280 (previously Article 209a) (2.1.), a new article concerning customs cooperation (2.2.); the opening of new possibilities with the introduction of a new title (2.3.); and more specific changes affecting the powers and duties of the institutions (2.4.). Lastly, a summary of changes is offered (2.5.).

2.1. Article 280

Article 280, introduced by the Maastricht Treaty, has proved disappointing. Firstly the principle of assimilation it contains has been described as largely ineffective (*see* Chapter 8). Secondly it has never been used as a legal basis. The Amsterdam amendments have tackled both issues.

2.1.1. Assimilation Reinforced

The new Article 280(1) and (2) requires the measures taken by the Member States to counter fraud and other illegal activities not only to be assimilated to national measures, but also to act as deterrent and to be such as to afford effective protection in the Member States. This requirement constitutes a logical progression, since it was already established by the jurisprudence of the European Court of Justice. Article 280(3) replaces the second paragraph of Article 209a, and continues to require the Member States to coordinate their action aimed at protecting the financial interests of the Community against fraud by organizing, together with the Commission, close and regular cooperation between the competent authorities.

2.1.2. Qualified Majority for Anti-fraud Legislation

The main change to Article 280 is contained in paragraph (4). It empowers the Council to adopt the necessary measures 'in the fields of the prevention of and fight against fraud affecting the financial interests of the Community with a view to affording effective and equivalent protection in the Member States', by acting in accordance with the procedure in Article 251 (previously Article 189b). Such measures must not concern the application of national criminal law and the national administration of justice. This creates a new legal basis for Community anti-fraud measures, to be taken on QMV and with the fullest participation of the EP, whilst respecting sovereign sensitivities. The Commission and the EP, however, had hoped that measures concerning national criminal laws would not be excluded.

2.1.3. Monitoring of Article 280

The Commission, in cooperation with the Member States, now has the duty to submit to the Council and the EP a report on the measures taken for the implementation of this article. This monitoring, provided for in the fifth paragraph of the amended article, should enable progress to be gauged annually.

2.2. Customs Cooperation

Newly inserted Article 135 requires the Council to take measures to strengthen customs cooperation. Again, such measures must not concern the application of national criminal law and the administration of justice. Given that this requirement is fulfilled, the Council may act in accordance with the procedure referred to in Article 251.

2.3 Flexibility and the New Title

The Amsterdam amendments to the Treaty introduce a title on freedom, security and justice, in which the free movement of persons is assure in conjunction with appropriate measures with respect to external border controls, immigration, asylum and the prevention and combatting of crime.[2]
Closer cooperation is possible, provided that the cooperation proposed:

(a) does not concern areas which fall within the exclusive competence of the Community;
(b) does not affect Community policies, actions or programmes;
(c) does not concern the citizenship of the Union or discriminate between nationals of Member States;
(d) remains within the limits of the powers conferred upon the Community by this Treaty;
(e) and does not constitute a discrimination or a restriction on trade between Member States and does not distort the conditions of competition between the latter.

---

2. Title IV on visas, asylum, immigration and other policies related to the free movement of persons.

This new title makes provisions for cooperation in civil and administrative matters. Its Article 61(c) and (d) provide that in order to establish an area of freedom, security and justice, the Council shall adopt measures in the field of judicial cooperation and appropriate measures to encourage and strengthen administrative cooperation. Article 65, inserted in the new title on free movement of persons, asylum and immigration replaces a previous mention in the third pillar under Article K.1(6). It provides, *inter alia*, for the possibility of taking measures to eliminate obstacles to the good functioning of civil proceedings by promoting the compatibility of the rules of civil procedure applicable in the Member States. Under Article 66, measures to ensure cooperation between the relevant departments of the administrations of the Member States, as well as between those departments and the Commission, can be taken by the Council.

Measures under Articles E and F must be taken in accordance with Article G, which requires unanimity to be maintained for a transitional period of five years (i.e. until 2004). The unanimity requirement will thereafter be reconsidered by the Council. After consulting the EP, the Council will have to decide whether it wants to make all or part of the areas covered in the title subject to the procedure referred to in Article 251. So it seems that QMV has, for all intents and purposes, been postponed indefinitely for measures harmonizing administrative and civil laws, and with an affinity with the new title.

2.4. Summary and Commentary

In 1999, after the entry into force of the Amsterdam amendments to the Treaties, Article 280(4) is to be used in conjunction with Article 251 to take Community measures to fight fraud and other illegal activities, as long as such measures do not concern criminal law and the administration of justice in the Member States. A new article on customs cooperation, also to be used in conjunction with Article 251, contains the same prerequisite. Remembering that both the 'PIF' Regulation and the on-the-spot checks regulation both had to be adopted under Article 308 (previously Article 235) by unanimity, and after an opinion from the EP (but without the ECA being consulted), the new Article 280 must constitute progress in the sense that it will make it possible to adopt anti-fraud measures more expeditiously under QMV, and with a fuller participation of the EP and after the ECA has been consulted.

3. JUSTICE AND INTERNAL AFFAIRS SPHERE

The requirement for an unanimous vote by the Council, the lack of involvement by the EP in the legislative process, the lack of enforceability and snail-paced ratification have often been described as impediments to the construction of an effective and democratic European legal space (*see* previous chapter). Three of these criticisms have been addressed in the amended Treaty. Flexibility has also been added as an option.

The stated aims of cooperation in Justice and Internal Affairs are expressed in Article 31 (previously Article K.3). New instruments are outlined in Article 34 (previously Article K.6) and comprise common positions, framework decisions, decisions and conventions.

3.1. Enforceability

Framework decisions are to be taken for the purpose of approximating the laws and regulations of the Member States, are binding on the Member States as to the results to be achieved, although they do not entail direct effect. Decisions which are aimed at measures which exclude the approximation of laws, are to be binding, although like framework decisions, they do not entail direct effect. Through Article 35(6) (previously Article K.7(6)) the ECJ has acquired jurisdiction over both types of instruments.

3.2. Involvement of the European Parliament

The EP must be consulted in relation to framework decisions, decisions and conventions (Article 39, previously Article K.11). Its opinion must be delivered within a three-month time limit.

3.3. Council: Voting Requirements

All instruments are to be adopted by the Council acting unanimously, although measures necessary to implement decisions and conventions are to be adopted by a majority of two thirds.

3.4. Speeding Up Ratification

In the draft Treaty, conventions are to enter into force as soon as they have been adopted by two thirds of the contracting parties.

3.5. Flexibility

Article 40 (previously Article K.12) introduces flexibility in Justice and Internal Affairs by stating that Member States which intend to establish closer cooperation between themselves may be authorized to make use of the institutions, procedures and mechanisms laid down by the Treaties to enhance cooperation. The authorization in question is granted by the Council upon a qualified majority vote, at the request of the Member States concerned. If a Member State has an objection to QMV, the matter can be referred to the Council for decision by unanimity.

4. IMPACT OF AMSTERDAM ON THE INSTITUTIONS

Amendments to the Treaties relating to the composition and organization of the institutions have been omitted from this section. Other changes which potentially have a more direct impact on the protection of the financial interests of the European Union are outlined below.

4.1. The European Court of Auditors (ECA)

The ECA sees its role as an institution consolidated and widened. This is done by requiring the ECA to be consulted under Article 280, by including the ECA in provisions where other European institutions are mentioned, by giving the Statement of Assurance a role in the discharge of the budget, by expanding the powers of the ECA to carry out on-the-spot audit checks and by improving its access to documents.

4.1.1. Automatic Consultation

In its pre-IGC report, the ECA requested that it should automatically be consulted at the drafting stage of relevant legislation, and it deplored the fact that it had not been consulted with respect to the 'PIF' Regulation in 1995. Following the Amsterdam amendments, the ECA will have to be consulted whenever Articles 280/251 are used as a conjoint legal basis for measures in the fields of the prevention and of fight against fraud affecting the financial interests of the Community.

4.1.2. Inclusion of the ECA in Provisions of the Treaties Relating to the Powers and Duties of the Institutions

Article 5 (previously Article E), which requires the institutions to exercise their powers under the conditions and for the purposes provided for by the Treaties, has been amended to include the ECA. This has the effect of acknowledging its extended role in auditing expenditure under the second and the third pillar. The ECA has also been added to Article 173 EC. The ECA can now protect its prerogatives in the same way as the European Parliament, Council, Commission and the European Central Bank (ECB) have done hitherto.

4.1.3. The Statement of Assurance (SoA)

Under the amended Article 248(1) (previously Article 188c(1)) second paragraph, the SoA, which is produced annually by the ECA, must now be published in the *Official Journal*. Furthermore the SoA has been added to Article 276(1) (previously Article 206(1)) of the Treaty, which means that it must now be examined by the European Parliament, together with the annual report of the ECA and any special reports from the ECA, in the process leading to the granting of a discharge to the Commission in respect of the implementation of the budget.

4.1.4. On-the-spot Audit Checks

The powers of the ECA to carry on checks has been expanded. The ECA can now carry out checks 'on the premises of any body which manages revenue or expenditure on behalf of the Community ... including on the premises of any natural or legal person in receipt of payments from the budget'.[3] Furthermore, the national audit bodies of the Member States now have to cooperate in a 'spirit of trust' with the ECA, whilst maintaining their independence.

4.1.5. Access to Records

Under the new Article 248(3) (previously Article 188c(3)), second paragraph, the duty to forward to the ECA, at its request, any document or information necessary to carry out its tasks now extends not only to other institutions of the Community and the national audit bodies, but also to any bodies managing revenue or expenditure on behalf of the Community, and any natural or legal person in receipt of any payment from the budget. Furthermore, an additional paragraph has been added to Article 188c(3), which states that in respect of the EIB's activity in managing Community expenditure and revenue, the ECA's rights of access to information held by the Bank shall be governed by an agreement between the ECA, the Bank and the Commission. In the absence of an agreement, the ECA must nevertheless have access to information necessary for the audit of Community expenditure and revenue managed by the Bank.

The request of the ECA to play an investigative role in disciplinary proceedings appears not to have been heeded. It must also be noted that the ECA has not been included in the new Article 255. Bearing in mind that not all the special reports of the ECA are published, this seems an unfortunate oversight.

4.2. The European Court of Justice (ECJ)

Article 46 (previously Article L) has now been amended to give the ECJ jurisdiction to rule in disputes arising from Title VI provisions, under the provisions provided by Article 35 (previously Article K.7).

The Maastricht Treaty only provided the possibility for conventions to confer on the ECJ the jurisdiction to interpret provisions and to rule on any disputes regarding their application, in accordance with such arrangements as they may lay down.[4] The Jurisdiction of the ECJ in Title VI has hitherto remained controversial, and has caused considerable delays.

---

3. Article 248(3), previously Article 188c(3) first paragraph, Draft Treaty of Amsterdam.
4. Article 30, previously Article K.3(2)(c) third paragraph of draft Treaty of Amsterdam, *op. cit.*

The consolidated Amsterdam Treaty states that the ECJ is to have no jurisdiction to review the validity or proportionality of operations carried out by the police or other law enforcement agencies in the Member States.[5] However, the ECJ would have jurisdiction to review the legality of framework decisions[6] and decisions in actions brought by a Member State or the Commission on the usual grounds. The ECJ also has jurisdiction to rule on disputes between Member States regarding the interpretation or the application of acts adopted under Article 34.[7] The Court will also have jurisdiction to rule on any dispute between the Member States and the Commission regarding the interpretation or the application of conventions established under Article K.6(2)(b).

4.3. The Commission

The first paragraph of Article 205 (previously Article 148) has been amended and now requires Member States to cooperate with the Commission to ensure that the budget appropriations are used in accordance with the principles of sound financial management. In its pre-IGC report, the Commission had deplored the fact that although it had a duty to safeguard EC finances, only the Member States were in a position to do so. The amended Article 205 goes some way towards addressing this conundrum.

4.4. The Council

The use of qualified majority voting has now been extended to some existing and to some new provisions. Two are of particular interest. The first is Article 280, which has been amended extensively, and the second is a new article on customs cooperation, Article 135. Another important amendment relates to public access to Council documents, where Article 207(3) has been amended in order to apply the new Article 255(3).

4.5. The European Parliament

The role of the EP has been increased in the Community sphere (*see* Article 280, for example), but it is also set to acquire a role in Justice and Internal Affairs. Article 39(2) (previously Article K.11(2)) places a duty on the presidency of the Council and the Commission to inform the EP regularly of discussion in the areas of Justice and Home Affairs. Lastly, according to Article 39(3) (previously Article

---

5. Article 35(5), previously Article K.7(5).
6. Article 34 provides for the adoption, under unanimity, of framework decisions for the purpose of approximation of the laws and regulations of the Member States.
7. (a) common positions; (b) framework decisions which are binding as to the result to be achieved; (c) decisions which are binding but do not entail direct effect; (d) conventions which enter into force once adopted by at least half the Member States, their implementing measures being adopted by a majority of two thirds.

K.11(3)), the EP may ask questions of the Council or make recommendations to it. Furthermore the EP must hold an annual debate on the progress made in Justice and Internal Affairs.

5. DISCUSSION: IMPACT ON THE EUROPEAN LEGAL SPACE

As far as the amendments of the draft Amsterdam Treaty are concerned, which impact on the protection of the financial interests of the European Union, and the construction of the legal space, the results of the IGC can only be described as mixed.

One welcomes amendments concerned with the powers and duties of the ECA, the increased involvement of the EP in the first and third pillar (which can only increase the legitimacy of anti-fraud measures), the introduction of QMV for certain anti-fraud measures and for customs cooperation. Greater transparency (in the third pillar in particular!) is very much welcomed.

But the draft revisions merit closer, and more critical scrutiny.

Firstly, the principle of 'flexibility' is interesting, but as stated in 1.1., it is only to be used as a last resort, where the objectives of the Treaties cannot be achieved any other way. In any case such an approach seems inappropriate for the protection of the budget – since what is required, for the sake of effectiveness, is that all economic operators receive equal treatment across the European Union.

Secondly, unanimity remains in key areas. This is the case in Justice and Internal Affairs, in spite of the qualitative changes related earlier. Unanimity may also lead to slow progress within the new title, in the field of cooperation in civil and administrative matters.

Thirdly, its seems that it may prove easier, in the period after 1999, to agree measures to combat fraud under the new Article 280, and to enhance customs cooperation under the new article – but only if these measures do not concern the application of national law and the national administration of justice. This proviso has the effect of limiting the scope of Article 280 in particular, and appears to rule it out as a legal basis for the Corpus Juris.[8]

Community measures to fight fraud will also have to abide with the newly-worded principle of subsidiarity, which introduces very stringent tests for the legislator to satisfy.

These difficulties are not unsurmountable but they are certainly challenging. Challenging, too, is the increasing complexity of the legal space, which makes the need for a well-articulated anti-fraud strategy paramount.

Have the amendments to the Treaties given us the tools to protect the budget after enlargement? In Chapter 7, I envisaged three enlargement 'scenarios': firstly, the possibility of a classical membership enlargement; secondly, a partial membership enlargement, and thirdly the possibility of a 'mixed membership' enlargement, which may cause the most problems in protecting common funds. With classical enlargement, which implies full membership, measures to protect the budget are

---

8. *But see* K. Tiedemann, 'Pour un espace juridique commun après Amsterdam' (1997) *AGON* number 17, pp. 12–13.

taken on gradually, as part of the *acquis* and according to a timetable. This means that all measures to protect the budget are adopted *en bloc* by the new entrants. Partial membership, in contrast, might call for flexible arrangements in areas covered by the membership only. A mixed membership might cause the most problems, since a complex reorganization of funds, involving parallel systems, would open the need for parallel and substantively distinct EU legislation to protect the tax payer. This in turn might lead to anomalies and delays, and to an (even more) uneven control space.

The increased complexity of the new legal space, and the unsuitability of 'flexible' arrangements to give a satisfactory answer to the protection of the budget after enlargement, will no doubt reinforce the view held in some quarters that the Corpus Juris, should an acceptable legal basis be found, could be the only solution to a fair and effective protection of the budget. Indeed the relative simplicity of the Corpus Juris might also appeal. To adopt this view, however, would represent a tilt towards a predominantly repressive approach, by means of criminal law. Such an approach to financial crime, it must be remembered, is not universally recognized as effective.

Conclusion

From the institutional point of view, the protection of the financial interests of the European Communities is one area where the European Court of Justice cannot be accused of activism, but where the interests of the European Parliament and of the Commission have fruitfully coincided in the 1990s. Provoked by the powerful duo, the Council has acted, albeit slowly, due to the requirement for unanimity that anti-fraud measures usually demand.

The author argues that economically and fiscally radical approaches which focus on reducing opportunities for fraud and corruption should be prioritized. This means, first and foremost, completing the internal market. In this the proper implementation of Article 99 EC could go some way towards reducing opportunities for crime. A structural approach to the protection of VAT resources, for example, must include a move to the definitive system, together with further harmonization of indirect taxation. The persisting disparities in excise rates, although not having a direct effect on Community finance, encourage a black market in sensitive products, which in turn undermines EC income.

As far as import duties are concerned, the whole of which accrue to the budget, 'europeanizing' national Customs authorities by increasing their identification with the task of collecting common revenue might seem an important step. This could go some way towards ensuring that Customs' powers of deterrence are restored in the internal market environment, and beyond. In these areas of the budget (VAT, import duties), where the Member States exercise their sovereign tax-raising powers, the penetrating powers of the Commission to perform inspections are likely to be resented, and constructive but relatively hands-off approaches need to be prioritized at Community-level.

On the expenditure side of the budget, the enforcement space remains very uneven, with most checks and inspections falling on to the EAGGF Guarantee Section, and most anti-fraud appropriations spent there too. The Structural Funds remain fairly un-policed, and the Member States tend to escape financial liability for the misappropriation of funds. This is worrying in view of the plan which has been mooted of giving Structural Funds an enhanced role in the future, and a larger share of the budget, in anticipation of the next wave of enlargement. The type of Structural Funds held to be best suited for the post-1999 period are transnational Community initiatives. Transnational initiatives seem to have been particularly vulnerable to fraud in the past, and to increase their use would in turn entail new legislation and more work for (an enlarged?) UCLAF, whose job it is to coordinate trans-national investigations. Any such move (towards more Structural Funds of a transnational nature), the author believes, should be accompanied beforehand by an American-style multi-disciplinary 'Criminal Impact Assessment', to which the

European Court of Auditors could be a major contributor. That way, criminogenic schemes could be detected *in utero*, and either avoided altogether or re-drafted to reduce the obvious (or less obvious) opportunities for crime they create.

Tighter financial accountability and a credible anti-corruption strategy could help achieve some protection of vulnerable sectors, such as procurement expenditure. A credible anti-corruption strategy, however, means paying attention to the role of political corruption as well as corruption involving *fonctionnaires*, confronting squarely the issue of immunities and of financial liability, as well as generally dealing with the wider international and organized crime dimensions of this phenomenon. Riding on the political impetus to consolidate the European Project prior to monetary union, and looking back at the amount of creative law-making that has already occurred to protect the budget, further progress should be possible.

It has not been the objective of this work to address 'pillars' questions. Nevertheless it is to be hoped that the in-depth understanding offered here of Community control in the protection of the financial interests of the European Communities will contribute to the wider debate on crime in the Union. The danger of white-collar crime, flourishing in the 'grey zone' where otherwise legal and unambiguously criminal activities occur, must be more effectively addressed. More can be done at Community level to reduce the opportunities for a rise in crime that too easily could swamp third pillar action. It is in this wider context that the Corpus Juris represents the most ambitious attempt to deepen the legal space. That level of ambition is both its great virtue and its potential Achilles' heel. The draft Treaty of Amsterdam brings improvements, but also increased complexity to a European Legal Space where Member States seem determined to safeguard their sovereignties in the area of criminal law and criminal procedure.

In conclusion, it is maintained that the interests of the European tax payer and citizen could be served by greater economic and fiscal integration. Necessary measures include the completion of the internal market and the integration of Customs forces. In other words, the centre of gravity for effective action should be economic and fiscal radicalism in the classical, Treaty of Rome tradition, without which the criminal law radicalism epitomized in the Corpus Juris would be icing without any cake.

APPENDICES

Appendix A. Glossary of Terms and Abbreviations

CAP	Common Agricultural Policy
CCC	Community Customs Code
CCEEs	Countries of Central and Eastern Europe
CCT	Common Customs Tariff
CEMA	Customs and Excise Management Act
CFSP	Common Foreign and Security Policy
CIS	Customs Information System
CJ	Corpus Juris
COCOLAF	Comité Consultatif pour la coordination dans le domaine de la lutte Anti-Fraude (French acronym), in English: Advisory committee for the coordination of fraud prevention
CPS	Crown Prosecution Service
CFS	Community Support Framework
DPP	Director of Public Prosecution
DTI	Department of Trade and Industry
EAGGF	European Guarantee and Guidance Fund
EC	European Community (term used since the entry into force of the treaty on European Union)
ECJ	European Court of Justice
ECU	European Currency Unit
EIB	European Investment Bank
EDF	European Development Fund
EFTA	European Free Trade Association
EP	European Parliament
ESF	European Social Fund
EUA	European Unit of Account
FIFG	Financial Instrument for Fisheries Guidance
FCPC	Foreign Corrupt Practices Act (US)
GATT	General Agreement on Tariffs and Trade
GNP	Gross National Product
GSP	Generalized System of Preferences
IACS	Integrated Administrative and Control System
IBAP	Intervention Board in Agricultural Products
IGC	Intergovernmental Conference
IRENE	Irrégularités, Enquêtes, Exploitation – Irregularities, Investigations, Exploitation
IRU	International Road Transport Union
JHA	Justice and Home Affairs
MAFF	Ministry for Agriculture Fisheries and Food
MPE	Ministère Public Européen: European Prosecution Service

OJ	*Official Journal of the European Communities* (O.J. L: series L, legislation; O.J. C: series C, communications)
OOPEC	Office of the Official Publications of the European Communities
'PIF'	Protection des intérêts financiers de la communauté; in English protection of the financial interests of the European Communities
SAD	Single Administrative Document
SCENT	System for a Customs Enforcement NeTwork
SEM 2000	Programme to improve financial management launched by the Commission in 1995. Its full name is Sound and Efficient Financial Management, SEM 2000
SFO	Serious Fraud Office
SME	Small and medium sized enterprise
SOA	Statement of Assurance
SOID	Scottish Office Industry Department
SPD	Single Programming Document
TCI	Temporary Committee of Inquiry
TECA	Trade and Economic Cooperation Agreement
TIR	Transport International Routier – in English International Road Transport
TPCC	Trade Promotion Co-ordinating Committee
UA	Unit of Account
UCLAF	Coordinating unit for the fight against fraud
VAS	Verification and Audit Section
VAT	Value Added Tax
WTO	World Trade Organization

Appendix B. Council Regulation 2988/95

Council Regulation 2988/95 of 18 December 1995 on the protection of the European Communities' financial interests, O.J. (1995) L 312/1.

THE COUNCIL OF THE EUROPEAN UNION,

Having regard to the Treaty establishing the European Community, and in particular Article 235 thereof,

Having regard to the Treaty establishing the European Atomic Energy Community, and in particular Article 203 thereof,

Having regard to the proposal from the Commission,[1]

Having regard to the opinion of the European Parliament,[2]

Whereas the general budget of the European Communities is financed by own resources and administered by the Commission within the limit of the appropriations authorized and in accordance with the principle of sound financial management; whereas the Commission works in loose cooperation with the Member States to that end;

Whereas more than half the Community expenditure is paid to beneficiaries through the intermediary of the Member States;

Whereas detailed rules governing this decentralized administration and the monitoring of their use are the subject of differing detailed provisions according to the Community policies concerned; whereas acts detrimental to the Communities' financial interests must, however, be countered in all areas;

Whereas the effectiveness of the combating of fraud against the Communities' financial interests calls for a common set of legal rules to be enacted for all areas covered by Community policies;

Whereas irregular conduct, and the administrative measures and penalties relating thereto, are provided for in sectoral rules in accordance with this Regulation;

Whereas the aforementioned conduct includes fraudulent actions as defined in the Convention on the protection of the European Communities' financial interests;

Whereas Community administrative penalties must provide protection for the said interests; whereas it is necessary to define general rules applicable to these penalties;

Whereas Community law has established Community administrative penalties in the framework of the common agricultural policy; whereas such penalties must be established in other fields as well;

---

1. O.J. No. C 216, 6.8.1994, p. 11.
2. O.J. No. C 89, 10.4.1995, p. 83 and opinion delivered on 30 November 1995 (not yet published in the *Official Journal*).

Whereas Community measures and penalties laid down in pursuance of the objectives of the common agricultural policy form an integral part of the aid systems; whereas they pursue their own ends which do not affect the assessment of the conduct of the economic operators concerned by the competent authorities of the Member States from the point of view of criminal law; whereas the effectiveness must be ensured by the immediate effect of Community rules and by applying in full Community measures as a whole, where the adoption of preventive measures has not made it possible to achieve that objective;

Whereas not only under the general principle of equity and the principle of proportionality but also in the light of the principle of *ne bis in idem*, appropriate provisions must be adopted while respecting the *acquis communautaire* and the provisions laid down in specific Community rules existing at the time of entry into force of this Regulation, to prevent any overlap of Community financial penalties imposed on the same persons for the same reasons;

Whereas, for the purposes of applying this Regulation, criminal proceedings may be regarded as having been completed where the competent national authority and the person concerned come to an arrangement;

Whereas this Regulation will apply without prejudice to the application of the Member States' criminal law;

Whereas Community law imposes on the Commission and the Member States an obligation to check that Community budget resources are used for their intended purpose; whereas there is a need for common rules to supplement existing provisions;

Whereas the Treaties make no provision for the specific powers necessary for the adoption of substantive law of horizontal scope on checks, measures and penalties with a view to ensuring the protection of the Communities' financial interests; whereas recourse should therefore be had to Article 235 of the EC Treaty and to Article 203 of the EAEC Treaty;

Whereas additional general provisions relating to checks and inspections on the spot will be adopted at a later stage,

HAS ADOPTED THIS REGULATION:

TITLE I
General principles

Article 1

1. For the purposes of protecting the European Communities' financial interests, general rules are hereby adopted relating to homogenous checks and to administrative measures and penalties concerning irregularities with regard to Community law.

2. 'Irregularity' shall mean any infringement of the provisions of Community law resulting from an act or omission by an economic operator, which has, or would have, the effect of prejudicing the general budget of the Communities or budgets managed by them, either by reducing or losing revenue accruing from own resources collected directly on behalf of the Communities, or by an unjustified item of expenditure.

Article 2

1. Administrative checks, measures and penalties shall be introduced in so far as they are necessary to ensure the proper application of Community law. They shall be effective, proportionate and dissuasive so that they provide adequate protection for the Communities' financial interests.

2. No administrative penalty may be imposed unless a Community act prior to the irregularity has made provision for it. In the event of a subsequent amendment of the provisions which impose administrative penalties and are contained in Community rules, the less severe provisions shall apply retroactively.

3. Community law shall determine the nature and scope of administrative measures and penalties necessary for the correct application of the rules in question, having regard to the nature and seriousness of the irregularity, the advantage granted or received and the degree of responsibility.

4. Subject to the Community law applicable, the procedures for the application of Community checks, measures and penalties shall be governed by the laws of the Member States.

Article 3

1. The limitation period for proceedings shall be four years as from the time when the irregularity referred to in Article 1(1) was committed. However, the sectoral rules may make provision for a shorter period which may not be less than three years.

In the case of continuous or repeated irregularities, the limitation period shall run from the day on which the irregularity ceases. In the case of multiannual programmes, the limitation period shall in any case run until the programme is definitely terminated.

The limitation period shall be interrupted by any act of the competent authority, notified to the person in question, relating to investigation or legal proceedings concerning the irregularity. The limitation period shall start again following each interrupting act.

However, limitation shall become effective at the latest on the day on which a period equal to twice the limitation period expires without the competent authority having imposed a penalty, except where the administrative procedure has been suspended in accordance with Article 6(1).

2. The period for implementing the decision establishing the administrative penalty shall be three years. That period shall run from the day on which the decision becomes final.

Instances of interruption and suspension shall be governed by the relevant provisions of national law.

3. Member States shall retain the possibility of applying a period which is longer than that provided for in paragraphs 1 and 2 respectively.

TITLE II
Administrative measures and penalties

Article 4

1. As a general rule, any irregularity shall involve withdrawal of the wrongly obtained advantage:
   – by an obligation to pay or repay the amounts due or wrongly received,
   – by the total or partial loss of the security provided in support of the request for an advantage granted or at the time of the receipt of an advance.

2. Application of the measures referred to in paragraph 1 shall be limited to the withdrawal of the advantage obtained plus, where so provided for, interest which may be determined on a flat-rate basis.

3. Acts which are established to have as their purpose the obtaining of an advantage contrary to the objectives of the Community law applicable in the case by artificially creating the conditions required for obtaining that advantage shall result, as the case shall be, either in the failure to obtain the advantage or in its withdrawal.

4. The measures provided for in this Article shall not be regarded as penalties.

Article 5

1. Intentional irregularities or those caused by negligence may lead to the following penalties:
(a) payment of an administrative fine;
(b) payment of an amount greater than the amounts wrongly received or evaded, plus interest where appropriate; this additional sum shall be determined in accordance with a percentage to be set in the specific rules, and may not exceed the level strictly necessary to constitute a deterrent;
(c) total or partial removal of an advantage granted by Community rules, even if the operator wrongly benefitted from only a part of that advantage;
(d) exclusion from, or withdrawal of, the advantage for a period subsequent to that of the irregularity;
(e) temporary withdrawal of the approval or recognition necessary for participation in a Community aid scheme;
(f) the loss of a security or deposit provided for the purpose of complying with the conditions laid down by rules or the replenishment of the amount of a security wrongly released;
(g) other penalties of a purely economic type, equivalent in nature and scope, provided for in the sectoral rules adopted by the Council in the light of the specific requirements of the sectoral rules adopted by the Council in the light of the specific requirements of the sectors concerned and in compliance with the implementing powers conferred on the Commission by the Council.

2. Without prejudice to the provisions laid down in the sectoral rules existing at the time of entry into force of this Regulation, other irregularities may give rise only to those penalties not equivalent to a criminal penalty that are provided for in

paragraph 1, provided that such penalties are essential to ensure correct application of the rules.

Article 6

1. Without prejudice to the Community administrative measures and penalties adopted on the basis of the sectoral rules existing at the time of entry into force of this Regulation, the imposition of financial penalties such as administrative rules may be suspended by decision of the competent authority if criminal proceedings have been initiated against the person concerned in connection with the same facts. Suspension of the administrative proceedings shall suspend the period of limitation provided for in Article 3.

2. If the criminal proceedings are not continued, the suspended administrative proceedings shall be resumed.

3. When the criminal proceedings are concluded, the suspended administrative proceedings shall be resumed, unless that is precluded by general legal principles.

4. Where the administrative procedure is resumed, the administrative authority shall ensure that a penalty at least equivalent to that prescribed by Community rules is imposed, which may take into account any penalty imposed by the judicial authority on the same person in respect o the same facts.

5. Paragraphs 1 to 4 shall not apply to financial penalties which form an integral part of financial support systems and may be applied independently f any criminal penalties, if and in so far as they are not equivalent to such penalties.

Article 7

Community administrative measures and penalties may be applied to the economic operators referred to in Article 1, namely the natural or legal persons and the other entities on which national law confers legal capacity who have committed the irregularity and to those who are under a duty to take responsibility for the irregularity or to ensure that it is not committed.

TITLE III
Checks

Article 8

1. In accordance with their national laws, regulations and administrative provisions, the Member States shall take the measures necessary to ensure the regularity and reality of transactions involving the Communities' financial interests.

2. Measures providing for checks shall be appropriate to the specific nature of each sector and in proportion to the objectives pursued. They shall take into account existing administrative practice and structures in the Member States and shall be determined so as not to entail excessive economic constraints or administrative costs.

The nature and frequency of the checks and inspections on the spot to be carried out by the Member States and the procedure for performing them shall be determined as necessary by sectoral rules in such a way as to ensure uniform and effective application of the relevant rules and in particular to prevent and detect irregularities.

3. The sectoral rules shall include the provisions necessary to ensure equivalent checks through the approximation of procedure and checking methods.

Article 9

1. Without prejudice to the checks carried out by the Member States in accordance with their national laws, regulations and administrative provisions and without prejudice to the checks carried out by the Community institutions in accordance with the EC Treaty, and in particular Article 188C thereof, the Commission shall, on its responsibility, have checks carried out on:
(a) the conformity of administrative practices with Community rules;
(b) the existence of the necessary substantiating documents and their concordance with the Communities' revenue and expenditure as referred to in Article 1;
(c) circumstances in which such financial transactions are carried out and checked.

2. In addition, it may carry out checks and inspections on the spot under the conditions laid down in the sectoral rules.
Before carrying out such checks and inspections, in accordance with the rules in force, the Commission shall inform the Member State concerned accordingly in order to obtain any assistance necessary.

Article 10

Additional general provisions relating to checks and inspections on the spot shall be adopted later in accordance with the procedures laid down in Article 235 of the EC Treaty and Article 203 of the EAEC Treaty.

Article 11

This Regulation shall enter into force on the third day following its publication in the *Official Journal of the European Communities.*
This Regulation shall be binding in its entirety and directly applicable in all Member States.

Done at Brussels, 18 December 1995.
For the Council
The President
J. Borrell Fontelles

Appendix C. Corpus Juris

I – CRIMINAL LAW

Article 1 – Fraud in the Community budget

1. Fraud affecting the Community budget of the European Communities constitutes a offence, both in the area of expenditure and in the area of receipts, when one of the following acts has been carried out either intentionally or by recklessness or by gross negligence:
a)   in connection with a grant or subsidy or the settlement of a fiscal debt, presenting the competent authority with declarations which in important respects are incomplete, or based on false documents, in such a way as to risk harm to the Community budget;
b)   in the same context, omitting to provide information to the competent authorities in breach of a requirement to provide such information;
c)   diverting Community funds (subsidies or grants) obtained legally.

2. Any person who corrects or completes a false declaration, or withdraws an application on the basis of false documents, or who informs the authorities about facts that he has omitted to reveal, before the act has been discovered by these authorities, is not punishable.

Article 2 – Market-rigging

To rig the market when a decision is being made as to who shall be awarded a contract constitutes a criminal fraud where this is liable to harm the financial interests of the Communities. The fraud consists of a secret agreement between competitors over offers or treats or promises towards competitors, or deceiving tem, or colluding with the official responsible for the decision.

Article 3 – Corruption

1. For the purposes of the present text the term official covers any official whether 'European' or 'national'.
A 'European official' means
a)   any person who is an official or an agent employed under contract as understood by the Staff Regulations;
b)   any person laced at the disposal of the European Communities by the Member States or by any private organisation, who exercises functions equivalent to those exercised by officials or other agents of the European Communities.

The expression 'national official' is interpreted by reference to the meaning of 'official' or 'public officer' under the national law of the Member State where the person in question holds this title for the purposes of application of its criminal law.

2. Acts of passive and active corruption are criminal offences if they harm or might harm the financial interests of the European Communities.

3. Passive corruption is where an official solicits or accepts, directly or via a third person, any offer, promise or other advantage of whatever nature:
a) in order to carry out a official act or act relating to his duties, in breach of his official obligations;
b) in order not to carry out an official act or act relating to his duties, which he is officially required to perform.

4. Active corruption means where any person makes or gives, directly or via a third person, any offer, promise or any other advantage, of whatever nature, to an official, in his own interests or in the interests of a third person:
a) to induce him to carry out an official act or act in relation to his duties, in such a way as to contravene his official duties;
b) to induce him not to carry out an official act or act relating to his duties which his official duties require him to carry out.

Article 4 – Abuse of office

1. A Community official commits a criminal offence:
a) if he makes a decision on the award of a subsidy, grant or an exemption from duty in favour of a person who clearly has no right to it;
b) if he intervenes, directly or indirectly, in the awarding of subsidies, grants or exemption from duty in relation to any business or operation in which he has some personal interest.

2. The penalty is increased when the damage caused is greater than 100,000 ECUs.

Article 5 – Misappropriation of funds

1. It is a criminal offence for Community officials to commit a breach of trust in administering funds from the Community budget. The offence is committed when a Community official formally authorised to allocate funds from the Community budget, or to contract out requirement on behalf of the Community, abuses his powers by harming those interests entrusted to him.

2. The penalty is increased when the damage caused amounts to more than 100,000 ECUs.

Article 6 – Disclosure of secrets pertaining to one's office

1. It is a criminal offence for an official improperly to reveal secrets pertaining to his office, when the secret concerns information acquired in, or by virtue of, his professional activity, particularly when monitoring receipts or awarding grants and subsidies.

2. This provision is not applicable in cases where the law, or a regulation, imposes or authorises disclosure of the secret, or if there is the consent of the person who is guardian of the secret.

Article 7 – Money laundering and receiving

1. It is criminal offence to launder the fruits or the profits of offences described in articles 1 to 6.

Laundering means:

a) the conversion or transfer of goods resulting from any of the criminal activities mentioned in the previous paragraph or participation in such activity with the aim of concealing or disguising the illicit origins of the said goods or of helping any person involved in this activity to escape the legal consequences of his acts;

b) the concealing or disguising of the nature, origin, site, placing, disposal, movements or the real ownership of goods or rights resulting from any criminal activity mentioned in the previous paragraph, or participation in such an activity.

2. It is criminal offence to receive products or profits from the offences set out in Articles 1 to 6.

Receiving means the acquisition, keeping or use of goods from any of the criminal activities mentioned in the previous paragraph or participation in such an activity.

Article 8 – Conspiracy

1. A conspiracy which harms the Community budget constitutes a criminal offence.

2. A conspiracy is when two or more persons work together, setting up the necessary organisation, with a view to carrying out one or more of the offences set out in Articles 1 to 7.

Article 9 – Penalties

1. The principal penalties, common to all offences set out in Articles 1 to 8, are as follows:

a) for natural persons, a custodial sentence for a maximum of five years and/or a fine of up to one million ECUs, which may be raised to five times the amount involved in the offence;

b) for bodies corporate, legal supervision for a maximum of five years and/or a fine of up to one million ECUs, which may be raised to five times the amount involved in the offence;

c) confiscation of the instruments, fruits and profits of the offence;

d) publication of the conviction.

2. Additional penalties for the same offences are as follows:

a) for an offence under Article 1, exclusion from future subsidies for five years at most;

b) for an offence under Article 2, exclusion from future contracts for five years at most;

c) for offences under Articles 3 to 6, ban from Community and national public office for up to five years.

Article 10 – Mens Rea

All the offences set out above (Articles 1 to 8) require intention or fraud, with the exception of Community fraud (Article 1) for which recklessness or gross negligence is sufficient.

Article 11 – Error

1. Mistake about the essential elements of the offence excludes fraud; but recklessness and gross negligence may nevertheless be sanctioned in the case of Community fraud (*see* above Article 1).

2. Mistake about the existence of a legal prohibition or its interpretation excludes liability if it would have inevitably been committed by a careful, sensible person. If the mistake was avoidable, the penalty will be reduced, which means that the judge may not impose the maximum penalty (*see* above, Article 9).

Article 12 – Individual criminal liability

1. Any person may be held responsible for the offences defined above (Articles 1 to 8) as a principal offender, inciter or accomplice:
a) as principal offender, if he commits the incriminating facts or participates, as co-offender, in committing an offence;
b) as an inciter if he, by means of a bribe, promise, threat, order, abuse of authority or power provokes the offence or gives instructions for it to be committed;
c) as an accomplice if he knowingly, by providing assistance, facilitates the preparation or the commission of the offence.

Article 13 – Criminal liability of the head of a business

1. If one of the offences defined above (Articles 1 to 8) has been committed for the benefit of a business by a person subject to their authority, the head of the business is also criminally liable, and any other person with powers of decision or control within the business, if he has knowingly given orders, allowed the offence to be committed or omitted to exercise the necessary supervision.

2. The delegation of powers and criminal liability is only valid as a defence if it is partial, precise and specific, if it corresponds to a structure necessary for the running of the business and if the delegatees are really in a position to be able to fulfil the functions delegated to them. Such delegation does not exclude the general responsibilities of monitoring, supervision and selection of personnel, and does not include matter proper to the head of the business such as general organisation of work within the business.

Article 14 – Criminal liability of organisations

1. The offences defined above in Articles 1–8 above may be committed by corporations, ad also by other organisations which are recognised by law as competent to hold property in their own name, provided the offence is committed for the benefit of the organisation by some organ or representative of the

organisation, or any person acting in its name and having power, whether by law or merely in fact, to make decisions.

2. Where it arises, the criminal responsibility of an organisation does not exclude that of any natural person as author, inciter or accomplice to the same offence.

Article 15 – Extent of the penalty

The penalties applicable to the offences set out above (Article 1 to 8) are to be imposed in accordance with the seriousness of the act, the fault of the offender and the extent of his participation in the offence. In particular the previous life of the accused, any previous offences, his character, his economic and social situation, and his efforts to make amends for the damage caused will all be taken into account.

Article 16 – Aggravating circumstances

1. The following constitute aggravating circumstances:
a)   the fraudulent result sought is achieved;
b)   the amount of the fraud or profit sought through the offence exceeds 200,000 ECUs;
c)   the offence is carried out in the context of a conspiracy.

2. Where aggravating circumstances exist, a custodial sentence (or as the case may be, placing under legal supervision) is mandatory, and the maximum length of the penalty incurred is increased to seven years.

Article 17 – Penalties incurred in the case of concurrent offences

1. Where one person is liable for several offences as defined above (Articles 1 to 8), a single penalty shall be applied, determined on the basis of the penalty which would have been incurred for the most serious offence, and increased by up to three times that amount; a penalty determined in this way shall not exceed the sum of the penalties which could have been inflicted separately for each offence.

2. When a single act constitutes a criminal offence under both Community regulations and national laws, only Community regulations are to be applied.

3. In all other cases of concurrent offences, the competent authority must, in determining the penalty, take into account penalties already imposed for the same act.

II – CRIMINAL PROCEDURE

Article 18 – Status and structure of the European Public Prosecutor (E.P.P.)

1. For the purposes of investigation, prosecution, trail and execution of sentences concerning the offences set out above (Article 1 to 8), the territory of the Member States of the Union constitutes a single legal area.

2. The E.P.P. is an authority of the European Community, responsible for committal to trial, presenting the prosecution case at trial and the execution of

sentences concerning the offences defined above (Articles 1 to 8). It is independent as regards both national authorities and Community institutions.

3. The E.P.P. consists of a European Director of Public Prosecution (E.D.P.P.) whose offices are based in Brussels and European delegated Public Prosecutors (E.Del.P.P.) whose offices are based in the capital of each Member State, or any other town where the competent court sits on application of Article 26.

4. The E.P.P.is indivisible and interdependent:
a) indivisibility implies that any act undertaken by one of its members is taken as done by the E.P.P.; that all acts fall within the competence of the E.P.P. (particularly powers of investigation as set out under Article 20) may be undertaken by nay one of its members; and that, with the agreement of the E.D.P.P., or in emergencies where he retrospectively approves, any of the E.del.P.P.s, may exercise his duties on the territory of any of the Member States, in collaboration with the offices of the E.del.P.P. in that Member State;
b) interdependence requires, on the part of the different E.Del.P.P.s, an obligation to assist each other.

5. National Public Prosecutors (N.P.P.) are also under a duty to assist the E.P.P.

Article 19 – Seizing of the E.P.P. and opening of proceedings

1. The E.P.P. must be informed of all acts which could constitute one of the offences defined above (Articles 1 to 8), by the national authorities (police, public prosecutors, *juges d'instruction*, agents of national administrations such as tax or Customs authorities) or the competent Community body, the Commission's Anti-Fraud Unit (UCLAF). It may also be informed by denunciation from any citizen or by a complaint from the Commission. National authorities must seize the European Prosecution Service at latest when the suspect is formally 'under investigation', under Article 29(2), or when coercive measures are employed, particularly arrest, searches and seizures or when a person's telephone is to be tapped.

2. If an investigation conducted by a national authority reveals that one of the offences above has been committed (Articles 1 to 8), the dossier must be immediately submitted to the E.P.P.

3. However the E.P.P. learns about the facts, it may become officially seized either by the national authorities or by acting on its own initiative.

4. The decision to prosecute, which means opening an investigation, may be taken by the E.P.P. whatever the sum of the fraud involved. The E.P.P., bound by the legality principle, must bring a prosecution if it appears that one of the offences (Articles 1 to 8) has been committed. It may, however, by a decision with special grounds communicated immediately to the person who has informed it, or denounced it to its officials or laid a complaint
a) either refer offences which are not serious or which affect principally national interests to the national authorities;
b) or drop the case, if the accused, having admitted guilt, has made amends for the damage caused and, as the case may be, returned funds received illegally;

c) or grant an authorization for settlement to a national authority which has applied for it, according to the conditions set out below (Article 22(2b)).

Article 20 – Powers of investigation of the E.P.P.

1. In order to discover the truth and to bring the case to a point where it may be tried, the E.P.P. conducts investigations into the offences defined above (Articles 1 to 8) looking for evidence of innocence as well as for evidence of guilt (*à charge et à décharge*). Its powers are divided between the European Director of Public Prosecutions (E.D.P.P.), the European Delegated Public Prosecutors (E.Del.P.P.) and, as may be, national authorities appointed for this purpose, according to the following rules.

2. The E.D.P.P.'s own powers include:
a) overseeing investigation and their delegation to one or more E.Del.P.P., in accordance with the conditions and restrictions set out below (Article 20(3));
b) the coordination of investigations undertaken by the E.Del.P.P. as well as by national police forces and competent national administrations and, as may be, UCLAF; this coordination may take the form of oral or written recommendations to the relevant authorities;
c) the right to call in cases where the investigation reveals that they concern in whole or in part offences defined above (Articles 1 to 8).

3. All the following powers may either be exercised by the E.D.P.P. or delegated to E.Del.P.P., where there is an investigation into offences set out in Articles 1 to 8:
a) questioning of the suspect, under conditions which respect his rights as set out below (Article 29);
b) collection of documents and/or computer-held information necessary for the investigation and, if need be, visits to the scene of the offence;
c) request addressed to the judge to order an expert enquiry under the conditions set out below (Article 31);
d) searches, seizures and telephone tapping ordered in accordance with the rule below (Article 25), on authorization from a judge or with his subsequent permission, and undertaken with respect for the rights of the accused (Article 31);
e) hearings of witnesses who agree to cooperate with the law and, as may be, witnesses obliged to appear in accordance with the conditions below (Article 25);
f) notification of charges to the accused, with respect for the rights set out below (Article 29);
g) to make requests for a person's remand in custody or remand on bail subject to conditions, for a period of up to 6 months, renewable for 3 months, where there are reasonable grounds to suspect that the accused has committed one of the offences defined above (Articles 1 to 8) or good reasons for believing it necessary to stop him committing such an offence or from fleeing after committing it; this order, in writing and giving reasons, must be addressed to the competent national legal authorities in accordance with the rules below

(Articles 24 and 25), the execution of the measures being organised in the country where the arrest was made.

4. Powers delegated to the E.Del.P.P. may be partially subdelegated (limited *ratione materiae et ratione temporis*) to a national authority (prosecuting authority, police, or any other competent administration such as the tax or customs authorities) who will be bound to respect all the rules contained in this European Corpus.

Article 21 – Closure of the preparatory stage

1. When he considers investigations to be completed, the E.Del.P.P. decides, under the authority of the E.D.P.P., either to make a decision not to prosecute, or to bring the case to court.

2. The decision not to prosecute is notified to the European Commission and to any body or person who informed the E.P.P., denounced the offence to its officials or brought a complaint, as defined above (Article 19(4)).

3. The decision to bring the case to court, notified under the same conditions as non-prosecution (Article 21(2), includes the name and address of the accused, a description of the acts and the offence so committed, and also states where the case is to be tried. It passes into the control of the competent national legal authority in accordance with the rules set out below (Article 25) which, after establishing the lawfulness of the proceedings, seizes the court with jurisdiction and sends a summons to the accused stating the date and the time he is to appear.

Article 22 – Bringing and terminating a prosecution

1. For the offences set out above (Articles 1 to 8), the E.P.P. prosecutes at the court of trial (selected as indicated hereafter, Article 26), according to the laws in the relevant State. The national prosecuting party may if appropriate prosecute with him, if national interests are also under threat. In such a case, notices and summons are also addressed to the national prosecuting party and the dossier is sent out to it in good time.

2. For the same offences, the prosecution is extinguished (ruling out any national pardon or amnesty) on the death of the defendant (or if it concerns a group, the dissolution of the group), or by the expiry of the limitation period or by settlement:
a)   there is a limitation period of five years, calculated from the day when the offence was committed if within this time there has been no investigation or prosecution; if investigation or prosecution have taken place, the offence is only time-barred from five years after the last act of investigation or prosecution. In all cases, notification of the charges to the suspect interrupts the limitation period;
b)   settlement is ruled out in the case of repeated offences, where arms or forgery were used, or if the sum involved is 50,000 ECUs or more. In other cases, it may be proposed by the national authorities to the E.P.P., both for cases under national jurisdiction and for cases under European jurisdiction, according to the following conditions: the defendant freely admits his guilt, the authorities have sufficient evidence of guilt to justify committal to trial, the decision to come to a settlement is made publicly, and the agreement concluded respects the

principle of proportionality. In the case of refusal, the E.P.P. must, if there are grounds, call in the case.

Article 23 – Execution of sentences

1. When a conviction becomes definitive, it is immediately communicated by the E.P.P. to the authorities of the Member State which is appointed as the place of execution of the decision; certain penalties such as confiscation, removal of rights or publication of the conviction may be carried out in one or more places other than the place of imprisonment. The E.P.P. is responsible, alongside the competent national authority, for ordering and overseeing the implementation of the sentence if this is not automatic. In principle, execution of the penalties is governed by the laws in force in the Member State appointed as place of execution of the sentence. However, the E.P.P. oversees the application of the following common rules across the whole territory of the States of the European Union:

a) any period spent in custody by the accused on account of the same acts, in any State and at any point of the procedure, is deducted from the custodial sentence pronounced by the court of judgment;

b) no person may be prosecuted or criminally convicted in a Member State by reason of one of the offences defined above (Articles 1 to 8) for which he has already been either acquitted, or convicted by a final judgment, in any of the Member States of the European Union;

c) any sentencing decision relating to one of the offences outlined above (Articles 1 to 8) must take into account in determining the penalty the rules set out above (Article 17) on concurrent offences.

2. The E.P.P. may, if there are grounds, authorise a transfer if a convicted person with a custodial sentence asks to be imprisoned in a Member State other than the one named by the conviction.

Article 24 – Competence ratione loci

1. In the single legal area as defined in Article 18(1), competence *ratione loci* is exercised according to the following rules:

a) members of the E.P.P. appointed by the E.D.P.P. to bring prosecution and conduct investigations into cases in accordance with the conditions set out above (Article 18 *et seq.*) have competence across the entire territory of the European Union (*cf.* Article 18(4a));

b) a European warrant for arrest, issued on the instructions of the E.P.P. by a national judge (*cf.* Article 20(2e)) is valid across the whole territory; any person arrested thus may be transferred to the territory of a State where he is required to be (during the preparatory stage or at trial);

c) judgments relating to the offences set out above made by the courts of any of the Member States are valid across the whole territory of the Union.

2. If investigations require legal cooperation of any kind from a third State, the E.P.P. requests the national authorities of the principal country where investigations are taking place to apply to the third State concerned, following the procedure laid down by the national and international legal instruments in force.

Article 25 – Preparatory stage

1. The preparatory stage of proceedings, opened with regard to the offences defined above (Articles 1 to 8), lasts from the initial investigations conducted by the E.P.P. until the decision to commit the case to trial (above Article 21(3)). Throughout this stage, judicial control is exercised by an independent and impartial judge, the 'judge of freedoms', appointed by each Member State from the court where the E.Del.P.P. is based. This judge is also competent to rule on whether the Commission is entitled to constitute itself a *'partie civile'* (*cf.* Article 30) and also to order, as needed, measures to preserve matters or things which are subject of the case, when the necessity for this cannot be seriously disputed, and when such measures are necessary to preserve civil interests and proportional to them.

2. During the course of an investigation into the offences set out above (Articles 1 to 8), the coercive measures listed under Article 20(3) are admissible. However, any measure restricting rights and fundamental freedoms recognised by the European Convention on Human Rights which is taken at this stage and which affects a witness or the accused must first be authorised by the judge of freedoms, who checks that the measure is lawful and regular as well as that the principles of necessity and proportionality are respected; however, an *a posteriori* authorization in the following forty-eight hours is allowed in an emergency, particularly where clues might disappear, where the offence is in the process of being committed, or where there is a risk that the suspect will escape from the law.

3. At the end of the preparatory stage, if he decides to commit the case to trial (*cf.* Article 21(1&2)), the E.D.P.P. submits this decision to the judge of freedoms who checks the lawfulness of all the proceedings, excludes if necessary any evidence obtained in breach of the rules below (Article 32) and seizes the court of trial according to the rules set out hereafter (Article 26).

Article 26 – Trial

1. The offences set out above (Articles 1 to 8) are tried by national, independent and impartial courts, appointed by each Member State according to the rules on competence *ratione materiae* of the national law, sitting at the centres where the E.Del.P.P. is based. The courts must consist of professional judges, specialising wherever possible in economic and financial matters, and not simple jurors or lay magistrates.

2. Each case is judged in the Member State which seems appropriate in the interests of efficient administration of justice, any justice, any conflict of jurisdiction being settled according to the rules set out hereafter (Article 28). The principle criteria for the choice are the following:
a) the State where the greater part of the evidence is found;
b) the State of residence of nationality of the accused (or the principal persons accused);
c) the State where the economic impact of the offence is the greatest.

3. On application of the general rule on the subsidiarity of national law (Article 35), national courts must refer to the rules in the European corpus and, if there is a lacuna, apply the national law. They are bound in all cases to give grounds for the

penalty by reference to circumstances pertaining to the particular case, applying the rules set out above (Articles 15 to 17).

Article 27 – Appeal to national courts

1. Any conviction pronounced against a person declared guilty of one of the offences set out above (Articles 1 to 8) must be subject to appeal by the convicted person leading to the case being retried, in law and in fact, by a higher court of the State where the conviction was pronounced at first instance; the higher court must apply, as the court of first instance, the rules set out in the European corpus and, in the case of a lacuna, must apply national law.

2. In the case of total or partial acquittal, appeal is also open to the E.P.P. as a prosecuting party; the Commission may be joined to it, as *partie civile*, on the basis of civil interests only.

3. In the case of appeal by the convicted person alone, the court seized may not pronounce a stiffer penalty.

Article 28 – Appeal to the European Court of Justice (ECJ)

1. The Court of Justice has jurisdiction to rule on offences as defined above (Articles 1 to 8) in three cases:
a) preliminary questions on the interpretation of the corpus and any application measures;
b) on the request of a Member State or the Commission on any dispute concerning the application of the corpus;
c) on the request of the E.P.P. or a national authority on conflicts of jurisdiction regarding application of the rules on the principle of European territoriality, concerning both the public prosecution service (Articles 18 and 24) and the exercise of judicial control by national courts (Articles 25 to 27).

2. When a question of interpretation is raised or a conflict of jurisdiction brought before a court of one of the Member States, this court may, if it considers that a decision on this point is necessary in order to give its judgment, call on the Court of Justice to rule on the issue.

3. When an issue or conflict such as this is raised in a case pending before a national court whose decisions are not subject to appeal in national law, this court is bound to seize the Court of Justice.

Article 29 – Rights of the accused

1. In any proceedings brought for an offence as set out above (Articles 1 to 8), the accused enjoys the rights of the defence guaranteed by Article 6 of the European Convention on Human Rights and Article 10 of the UN National Covenant on Civil and Political Rights.

2. A person may not be heard as a witness but must be treated as accused from the point when any step is taken establishing, denouncing or revealing the existence of clear and consistent evidence of guilt and, at the latest, from the first questioning by an authority aware of the existence of such evidence.

3. From the time of his first questioning, the accused has the right to know the content of the charges against him, the right to be assisted by a defence lawyer of his choice, and, if necessary, an interpreter. He has the right to remain silent.

Article 30 – Rights of the Commission as partie civile

1. Where the Community is the victim of damage directly caused by one of the offences set out above (Articles 1 to 8), the European Commission may constitute itself *partie civile* before the competent judge, either at the preparatory stage, or at the opening of the trial. It may ask the judge to take preservation measures and, as the case may be, order compensation for the damage.

2. Once the *partie civile* is declared admissible, the Commission is entitled to the rights and prerogatives of a party to the proceedings: receiving the dossier, notification of procedural steps, assistance by a lawyer, presence at the hearing, participation in the administering of the evidence, exercise of the right to appeal as far as its civil interests are concerned (*cf.* Article 27).

Article 31 – Burden of proof

1. Any person accused of one of the offences set out above (Articles 1 to 8) is presumed innocent until his guilt has been established legally by the final judgment which has acquired the authority of *res judicata*.

2. Subject to the obligation to produce certain documents which may be required under national or Community law, no person is obliged actively to contribute, directly or indirectly, in establishing his own guilt.

Article 32 – Admissible evidence

1. In Member States of the European Union, the following evidence is admitted:
a) testimony, either direct, or presented at the trial via an audiovisual link if the witness is in another Member State, or recorded by the E.P.P. in the form of a 'European deposition'. For the latter, the witness must be examined before the judge, the defence lawyer must be present and allowed to put questions, and the operation must be recorded on video;
b) questioning of the accused, whether direct or recorded by the E.P.P. in the form of a 'European interrogation report'. For the latter the questioning must take place before the judge, the accused must be assisted by a defence lawyer of his choice (who has received the dossier in good time and at the latest 48 hours before the questioning) and, if necessary, by an interpreter; in addition, the operation must be recorded on video;
c) statements made by the accused, outside the interrogations previously mentioned, as long as they have been made before the competent authority (E.P.P. or judge), and the accused has first been informed of his right to silence and his right to be assisted by a defence lawyer of his choice and that the statements have been recorded in some way;
d) documents presented by an official accountant, appointed by the competent court from individuals or corporations appearing on a European list approved

by the Member States on the proposal of the E.P.P., either during the preparatory stage, or at the beginning of the trial;

e) documents that the accused has been required to produce in a preliminary administrative investigation, unless such an obligation is accompanied by criminal sanctions.

2. These provisions do not exclude the validity of other forms of evidence considered as admissible under the national law in force in the State of the court of judgment.

Article 33 – Exclusion of evidence illegally obtained

1. In proceedings for one of the offences set out above (Articles 1 to 8) evidence must be excluded if it was obtained by Community or national agents either in violation of the fundamental rights enshrined in the ECHR, or in violation of applicable national law without being justified by the European rules previously set out.

2. The national law applicable to determine whether the evidence has been obtained legally or illegally must be the law of the country where the evidence was obtained. When evidence has been obtained legally in this sense, it should not be possible to oppose the use of this evidence because it was obtained in a way that would have been illegal in the country of use. But it should always be possible to object to the use of such evidence, even where it was obtained in accordance with the law of the country where it was obtained, if it has nevertheless violated rights enshrined in the ECHR or the European rules (Articles 31 and 32).

Article 34 – Publicity and secrecy

1. Investigations carried out under the authority of the E.P.P. are secret and authorities participating in these investigations are bound to respect the rule of professional secrecy.

2. Hearings before the judge of freedoms may be published if all parties consent to it, unless publicity would be likely either to harm either the smooth running of the investigation, or to damage the interests of a third party, or endanger public order or morals. In any case, the media are banned from publishing information at this stage relating to the evidence.

3. The judgment must be given publicly, but access to the court may be denied to the press and the public, during all or part of the proceedings, under the conditions stipulated in Article 6(1) ECHR. Publicity may include recording and broadcasting the proceedings audiovisually if the national law of the State concerned allows it and under the conditions which it imposes.

Article 35 – Subsidiarity of national law with regard to the European corpus

The corpus of rules set out above concerning both substantive law (Articles 1 and 17) and procedure (Articles 18 to 34) applies across all the territory of Member States of the European Union. Where there is lacuna in the corpus, the law applied is that of the place where the offence is prosecuted, committed to trial or, as the case may be, where the sentence is carried out.

Appendix D. Table of Cases

66/82, *Fromençais* v. *Forma*, [1983] ECR 395, page 60.

C-240/90, *Germany* v. *Commission*, [1992] ECR I-5383, pages 20, 57, 58, 94, 136.

18/76, *Germany* v. *Commission (EAGGF)* [1979] ECR 343, pages 57, 133.

C-167/94, *Grau Gomis*, judgment of 7 April 1995, nyr, page 53.

180/87, *Hamill* v. *Commission*, [1988] ECR 6141, pages 276, 277.

148/77, *Hansen* v. *Hauptzollamt Flensburg*, [1978] ECR 1787; [1979] 1 CMLR 604, page 55.

46/87 and 227/88, *Hoechst AG* v. *Commission*, [1989] ECR 2859, page 60.

85/76, *Hoffman-La Roche* v. *Commission (vitamins case)*, [1979] ECR 461, page 60.

T-36/91, *ICI*, judgment of 29 June 1995, nyr, page 60.

11/70, *Internationale Handelsgesellschaft* v. *Einfuhr- und Vorratstelle für Getreide und Futtermittel* [1970] ECR 1125, page 57.

C-199/90, *Italtrade* v. *AIMA*, [1990] ECR I-5545, page 57.

C-34/89, *Italy* v. *Commission (olive oil production aid)*, [1990] ECR I-3603, [1992] 2 CMLR 797, pages 55, 181.

222/84, *Johnston* v. *Chief Constable of the RUC*, [1986] ECR 1651 at 18, page 60.

63/83, *R* v. *Kirk*, [1984] ECR 2689, page 59.

117/83, *Könecke GmbH and Co KG* v. *Bundesanstalt für Landwirtschaftliche Marktordnung*, [1984] ECR 3291, pages 22, 59.

25/70, *Einfuhr- und Voratsstelle für Getreide und Futtermittel* v. *Köster, Berodt & Co*, preliminary ruling, [1970] ECR 1161, page 21.

230/81, *Luxembourg* v. *European Parliament ('seat' case)*, [1983] ECR 255, page 55.

137/85, *Maizena* v. *BALM*, [1987] ECR 4587, pages 57, 59.

181/84, *R.* v. *Intervention Board, ex parte Man (Sugar) Ltd.*, [1985] ECR 2889, page 57.

C-352/92, *Milchwerke Köln/Wuppertal EG* v. *Hauptzollamt Köln-Rheinau*, [1994] ECR I-3385, page 55.

357/88, *Oberhausener* v. *BALM*, [1990] ECR 1669, page 57.

C-155/89, *Philipp Brothers*, [1990] ECR I-3265, page 57.

288/85, *Hauptzollamt Hamburg-Jonas* v. *Plange Kraftfutterwerke*, [1987] ECR 611, page 57.

64/63, *Potvin* v. *Van de Velde*, [1963] ECR 47, page 275.

C-319/90, *Pressler* v. *Germany*, [1992] ECR I-203, page 60.

33/76, *Rewe* v. *Landwirtschaftskammer für das Saarland*, [1976] ECR 1989, page 174.

158/79, *Rougemous* v. *Council*, [1982] ECR 4379, page 277.

9/69, *Sayag and another* v. *Leduc and others*, [1969] ECR 329, page 276.

C-9/89, *Spain* v. *Council*, [1990] ECR 1383, page 62.

1/88, *S.A Générale de Banque* v. *Commission*, [1988] ECR 857, page 275.

49/76, *Überseehandel* v. *Handelskammer Hamburg*, [1977] ECR 41, page 78.

1/87, *Universe Tankship Incorporated* v. *Commission*, [1987] ECR 2807, page 275.

114/78, *Yoshida GmbH* v. *I.H.K.*, [1979] ECR 151, page 78.

C-2/8, *Zwartveld and others* v. *Commission*, [1990] ECR I-3365, page 63.

Appendix E. Bibliography of Official Publications

COUNCIL OF EUROPE

Council of Europe, *Administrative, civil and penal aspects, including the role of the judiciary, of the fight against corruption* (1995) proceedings of 19th conference of European Council Ministers, Valetta, Malta, 14–15 June 1994.

Council of Europe, *Draft programme of action against corruption* (1995) by the multidisciplinary group on corruption, October.

THE EUROPEAN INSTITUTIONS

European Commission, *Community Structural Funds 1994–99* (1993) OOPEC.

European Commission, *Comparative analysis of the reports supplied by the Member States on national measures taken to combat wastefulness and the misuse of Community resources* (1995).

European Commission, *Fraud in the transit procedure, solutions foreseen and perspectives for the future* (1995) COM(95) 108.

European Commission, *Préparation CIG 1996 contribution du conseil, information aux délégations extérieures de la Commission* (1995) info-note number 20/95.

European Commission, *Préparation CIG 1996 contribution du Parlement Européen, information aux délégations extérieures de la Commission* (1995) info-note number 26/95.

European Commission, *Protecting the financial interests of the European Community, the fight against fraud* (1994) OOPEC.

European Commission, *Protecting the Community's financial interests, The fight against fraud – Annual report 1995* (1996) COM(96) 173.

European Commission, *Protecting the Community's financial interests, Synthesis document of the comparative analysis of the reports supplied by the Member States on national measures taken to combat wastefulness and the misuse of Community resources* (1995) COM(95) 556.

European Commission, *Rapport Intermédiaire sur le transit* (1996) SEC(96) 1739.

European Commission, *Reform of the CAP and its implementation* (1993) DG for agriculture.

European Commission, *Report of the Committee of budgets on the Commission Proposal to the Council for amending Council Regulation 1552/89* (1993).

European Commission, *Report of the study on the systems of administrative and criminal penalties of the Member States and general principles applicable to Community penalties* (1993) SEC(93) 1172 ('Delmas-Marty Report').

European Commission, *Report on the application of Council Regulation 1552/89 implementing Decision 88/376 on the system of Communities' own resources* (1992) COM(92) 530.

European Commission, *Report on the functioning of the inspection arrangements for traditional own resources* (1994) COM(93) 691.

European Commission, *Report on the operation of the Treaty of the European Union* (1995) SEC(95) 731.

European Commission, *Report on the recovery of traditional own resources in cases of fraud and irregularities* (1995) COM(95) 398.

European Commission, *Tableau comparatif des contributions du conseil, de la Commission, du P.E.* (1995) info-note number 32/95.

European Commission, UCLAF, *17 questions on fraud* (1996).

European Court of Auditors, *Annual Reports* concerning individual financial years, together with the institutions' replies:
  - for the 1977 financial year, [1978] O.J. C313
  - for the 1978 financial year, [1979] O.J. C326
  - for the 1979 financial year, [1980] O.J. C324
  - for the 1980 financial year, [1981] O.J. C344
  - for the 1981 financial year, [1982] O.J. C344
  - for the 1982 financial year, [1983] O.J. C357
  - for the 1983 financial year, [1984] O.J. C348
  - for the 1984 financial year, [1985] O.J. C326
  - for the 1985 financial year, [1986] O.J. C321
  - for the 1986 financial year, [1987] O.J. C336
  - for the 1987 financial year, [1988] O.J. C316
  - for the 1988 financial year, [1989] O.J. C312
  - for the 1989 financial year, [1990] O.J. C313
  - for the 1990 financial year, [1991] O.J. C324
  - for the 1991 financial year, [1992] O.J. C330
  - for the 1992 financial year, [1993] O.J. C309
  - for the 1993 financial year, [1994] O.J. C327
  - for the 1994 financial year, [1995] O.J. C303

European Court of Auditors, *Auditing the finances of the European Union* (1995).

European Court of Auditors, *Information note on the annual report of the Court of Auditors of the European Communities concerning the financial year 1993* (1994).

European Court of Auditors, *Observations de la Cour des Comptes sur la proposition de règlement (CE, EURATOM) relatif à la protection des intérêts financiers des Communautés ainsi que sur une proposition d'acte portant établissement de la convention relative a la protection des intérêts financiers des Communautés* (1995) COM (94) 214 final.

European Court of Auditors, *Préparation CIG 1996 contribution de la Cour des comptes, information aux délégations extérieures de la Commission* (1995).

European Court of Auditors, *Report to the Reflection Group on the operation of the Treaty on European Union* (1995).

European Court of Auditors, *Statement of Assurance concerning activities financed from the general budget for the financial year 1994* (1995).

European Court of Auditors, *The European Court of Auditors – Auditing the finances of the European Union* (1995).

European Parliament, *SEM 2000 Working document – Defining a methodological approach* (1996) Budgetary Control Committee PE 217.454.

European Parliament, *SEM 2000 Working document – Evaluation* (1996) Budgetary Control Committee PE 218.773.

European Parliament, *SEM 2000 Working document – Rationalising controls – Preventing fraud* (1996) Budgetary Control Committee PE 219.146.

European Parliament, *Contribution from FENEX* (1996) Committee of Inquiry into the Community Transit System, Rotterdam.

European Parliament, *Contribution by Jean Duquesne, president of ODASCE* (1996) Committee of Inquiry into the Community Transit System, Paris.

European Parliament, *Contribution submitted by the Bundesverband Spedition und Lagerei e.V.* (1996) Committee of Inquiry into the Community Transit System, Bonn.

European Parliament, *Contribution submitted by the Danish freight forwarders Association* (1996) Committee of Inquiry into the Community Transit System, Copenhagen.

European Parliament, *Contribution submitted by the UK Freight Transport Association* (1996) Committee of Inquiry into the Community Transit System.

European Parliament, *Hearing with commissioners Mario Monti and Anita Gradin* (1996) Committee of Inquiry into the Community Transit System.

European Parliament, *Progress Report number one*, rapporteur: Mr. Kellett-Bowman (1996) Committee of Inquiry into the Community Transit System.

European Parliament, *Reply from the Court of Auditors* (1996) Committee of Inquiry into the Community Transit System.

European Parliament, *Response from the Irish Permanent Representation to the European Union* (1996) Committee of Inquiry into the Community Transit System.

European Parliament, *Revised note on the TIR carnets and the 'Community' and 'Common' Transit procedures* (1996) Committee of Inquiry into the Community Transit System.

European Parliament, *Written statement by Commissioner Liikanen* (1996) Committee of Inquiry into the Community Transit System.

European Parliament, *Dankert Report* (1989) EP A2–20/89.

European Parliament, *De Keersmaeker Report* (1977) EP 531/76.

European Parliament, *Document de travail sur les modalités de l'exercice du droit d'enquête du Parlement Européen* (1995) PE 211.818.

European Parliament, *Gabert Report* (1984) EP 1–1346/83.

European Parliament, *Guermeur Report* (1987) EP A2–251/86.

European Parliament, *Options for a definitive VAT system* (1995) Economic Affairs Series.

European Parliament, *Rapport de la Commission du Contrôle Budgetaire sur les relations entre les organes de contrôle de budget communautaire* (1993) rapporteur John Tomlinson, A3–0320.

European Parliament, *Rapport: Commission de règlement, de la vérification des pouvoirs et des immunités* (1995) PE 210.700.

European Parliament, *Rapport: Commission de règlement, de la vérification des pouvoirs et des immunités* (1994) PE 210.750.

European Parliament, *Rapport: Commission de règlement, de la vérification des pouvoirs et des immunités* (1995) PE 212.084.

European Parliament, *Rapport: Les commissions parlementaires d'enquête des états membres de la CE* (1993) W3.

European Parliament, *Report of the Committee on civil liberties and internal affairs on combatting corruption in Europe* (1995) rapporteur: Heinke Salish, MEP.

European Parliament, *Theato Report* (1991) EP A3–0250/91.

UK OFFICIAL DOCUMENTS

Crown Prosecution Service, *Code for Crown prosecutors* (1994).

Employment Department, *Audit of European Social Fund projects* (1994).

Employment Department, *European Social Fund Guidance for 1995 applications – Objective 3* (1994).

Graham Report, *Insolvency law: an agenda for reform* (1994) Report chaired by David Graham, QC, JUSTICE.

H. M. Customs and Excise, *Customs, compounding, seizure and restoration* (1992) customers' booklet, HMSO.

H. M. Customs and Excise, *Annual Report for the year ended 31 March 1992* (1992) HMSO.

H. M. Customs and Excise, *Annual Report for the year ended 31 March 1994* (1994) HMSO.

HMSO Publications, *Open Government Code of practice on access to government information* (1994) HMSO.

HMSO Publications, *The civil service – Continuity and change* (1994) HMSO.

HMSO Publications, *The Civil Service* (1995) HMSO.

Hodgson Report (1984) 'Profits of crime and their recovery', Report of a Committee chaired by Sir Derek Hodgson, Heinemann, London.

Home Office, *Case screening by the Crown Prosecution Service How and why cases are terminated* (1994) Home Office Research Study 137, HMSO.

House of Lords Select Committee on the European Communities, *Financial control and fraud in the Community* (1994) 12th report, HMSO.

House of Lords Select Committee on the European Communities, *Fraud against the Community* (1989) 5th report, HMSO.

House of Lords Select Committee on the European Communities, *Fraud and mismanagement in the Community's finances* (1994) 6th report, HMSO.

House of Lords Select Committee on the European Communities, *1996 Inter-Governmental Conference* (1995) 21st report, HMSO.

House of Lords Select Committee on the European Communities, *1996 Inter-Governmental Conference – Minutes of evidence* (1995), 18th report, HMSO.

House of Lords Select Committee on the European Communities, *House of Lords Scrutiny of the inter-governmental pillars of the European Union* (1993) 28th report.

House of Lords Select Committee on the European Communities, *The fight against fraud with evidence* (1992) 13th report, HMSO.

Intervention Board for Agricultural Products (IBAP) Anti-Fraud Unit, *1993 Annual Report* (1994).

Keith Report (1983) Report of the Committee on enforcement powers of revenue departments, chaired by Lord Keith of Kinkel, HMSO.

Lord Chancellor's Department, *Judicial Statistics for the year 1993* (1994) HMSO.

Lord Chancellor's Department, *Judicial Statistics for the year 1992* (1993) HMSO.

Lord Chancellor's Department, *Judicial Statistics for the year 1991* (1992) HMSO.

MAFF, *European agriculture – The case for radical reform* (1995).

MAFF, *New independent report calls for radical reform of the Common Agricultural Policy* (1995) news release, 5 pages.

Scott Report (1996) 'Report of the Inquiry into the Export of Defence Equipment and Dual-Use Goods to Iraq and Related Prosecutions', chaired by Sir Richard Scott, HMSO.

Appendix F. Bibliography of Other Texts

J. Aigner, *Pour une Cour des comptes européenne* (1973) Luxembourg.

C. Amand, 'The future VAT regime in the European Union – The opinion of the tax consultants' (1995) *European Taxation*, July, pp. 219–222.

M. Andenaes, 'Enforcement of financial market regulation – Problems of parallel proceedings' (1995) PhD dissertation, Jesus College Cambridge.

M. Anderson et al., *Policing the European Union* (1995) Oxford.

J. Ashworth, 'Techniques for reducing subjective disparity in sentencing', in *Disparities in Sentencing – causes and solutions* (1989) Council of Europe, Strasbourg.

Association d'Etudes et de Recherches Pénales (AERPE), Luxembourg *La protection du budget communautaire et l'assistance entre états* (1995).

S. Arrowsmith, *An assessment of the legal techniques for implementing the procurement directives* (1996) W G Hart Legal Workshop, London.

M. Ayral, 'Contrôles communautaires dans les états sur l'exécution du budget des communautés' (1974) *Revue du Marché Commun*, pp. 462–466.

R. Baldwin, *Towards an integrated Europe* (1994) Council for European Policy Studies, London.

A. Bassi, 'Community frauds upon the ESF – The Italian experience' (1994) in *The legal protection of the financial interests of the Community – Progress and prospects since the Brussels seminar*, eds. European Commission, pp. 225–238.

I. Battistotti, *Protection des Intérêts financiers et Fonds Structurels* (1995) seminar paper.

J. Bliss, 'The Foreign Corrupt Practices of 1988: clarification or evisceration?' (1989) *Law and Policy in International Business*, pp. 441–469.

M. Bommensath, 'L'Europe au-delà de Maastricht et face à l'élargissement vers l'est' (1995) 387 *Revue du Marché Commun*, pp. 213–219.

P. Bourdieu, 'Droit et passe-droit, le champ des pouvoirs territoriaux et la mise en oeuvre des règlements' (1990) 81/82 *Actes de la Recherche en Sciences Sociales*.

S. Boyron, *Un pouvoir de contrôle confirmé: Les commissions temporaires d'enquête* (1995) report to the Commission Institutionnelle of the European Parliament.

S. Boyron, *Les commissions temporaires et les adaptations réglementaires nécessaires* (1995) report to the Commission Institutionnelle of the European Parliament.

T. Bunyan, 'Trevi, Europol and the European state' (1993) in *Statewatching the new Europe*, ed. T. Bunyan, Russell Press, pp. 15–36.

M. Bridges, 'Tax evasion – A crime in itself: The relationship with money laundering' (1996) 4:2 *Journal of Financial Crime*, pp. 161–168.

A. Buckwell, *Report on the feasibility of an agricultural strategy to prepare the countries of central and eastern Europe for EU accession* (1994).

P. Bugnot, 'La cour des comptes des communautés européennes – Premier bilan' (1982) *Revue du Marché Commun*, pp. 609–623.

Bundesministerium der Finanzen, *Formulation of the definitive scheme for imposing turnover tax on the intra-Community trade in goods and services and for a functional clearing procedure* (1994) Federal Ministry of Finance, Bonn.

T. Burns, *Better lawmaking? An evaluation of the law reform in the European Community* (1996) W G Hart Workshop, London.

A. Cadoppi, 'Towards a European Criminal Code?' (1996) 4:1 *European Journal of Crime, Criminal Law and Criminal Justice*, pp. 2–17.

M. Cappelletti, *The judicial process in comparative perspective* (1989) Clarendon Press, Oxford.

I. Caraccioli, 'L'importanza del diritto penale tributario in ambito europeo' (1995) 30 *Il Fisco*, pp. 7525–7526.

I. Caraccioli, *Vers un droit fiscal Européen* (1995) paper given at a Conference on the protection of the financial interests of the European Community, Dublin 1–2 June.

I. Caraccioli, 'Verso un diritto penal tributario europeo' (1995) 26 *Il Fisco*, pp. 6660–6663.

J. Carey, 'La cour des comptes européenne six ans après sa fondation' (1984) 19 *La Revue Administrative*, pp. 242–244.

J. Church and P. Phinnemore, *European Union and European Community, a handbook and commentary on the post-Maastricht Treaties* (1994) Harvester Wheatsheaf.

T. Christiansen, *Institutionalised contradictions of European governance: Politicised bureaucracy and multiple accountability in the European Commission* (1996) paper given at the Paris conference on the europeanization of public policies.

R. Cockfield and M. Mulholland, 'Tribunals, reviews and appeals: Sections 7 and 14–16, Finance Act' (1994) *British Tax Review*, pp. 282–285.

N. Collins, 'The European Community's farm lobby' (1990) 5 *Corruption and Reform*, pp. 235–257.

V. Contantinesco, 'L'article 5 CEE, de la bonne foi à la loyauté communautaire, du droit international au droit de l'intégration' (1987) *Liber Amicorum Pierre Pescatore*, eds. F. Capotorti, C-D Ehlermann, J. Frohwein, F. Jacobs, R. Joliet, T. Koopmans, R. Kovar.

J. Cosson, *Les industriels de la fraude fiscale* (1974) Editions du Seuil, Paris.

S. Cragg and G. Meyrick, 'An opportunity missed' (1996) *Legal Action*, October.

N. Courakis, 'Greece: Coping with EU fraud' (1996) 4:1 *Journal of Financial Crime*, pp. 78–84.

G. Dannecker (ed.), *Combatting subsidy fraud in the EC area* (1993) Bundesanzeifer, Köln.

M. Darras 'Le Parlement Européen et la protection juridique des intérêts financiers de la Communauté Européenne' (1992) *EC fraud*, ed. J. Van der Hulst, Kluwer.

F. D'Aubert, *Main basse sur l'Europe* (1994), PLON, Paris.

J. Davies and J. Willman, *What next? Agencies, departments, and the civil service* (1991) Institute for Public Policy Research, London.

K. Davis, *Discretionary justice: A preliminary enquiry* (1979) University of Illinois Press.

F. De Angelis, *Les problèmes liés à la décentralisation* (1996) paper given at a conference on the protection of the financial interests of the European Communities, held in Lille, 25–26 January.

H. De Doelder, 'The enforcement of economic legislation' (1994) in *Administrative law application and enforcement of Community law in The Netherlands*, ed. J. Vervaele, Kluwer, pp. 133–142.

F. De La Serre, 'L'élargissement aux PECO: Quelle differenciation?' (1996) 402 *Revue du Marché Commun*, pp. 642–655.

M. Delmas-Marty and E. Roche-Pire, *La criminalité des affaires et marché commun* (1980) PUF, Paris.

M. Delmas-Marty, 'La criminalité économique internationale: pour une politique criminelle à stratégie diversifiée' (1995) *Le Trimestre du Monde*, premier trimestre (Dossier Mafias et criminalité transnationale), pp. 83–90.

M. Delmas-Marty, *Droit Pénal des affaires* (1990) PUF, Paris.

M. Delmas-Marty, *Pour un droit commun* (1994) Seuil, Paris.

M. Delmas-Marty, 'White collar crime in Europe' (1980) in *Economic crime in Europe*, ed. L. Leigh, McMillan Press, London, pp. 78–105.

M. Delmas-Marty, *Vers un espace judicaire Européen, Corpus Juris portant dispositions pénales pour la protection des intérêts financiers de l'Union Européenne* (1996).

P. De Koster, *Obstacles causés par le régime d'immunités des fonctionnaires publics* (1995) paper given at a conference on the protection of the financial interests of the European Communities held at Sirmione, Italy, July.

L. De Moor, 'The Association of Lawyers for the Protection of the Financial Interests of the European Community' (1993) in *Europäische Einigung und Europäisches Strafrecht*, ed. U. Sieber, Carl Heymanns Verlag, pp. 29–33.

L. De Moor, 'The legal protection of the financial interests of the European Community' (1992) *EC fraud*, ed. J. Van der Hulst, Kluwer.

R. Derham, *Set-off* (1987) Clarendon Press, Oxford.

A. Doig and M. Graham, 'Fraud and the Intervention Board' (1993) 1:3 *Journal of Asset Protection and Financial Crime*, pp. 225–233.

A. Doig, 'A fragmented organizational approach to fraud in a European context – The case of the United Kingdom public sector' (1995) 3:2 *European Journal on Criminal Policy and Research*, pp. 48–64.

N. Dorn and S. White, 'Beyond "Pillars" and "Passerelle" debates: the European Union's emerging crime prevention space' (1997) 1 *Legal Issues of European Integration*.

U. Draetta, 'The European Union and the fight against corruption in international trade' (1995) 6 *Revue de Droit des Affaires Internationales* pp. 701–711.

M. Dunford, 'Winners and losers, the new map of economic inequality in the European Union' (1994) 1(2) *European Urban and Regional Studies*, pp. 95–114.

A. Easson, *The elimination of tax frontiers in 1992: One European market* (1989) EUI Florence.

P. Eglin, 'The dispute over the meaning and use of official statistics in the explanation of deviance' (1987) *Classic disputes in sociology*, eds. J. Hughes, J. Anderson and W. Sharrock, Allen and Unwin, London.

N. Emiliou, 'Implied powers and the legal basis of Community measures' (1993) 18 *European Law Review*, pp. 138–144.

N. Emiliou, 'Opening Pandora's box: the legal basis of Community measures before the Court of Justice' (1994) 19 *European Law Review*, pp. 488–507.

P. Everard and D. Wolter, *Glossary – Selection of terms and expressions used in the external audit of the public sector* (1989) OOPEC.

P. Farmer and J. Lyal, *EC tax law* (1994) Clarendon Press, Oxford.

R. Fennell, *The Common Agricultural Policy of the European Community* (1987) BSP Professional Books, London.

C. Fijnaut, 'Organized crime and anti-organized crime efforts in western Europe: an overview' (1991) in *Organized crime and its containment, a transatlantic initiative*, eds. C. Fijnaut and J. Jacobs, Kluwer.

E. Filkin, *Complaint and redress mechanisms in the public sector* (1994) paper given at the 1994 OECD Paris Symposium.

C. Flaesch-Mougin, 'La CEE et la lutte contre les fraudes au détriment du budget communautaire' (1983) 4 *Cahiers de Droit Européen*, pp. 393–436.

S. Fothergill, *The struggle over European funding* (1995) Local Government Information Unit, London.

D. Frisch, *The fight against international corruption: What the European Union can do* (1996) Transparency International workshop held in London on 4 July.

P. Garde, *Settlement in Danish law* (1995) OOPEC.

P. Garde, 'The suppression of fraud against the European Communities in Danish law and practice' (1989) in *The legal protection of the financial interests of the Community – Progress and prospects since the Brussels seminar of 1989*, pp. 212–217, Oak Tree Press, Dublin.

J. Gardiner, 'Defining Corruption' (1993) 7 *Corruption and Reform*, pp. 111–124.

L. Gormley, *Public Procurement, 1993: The European market – Myth or reality?* (1994) eds. D. Campbell and C. Flint, Kluwer.

C. Goybert, 'La fraude communautaire – Mythes et réalités' (1995) 388 *Revue du Marché Commun*, pp. 281–283.

W. Grant, 'Is agricultural policy still exceptional?' (1995) 66:3 *The Political Quarterly*, pp. 156–169.

G. Grebing, *The fine in comparative law – A survey of 21 countries* (1982) Cambridge Institute of Criminology, Occasional Papers number 9.

V. Greve and C. Gulman, 'Denmark: The system of administrative and penal sanctions' (1994) in *The system of administrative and penal sanctions in the Member States of the European Communities*, Volume 1, national reports, OOPEC.

S. Grüsser, S. White and N. Dorn, 'Free movement and welfare entitlement EU – drug users in Berlin' (1995) 5(1) *Journal of European Social Policy*, pp. 13–28.

C. Harding, *European Community investigations and sanctions* (1993) Leicester University Press.

C. Harding, 'The European Communities and control of criminal business activities' (1982) *International and Comparative Law Quarterly*, pp. 246–262.

J. Harrop, *The political economy of integration in the European Community* (1989) Gower.

R. Harwood, 'Corruption and public sector fraud – Prosecution by government agencies' (1996) 4:1 *Journal of Financial Crime*, pp. 51–54.

J. Heine, 'Community penalties in agriculture and fisheries – Legislative activity in the Commission' (1994) in *The legal protection of the financial interests of the Community – Progress and prospects since the Brussels seminar of 1989*, OOPEC.

International Chamber of Commerce, *Extortion and bribery in international business transactions* (1996) Revisions to the 1977 Report and rules of conduct to combat extortion and bribery.

G. Isaac, 'La rénovation des institutions financières des communautés européennes depuis 1970' (1977) 13 *Revue Trimestrielle du Droit Européen*, pp. 736–810.

G. Isaac, 'Les finances communautaires (année 1978 – premier semestre 1979)' (1980) 16 *Revue Trimestrielle du Droit Européen*, pp. 302–353.

D. Jupp, *Methods of criminological research* (1989) Unwin Hyman, London.

B. Knudsen, 'Global programme of the European Community's fight against fraud' (1994) in *The Legal protection of the financial interests of the Community – Progress and prospects since the Brussels seminar of 1989*, Oak Tree Press, Dublin.

C. Kok, 'The Court of Auditors of the European Communities: the other European court in Luxembourg' (1989) 26 *Common Market Law Review*, pp. 345–368.

T. Koopmans, 'Federalism: the wrong debate' (1992) 29 *Common Market Law Review*, pp. 1047–1052.

H. Labayle, 'La protection des intérêts financiers de la communauté' (1995) *Revue Europe*, March.

H. Labayle, *La transaction dans l'Union Européenne* (1996) (synthesis report for the studies carried out in the fifteen Member States concerning the settlement of fraud cases affecting the EC budget), OOPEC.

A. Lachat-Héritier, 'Commercial bribes: the Swiss answer' (1983) 5 *Journal of Comparative Business and Capital Market Law*, pp. 79–96.

B. Laffan, *Integration and cooperation in Europe* (1992) Routledge.

F. Lagerfeld, 'It's no longer criminal' (1994) 17 *Taxation*.

D. Lasok and J. Bridge, *Law and institutions of the European Communities* (1991) Butterworths, London.

G. Leguet, *La confusion dans la répartition des compétences dans le domaine des poursuites* (1996) paper given at a conference on the protection of the financial interests of the European Communities, held in Lille, 25–26 January.

L. Leigh, 'Crimes in bankruptcy' (1980) in *Economic crime in Europe*, ed. L. Leigh, McMillan Press, pp. 106–208.

L. Leigh and A. Smith, 'Some observations on European fraud laws and their reform with reference to the EEC' (1991) 6 *Corruption and Reform*, pp. 267–284.

L. Leigh, *Subvention frauds: the British experience* (1992).

P. Lelong, 'La Cour des comptes des Communautés européennes: sa mission, son bilan, L'Europe en formation' (1989) 274 *Les Cahiers du Fédéralisme*.

M. Levi, 'Fraudulent justice? Sentencing the business criminal' (1989) in *Paying for crime*, eds. P. Carlen and D. Cook, Open University Press, Milton Keynes, UK.

M. Levi, 'Serious fraud in Britain' (1995) in *Corporate crime: contemporary debates*, eds. F. Pearce and L. Snider, University of Toronto Press, pp. 181–198.

R. Levy, '1992: towards better budgetary control in the EC?' (1991) 6 *Corruption and Reform*, pp. 285–302.

R. Levy, 'The antibribery provisions of the Foreign Corrupt Practices Act of 1977: are they really as valuable as we think they are?' (1985) *Delaware Journal of Corporate Law*, 71–95.

J-C. Leygues, 'La commission de contrôle des communautés européennes' (1974) *Revue du Marché Commun*, 59–67.

L. Maublanc-Fernandez and J-P Maublanc, 'Chronique de jurisprudence fiscale européenne' (1995) 388 *Revue du Marché Commun*, pp. 320–325.

G. McClanahan, *Diplomatic immunity, principles, practices, problems* (1989) Hurst, London.

I. McLeod, I. Hendry and S. Hyett, *The External Relations of the European Communities* (1996) Clarendon Press, Oxford.

G. McFarlane, 'Customs Tribunals' (1994) *Importing Today*, May/June 1994, pp. 16–17.

D. McShane, *Global business, global rights* (1996), Fabian pamphlet 575, London.

L-P. Mahé, *Agriculture and enlargement of the European Union to include the central and eastern European countries: Transition with a view to integration or integration with a view to transition?* (1995) Report for DG I of the European Commission.

A. Makridimitris, *Reasoning and legality in administration* (1984) PhD thesis, University College, London.

S. Manacorda, 'La criminalité économique internationale: un premier bilan des instruments de politique criminelle' (1995) *Le Trimestre du Monde*, premier trimestre (Dossier Mafias et criminalité transnationale), pp. 59–81.

J-C. Marin, 'Legal protection of the Community's financial interests: experience and prospects since the Brussels seminar of 1989' (1994) in *Legal Protection of the Community's financial interests: Experience and prospects since the Brussels seminar of 1989*, Oak Tree Press, Dublin.

R. Merlin-Calzia, 'Le service central de prévention de la corruption comme possible instrument au service de la défense des intérêts financiers des communautés' (1995) *AGON*, July, 8–9.

R. Milas, 'Le budget communautaire sous analyse sytématique' (1988) *Revue du Marché Commun*, pp. 287–296.

A. Missir di Lusignano, 'La protection des intérêts financiers de la communauté' (1996) *Journal des Tribunaux Droit Européen*, 18 April.

J. Myard, *Combattre la fraude: un défi pour les quinze* (1996) Rapport d'information déposé par la délégation de l'Assemblée Nationale pour l'Union Européenne sur la proposition de règlement du conseil relatif aux contrôles et vérifications sur place de la Commission aux fins de la constatation des fraudes et irrégularités portant atteinte aux intérêts financiers des Communautés Européennes, French National Assembly Publications Kiosk.

R. Naylor, 'From underworld to underground enterprise crime, "informal sector" business and the public policy response' (1996) 24:2 *Crime, Law and Social Change*, pp. 79–150.

G. Nielsen, *Constitutional and administrative law in Danish law – A general survey* (1982) Bianco Lunos BogTrykkeri A/S, Copenhagen.

D. Norton, 'Smuggling under the CAP: Northern Ireland and the Republic of Ireland' (1986) 32:3 *Journal of Common Market Studies*, pp. 319–342.

D. O'Keefe, 'The Court of Auditors' (1994) in *Institutional dynamics of European integration Essays in honour of Henry G. Schermers*, Volume II, eds. D. Curtin and T. Heukels, Martinus Nijhoff Pubs, pp. 177–194.

D. Parkinson, *Value Added Tax in the EEC* (1981) Graham and Trotman Ltd, London.

N. Passas, *Milking consumers and taxpayers: Farm frauds in the European Community* (1993) mimeoed text, Temple University.

C. Pérez-Diaz, 'L'indulgence, pratique discrétionnaire et arrangement administratif' (1994) *Déviance et Société*, Vol. XVIII No. 4 pp. 397–430.

Public Concern at Work, Report on *Whistleblowing, fraud and the European Union* (1995).

D. Raponi, *L'I.V.A. comunitaria: Le tappe per il passagio al regime definitivo* (1996) paper given at a conference held in Venice and entitled L'I.V.A. e l'Unione Europea, Frodi, controlli, sanzioni, 24 February.

B. Rider, 'Civilising the law: the use of administrative proceedings to enforce financial services law' (1995) 3:1 *Journal of Financial Crime*, pp. 11–34.

J. Robinson, *The laundrymen* (1995), Pocket Books, London.

D. Rose, *In the name of the law: the collapse of criminal justice* (1996) Vintage.

D. Ruimschottel, *The EC budget: ten per cent fraud?* (1994) EUI Florence.

J. Rump, 'The legal protection of the Community's financial interests as seen by Customs investigators in Germany' (1993) in *Seminar on the protection of the financial interests of the Community – Progress and prospects since the Brussels seminar of 1989*, eds. European Commission, Oak Tree Press, Dublin.

M. Sacchettini, 'Un nouvel organe des communautés européennes: La cour des comptes' (1977) *Revue du Marché Commun*, pp. 344–347.

M. Shackelton, 'Budgetary policy in transition' (1991) in *The State of the EC*, eds. L. Hurwitz and C. Lequesne, Lynne Rienner Pubs, Colorado, pp. 65–79.

A. Sherlock and C. Harding, 'Controlling fraud within the European Community' (1991) 16 *European Law Review*, pp. 20–36.

C. Schmidt, 'Le protocole sur les privilèges et immunités des Communautés Européennes' (1991) *Cahier de Droit Européen*, pp. 61–100.

V. Schmitt, 'Dix ans de travaux de la cour des comptes européenne, essai de typologie' (1988) *Revue du Marché Commun*, pp. 282–286.

F. Schockweiler, *La répression des infractions au droit communautaire dans la jurisprudence de la cour – La protection du budget communautaire et l'assistance entre états* (1995) in Proceeds of a conference held in Luxembourg on 12 May, AERPE Luxembourg.

J. Schutte, 'Administrative and judicial co-operation in the fight against EC fraud' in *The Dutch approach in tackling EC fraud*, eds. M.S. Groenhuijsen and M.I. Veldt, Kluwer, pp. 127–134.

G. Slapper and D. Kelly, *The English legal system* (1993) Cavendish Publishing.

D. Southern, 'Set-off revisited' (1994) 6669 *New Law Journal*, pp. 1412–1414.

A. Spinelli, *The European adventure, Tasks for an enlarged Community* (1972) London, Charles Knight & Co.

D. Spinellis, *The phenomenon of corruption and the challenge of good governance* (1995) in Proceeds of OECD symposium, 13–14 March.

M. Spencer, *1992 and all that: Civil liberties in the balance* (1990) Civil Liberties Trust, London.

F. Stacey, *Ombudsmen compared* (1978) Clarendon Press, Oxford.

D. Strasser, 'La décharge, nouveau pouvoir du Parlement Européen, son application aux exercices 1977 et 1978' (1981) *Revue du Marché Commun*, pp. 109–129.

D. Strasser, 'La décharge donnée par le Parlement Européen pour les exercices 1977 et 1978' (1983) *Revue du Marché Commun*, pp. 124–167.

D. Strasser, *The finances of Europe* (1980) European perspectives series, Brussels.

D. Strasser, *The finances of Europe* (1991) OOPEC.

M. Sutton, 'Transition to the European Union?' (1994) in *Economies in transition Eastern Europe and the former Soviet Union*, London, Economist Intelligence Unit.

S. Tangermann and T. Josling, *Pre-accession agricultural policies for central Europe and the European Union* (1994) mimeoed text.

S. Tarditi and S. Senior-Nello, *Agricultural strategies for the enlargement of the European Union to central and eastern European countries* (1994) mimeoed text.

J. Terra and P. Wattel, *European Tax Law* (1992), Kluwer.

K. Tiedemann, 'La fraude dans le domaine des subventions: criminologie et politique criminelle' (1975) *Revue de Droit Pénal et de Criminologie*, pp. 129–140.

K. Tiedemann, 'La recherche criminologique en matiere de délinquance d'affaires – Etude des aspect internationaux de cette recherche' (1985) *Revue de Droit Pénal et de Criminologie*, pp. 707–726.

K. Tiedemann, 'Pour un espace juridique commun après Amsterdam' (1997) *AGON* number 17, pp. 12–13.

K. Thompson, 'Reforming the Common Agricultural Policy' (1995) 1 *European Access*.

H-G. Toft-Hansen, 'The law of procedure in constitutional and administrative law' (1982) in *Danish law – A general survey*, Bianco Lunos BogTrykkeri A/S, Copenhagen.

Transparency International, *The fight against corruption – What the European Union can do* (1995).

F. Tschofen, 'Article 235 of the Treaty establishing the European Economic Community: potential conflicts between the dynamics of lawmaking in the Community and national constitutional principles' (1991) 12:3 *Michigan Journal of International Law* (1991) pp. 471–509.

F. Tulkens, 'Les fraudes communautaires: un observatoire pénal européen' (1994) *Déviance et Société*, Vol. XVIII No. 2.

N. Tutt, *Europe on a fiddle* (1989) Helm, London.

UCLAF, 'Anti-fraud coordination in the EU' (1995) 3:2 *European Journal on Criminal Policy and Research*, pp. 65–74.

J. Usher, *Legal aspects of agriculture in the European Community* (1988) Clarendon Press, Oxford.

C. Van den Wyngaert, 'Criminal law and the European Communities: defining the issues' (1983) *Michigan Yearbook of International Law Studies*, pp. 247–270.

C. Van den Wyngaert, *Etude espace judiciaire européen, groupe thématique no. 2 – Règles de compétence et extra-territorialité* (1996).

J. Van Der Woude, 'Hearing officers and EC antitrust procedures – The art of making subjective procedures more objective' (1996) 33 *Common Market Law Review*, pp. 531–546.

P. Van Duyne, 'The phantom and threat of organised crime' (1996) 24:4 *Crime, Law and Social Change*, pp. 341–377.

W. Van Gerven, 'Bridging the gap between Community and national laws: towards a principle of homogeneity in the field of legal remedies?' (1995) 32 *Common Market Law Review*, pp. 679–702.

B. Vermeulen, 'The issue of fundamental rights in the administrative application and enforcement of Community law' (1994) in *Administrative law application and enforcement of Community law in the Netherlands*, Kluwer, pp. 39–80.

G. Vernimmen and A. Missir di Lusignano, Editorial of *AGON* (1995) 9.

J. Vervaele, *Fraud against the Community: The need for European fraud legislation* (1992) Deventer, Kluwer.

J. Vervaele, 'Fraude communautaire et sauvegarde du droit communautaire – Vers un droit pénal européen' (1994) *Déviance et Société* Vol. XVIII No. 2, pp. 201–210.

J. Vervaele, 'La communauté européenne face à la fraude communautaire: vers un "espace pénal comunautaire"?' (1990) *Revue de Science Criminelle et de Droit Pénal Comparé*, pp. 29–41.

J. Vervaele, *La fraude communautaire et le droit pénal européen des affaires* (1994) PUF, Paris.

J. Vervaele, 'La lutte contre la fraude communautaire: Une mise à l'épreuve de la loyauté communautaire des états membres?' (1991) *Revue de Droit Pénal et de Criminologie*, pp. 569–585.

J. Vervaele, 'L'application du droit communautaire – La séparation des biens entre le premier et le troisième piliers' (1996) *Revue de Droit Pénal et de Criminologie*, pp. 5–22.

J. Vervaele, 'Subsidy fraud' (1992) in *EC fraud*, ed. J. Van der Hulst, Kluwer.

J. Vervaele, 'Criminal law in the European Community: about myth and taboos' (1995) *AGON* number 7.

D. Villemot, *La TVA européenne – Les régimes de TVA applicables aux échanges avec les autres Etats membres de la CEE* (1994) PUF, Paris.

T. Vogler, 'Reflections on the creation of a unified criminal law' (1983) *Michigan Yearbook of International Law Studies*, pp. 271–277.

I. Ward, 'Making sense of integration: a philosophy of law for the European Community' (1993) *Journal of European Integration*, Volume XVII, No. 1, pp. 101–136.

G. Watson, 'From an adversarial to a managed system of litigation: a comparative critique of Lord Woolf's interim report' (1996) in *Achieving civil justice: Appropriate dispute resolution for the 1990s*, ed. R. Smith, Legal Action Group, London.

S. Weatherill, 'Implementation as a constitutional issue' (1995) in *Implementing EC law in the United Kingdom: Structures for indirect rules*, ed. T. Daintith, IALS London, Chancery Law Pubs, pp. 325–360.

S. White, 'A variable geometry of enforcement? Aspects of European Community budget fraud' (1995) 23 *Crime, Law and Social Change*, pp. 235–255.

S. White, 'Black listing: three questions' (1996) *AGON* No. 12, pp. 8–9.

S. White, 'Corruption: the EC fraud dimension' (1996) 4:2 *Journal of Financial Crime*, pp. 168–172.

S. White, 'EC fraud: what is VAT?' (1996) 3:3 *Journal of Financial Crime*, pp. 255–259.

S. White and N. Dorn, 'EC fraud, subsidiarity and prospects for the IGC: a regional dimension?' (1996) 3:3 *European Urban and Regional Studies*, pp. 262–266.

S. White, 'Proposed measures against corruption of officials in the EU' (1996) 21:6 *European Law Review*, pp. 465–476.

S. White, 'Recovering EC funds: the extra-judicial route' (1996) in *Fraud on the European budget*, Hume Papers on Public Policy, Vol. 4, No. 3, David Hume Institute, Edinburgh, pp. 61–69.

S. White, 'Reflections on the IGC and the protection of the financial interests of the EC' (1995) *AGON*, number 10, pp. 10–13.

S. White, 'The fight against international corruption: Towards a European strategy?' (1996) *AGON*, number 13, pp. 3–6.

S. White, 'The transit system in crisis: argument for European Customs?' (1996) 2 *Irish Journal of European Law*, pp. 225–237.

S. White, *The public interest as represented in English law: relevance for EC fraud* (1995) Proceeds of a conference held at Urbino, Italy.

S. White, *United Kingdom Report to DG XX of the European Commission for the 'Settlement Study' on the protection of the financial interests of the Community* (1995).

P. Wood, *English and international set-off* (1989) Sweet and Maxwell, London.

S. Woolcock, 'Public procurement' (1991) in *The state of the European Community – Policies, institutions and debates in the transition years*, eds. L. Hurwitz and C. Lequesne, Lynne Rienner Publishers, Longman.